Operational Guidelines
for Educational Facilities

Grounds

second edition

Published by

Printed in the United States of America.
International Standard Book Number: 1-890956-66-X

Editor: Steve Glazner
Project Manager: Anita Dosik
Design: John Reynolds Design
Cover Design: ImagePrep Design
Printing: Documation

Disclaimer

The concepts and guidelines presented in this publication are intended to assist facilities and grounds managers in the efficient and effective staffing of their grounds and landscaping operations. These are guidelines only and are not necessarily industry standards. Opinions expressed in this book are those of the authors and do not necessarily reflect the opinions of APPA. Mention of companies and products are for informational purposes only and are not intended by the publisher as an endorsement of any kind.

1643 Prince Street | Alexandria, Virginia 22314-2818 | U.S.A. | www.appa.org

Contents and Figures

Acknowledgments

This book is the second edition of what was first published as *Operational Guidelines for Grounds Management.* Alan Bigger, APPA Fellow and past APPA President, served as the editor-in-chief for the complete revision of the trilogy of APPA's popular publications, of which this is one, published together as *Operational Guidelines for Educational Facilities.* His knowledge of the educational facilities world, his nearly unlimited list of networking contacts, and his long experience as a writer and editor have all contributed to Alan's tremendous success in overseeing the massive effort to research, write, edit, and organize the content for all three books in the trilogy: Custodial, Grounds, and Maintenance.

Alan spent countless hours meeting with staff and task force chairs, in person and on conference calls, to make sure the content was right for each publication in the trilogy. He read and reread every single word numerous times, and acted as tie-breaker or decision maker for hundreds of questions and issues that arose throughout the revision process. He did all of this with great humor, sensitivity, and dogged determination. APPA's gratitude to Alan Bigger cannot fully be expressed in this acknowledgment.

APPA also thanks Tom Flood of Elon University for his leadership and service as task force chair for the Grounds book. Tom assembled an excellent team of writers and contributors who assessed the strong points of the first edition, updated and expanded chapters as needed, and wrote new chapters and case studies.

Many thanks go to Joseph C. Fisher of West Virginia University for his early guidance and suggestions for the improvement of all three books in the series. We also appreciate the assistance of Ernest Hunter of Hunter Consulting and Training for his thoughtful and detailed contributions.

The first edition of this book was published by APPA in cooperation with the National Recreation and Parks Association and the Professional Grounds Management Society, with assistance from the American Public Works Association. APPA gratefully acknowledges the collaboration among these associations. For this second edition, we thank PGMS for its support and for suggesting a number of its knowledgeable members to serve as authors and reviewers.

APPA also thanks the following for their contributions to the production and quality of this publication: Jane Rea of EEI Communications for thoughtful and consistent editing and proofreading, John Reynolds for going above and beyond in his design and layout, ImagePrep for its wonderful cover designs, and Documation for its printing expertise. Steve Glazner of APPA provided editorial direction for all three books and was the liaison with Alan Bigger and the task force chairs. Finally, APPA extends a warm thank-you to Anita Dosik, APPA's publications manager, who served as project manager for the trilogy, made and kept schedules, coordinated all production aspects of the books, and asked all the right questions at the right times.

Preface

By Alan S. Bigger, APPA Fellow, APPA Member Emeritus
Editor-in-Chief

In the late 1980s, a group of APPA physical plant directors started to discuss the possibility of developing staffing and operational guidelines for facilities management. The idea was driven by severe budget cuts that were forcing many directors to consider how to maintain their current levels of service in the face of cuts that threatened their ability to sustain quality services. Thus, the concept of operational guidelines was developed to assist directors of facilities with the management and staffing of their operations. The guidelines provided for concepts of levels of appearance and service that are consistent across all of APPA's operational guidelines. The first set of guidelines to be published was for custodial services (1992), followed by grounds (2001) and maintenance (2002).

Now, as then, facilities managers and directors are being asked to do more with less, and the new operational guidelines for grounds management is designed to assist with that effort. Building on the stellar work of the first edition, which included inputs from the National Recreation and Park Association, the American Public Works Association, and the Professional Grounds Management Society, the second edition has enhanced some of the original chapters as well as added new chapters to cover issues such as sustainability, snow removal, and the inventory of the assets of grounds management. The task force based the content of this book on data collected from APPA members and users of the APPA guidelines in an effort to provide current information for grounds managers in this decade.

Many people worked long and hard to revise and rewrite these guidelines. Tom Flood, task force chair for the book, coordinated the work of the task force and contributors, as well as contributing to several chapters himself. APPA staff, especially

Anita Dosik and Steve Glazner, were guiding lights in the process, a process that would never have come to fruition had it not been for their diligence and professionalism.

It is our hope that this revised edition will enable grounds professionals to manage effective and efficient operations that demonstrate their commitment to being good stewards of the assets assigned to them, as well as to a sustainable environment during the years ahead.

Alan S. Bigger
Editor-in-Chief of APPA's Operational Guidelines Trilogy
South Bend, Indiana
September 2011

Introduction

By Thomas Flood, ASLA, EFP
Task Force Chair

Professional grounds management is a great deal more than knowing "green side up"! Thirty years ago, Bill Murray portrayed a clueless assistant greenskeeper, Carl Spackler, in the cult movie classic *Caddyshack*. Despite my love of that comedic character (and my occasional desire to clean my office with a backpack blower), in my many years in the profession I have yet to find a grounds manager like him, and with good reason!

Over the past 30 years, the appearance of the campus landscape has grown in importance and esteem. It is now rare to run across anyone who still thinks of the grounds crew as Carl Spackler-like characters; the grounds manager is far more often seen as the "director of external marketing" and the grounds staff as admission recruiters or marketing personnel. The fact is that people do judge a book by its cover, and the appearance of our landscape and campus determines our customers' impressions of our institution to a large degree. People naturally assume that if the buildings and grounds appear well cared for, then the faculty and students must be well cared for, too. Grounds (and facilities) management is arguably the most important job at schools, colleges, and universities today.

Today's grounds manager has to be a scientist, a psychologist, an artist and designer, a business administrator, and an astute politician. This edition of *Operational Guidelines for Grounds Management* provides grounds managers with many of the resources necessary for efficient and effective operations. It has been revised and improved in some major ways since the original was published a decade ago. Not only does it contain revisions of many of the original chapters, the staffing guidelines, and level of service definitions, but major new sections have been added that expand the scope of this book into the areas of sustainability, landscape inventories, and snow removal, to name a few. We hope it will become an essential part of every grounds manager's library.

The book begins with a new and landmark work titled "Sustainable Grounds Operations." Ten years ago, the words sustainable and stewardship were seldom heard outside a very narrow circle. Although those of us with long experience in the landscape and grounds fields were "green" before green was cool, sustainability has now become mainstream. Yet the practices, procedures, materials, and equipment involved in sustainable grounds maintenance operations are still evolving. This chapter, and Chapter 2, which review the latest practices and technology in sustainable grounds operations as of 2011, focus on an area sure to evolve significantly before the next edition of this book.

The next chapter discusses organizational models for grounds organizations and the relative advantages and disadvantages for each, while Chapter 4 introduces the topic of staffing levels with a review of landscape inventory methods, systems, software, and benefits to the grounds manager. These issues of efficient organizations and inventorying assets are critical to effective and responsible management.

Chapter 5 provides an in-depth discussion of the classic APPA grounds staffing guidelines, with an introduction on how to use, and not use, the guidelines. The three case studies at the end of this chapter provide examples of how the guidelines can be used and modified to meet the needs of grounds management organizations at specific campuses. They offer valuable information on creating a staffing program to guide your management choices.

Of course, contracting out services is always an option, and chapter 6 presents some valuable information for those engaged in or considering outsourcing grounds management services. Chapters 7 through 9 offer a detailed review of benchmarking, the essentials of managing complex snow removal operations, and examples of grounds-specific position descriptions and why they are important. Last, don't overlook the appendices! There is a one-of-a-kind case study of the Quality Appearance Program at Duke University and a wealth of additional resources for the grounds manager.

I have often heard facility directors, construction managers, and contractors say that "the grounds director on my campus is really passionate about the job." This group of authors is no less so. It has been my pleasure to work with many of the original authors in revising their chapters and many new authors as well. These professionals come from a variety of backgrounds in the green industry—landscape architecture, horticulture, and academia—but all have in common a lifetime of experience that they are willing to share. Continued thanks goes out to the original authors whose work has stood the test of time, particularly Robert Getz and his fundamental development of a staffing calculation system that addresses many of the variables within grounds management, and Dennis Swartzell, who compiled the most complete glossary of green industry terms I have ever found (and which required few changes or additions). Special thanks to Marc Fournier, who has done yeoman's duty contributing new work to both editions, including significant research, contributions, and much editing and writing of the chapter on sustainable ground operations.

Authors

Alan S. Bigger, Editor-in-Chief, R.E.H, APPA Fellow, is a past APPA President and APPA Member Emeritus, formerly associated with Earlham College, the University of Notre Dame, and the University of Missouri - Columbia.

Thomas E. Flood, Grounds Chair, is assistant director of physical plant and director of landscaping and grounds at Elon University, Elon, North Carolina.

John Burns is manager, landscape services, at the University of Texas, Austin, Texas.

Stephanie DeStefano is grounds operations coordinator at American University, Washington, D.C.

Gerry Dobbs is grounds maintenance manager at Michigan State University, East Lansing, Michigan.

R. Marc Fournier, M.B.A., is assistant director for plant operations and sustainability at Lasell College, Newton, Massachusetts.

Robert A. Getz is an APPA Member Emeritus residing in Elgin, Illinois.

Frederic J. Gratto is assistant director of physical plant at the University of Florida, Gainesville, Florida.

Joseph Jackson is director, grounds and sanitation services, at Duke University, Durham, North Carolina.

John Lawter is associate director, plant building and grounds services, at the University of Michigan, Ann Arbor, Michigan.

Leonard O. Morrow is a retired professor at J. Sargeant Reynolds Community College in Richmond, Virginia.

Ellen Newell is associate director of facilities management at Arizona State University, Tempe, Arizona.

James B. Spengler is director of recreation, parks, and cultural activities for the City of Alexandria, Alexandria, Virginia.

Dennis L. Swartzell is co-owner of Horticulture Consultants Inc., Henderson, Nevada.

CHAPTER 1

Sustainable Grounds Operations

By R. Marc Fournier, Ellen Newell, and Stephanie DeStefano

The earth's climate has changed many times during the planet's history, with events ranging from ice ages to long periods of warmth. Historically, natural factors such as volcanic eruptions, changes in the earth's orbit, and the amount of energy released from the sun have affected the earth's climate. Regardless of cause or outcome, we, as individuals and as managers of our own little corners of the world, have a responsibility to be good and faithful stewards of the environment.

Beginning late in the 18th century, human (anthropogenic) activities associated with the industrial revolution have also changed the composition of the atmosphere. Recent research shows that these human activities are now disproportionately influencing the earth's climate. If we continue down this path, our actions will result in changes that will cause environmental, political, societal, and financial catastrophes.

Photo by Marc Fournier

Alaskan Glacier

Most grounds managers chose their profession because of their love for the environment. Yet, in our grounds operations, we add destructive greenhouse gases to the environment every day that contribute to climate change. We consume staggering amounts of fuel and emit pollutants from a wide variety of vehicles and power equipment. Are there ways we can improve our stewardship?

Existing and pending environmental regulations focused on reducing emissions and fuel use have stimulated manufacturers to develop innovative technologies and products that will be useful in grounds operations. Even with the realization that climate change is a real issue, consumer demand for these products is weak. In late 2010, distributors of grounds equipment indicated that the only demand has come from forward-thinking colleges, universities, municipalities, and government agencies. As representatives of educational institutions,, we must continue to be the leaders in developing and testing new technologies that will enable us to mitigate our effects on climate change.

We can develop strategies that mitigate the effects of our actions on climate change by making our operations more sustainable, and we can develop ways to adapt to the inevitable changes in climate that will occur due to our past actions. We have the opportunity to do the following:

- Design more efficient and cleaner technologies.
- Develop programs to combat invasive pests and plants that will thrive in a changed climate.
- Perform research into the changes that climate change will bring to our grounds environments.
- Use students, faculty, and staff to test new technologies and programs in real-world environments.
- Create a groundswell of cultural change in our industry.

We must strive to meet the needs of the present without compromising the ability of future generations to meet their own needs—*the very definition of sustainability.*

Beginning now, and in the years to come, it will benefit us as grounds professionals to design and implement environmentally responsible grounds operations, while concurrently educating our students and creating leaders of the future in our industry.

This chapter contains resources, information, ideas and helpful advice on how to do just that.

Environmental Organizations

Over the past decade or so, many new organizations have sprung up to help organizations design and implement sustainability in all facets of their operations. The following two are leaders in helping colleges and universities develop a more sustainable future.

The American College & University Presidents' Climate Commitment

The American College University Presidents' Climate Commitment (ACUPCC) is a high-visibility effort to address global climate disruption undertaken by a network of colleges and universities that have made institutional commitments to eliminate net greenhouse gas emissions from specified campus operations, and to promote the research and educational efforts of higher education to equip society to restabilize the earth's climate. Its mission is to accelerate progress toward climate neutrality and sustainability by empowering the higher education sector to educate students, create solutions, and provide leadership-by-example for the rest of society.

The ACUPCC provides a framework and support for America's colleges and universities to implement comprehensive plans in pursuit of climate neutrality. It recognizes the unique responsibility that institutions of higher education have as role models for their communities and in educating the people who will develop the social, economic, and technological solutions to reverse global warming and help create a thriving, civil, and sustainable society. ACUPCC institutions have agreed to do the following:

- Complete an emissions inventory.
- Within two years, set a target date and interim milestones for becoming climate neutral.
- Take immediate steps to reduce greenhouse gas emissions by choosing from a list of short-term actions.
- Integrate sustainability into the curriculum and make it part of the educational experience.
- Make the action plan, inventory, and progress reports publicly available.

The college and university presidents and chancellors who are joining and leading the ACUPCC believe that exerting leadership in addressing climate disruption is an integral part of the mission of higher education and will stabilize and reduce their long-term energy costs, attract excellent students and faculty, attract new sources of funding, and increase the support of alumni, business, and local communities.

The ACUPCC originated from planning sessions among a group of college and university presidents and their representatives, Second Nature, ecoAmerica, and AASHE (Association for the Advancement of Sustainability in Higher Education) at the AASHE conference in October 2006 at Arizona State University. Twelve presidents agreed to become founding signatories and launched the ACUPCC in early December 2006 by sending a letter to nearly 400 of their peers inviting them to join the initiative.

By March 31, 2007, 152 presidents and chancellors had become charter signatories of the ACUPCC. At that time, the expanded signatory group sent a packet of information to their peers at more than 3,500 institutions, asking them to sign the Commitment. In June 2007, with the signatory group up to 284 institutions, the ACUPCC was officially launched to the public at the first annual Climate Leadership Summit (www.presidentsclimatecommitment.org).

At the time of publication, 670 colleges and universities have signed on, and the ACUPCC has become the sustainability yardstick by which colleges and universities measure their progress.

Association for the Advancement of Sustainability in Higher Education

Another important organization helping higher education institutions is AASHE. AASHE is an association of colleges and universities that are working to create a sustainable future. Its mission is to empower higher education to lead the sustainability transformation. It does this by providing resources, professional development, and a network of support to enable institutions of higher education to model and advance sustainability in everything they do, from governance and operations to education and research.

AASHE defines sustainability in an inclusive way, encompassing human and ecological health, social justice, secure livelihoods, and a better world for all generations. Member institutions include colleges and universities throughout the world. In addition, businesses, nonprofit organizations, K–12 schools, higher education associations, system offices, and government agencies can join AASHE as associate members (www.aashe.org).

A major benefit of joining AASHE for colleges and universities is AASHE's Sustainability Tracking, Assessment & Rating System (STARS®), which enables institutions to benchmark progress in their sustainability initiatives and compare their progress with that of their peers.

STARS is a transparent, self-reporting framework for colleges and universities to gauge relative progress toward sustainability. STARS was developed by AASHE with broad participation from the higher education community. It is designed to do the following:

- Provide a framework for understanding sustainability in all sectors of higher education.
- Enable meaningful comparisons over time and across institutions using a common set of measurements developed with broad participation from the campus sustainability community.
- Create incentives for continual improvement toward sustainability.
- Facilitate information sharing about higher education sustainability practices and performance.
- Build a stronger, more diverse campus sustainability community.

The STARS framework is intended to engage and recognize the full spectrum of colleges and universities in the United States and Canada—from community colleges to research universities, and from institutions just starting their sustainability programs to long-time campus sustainability leaders. STARS encompasses long-term sustainability goals for already high-achieving institutions as well as entry points of recognition for institutions that are taking first steps toward sustainability.

STARS 1.0, which launched on January 19, 2010, after a three-year development process, is the first version of STARS in which participants can earn a rating.

U.S. Green Building Council and LEED®

Leadership in Energy and Environmental Design, commonly referred to as LEED, was developed by the U.S. Green Building Council (USGBC) in 1998 when the USGBC launched the first pilot project. The LEED green building rating system provides

Photo by Tom Flood

Lindner Hall, Elon University

building owners and operators a concise framework for identifying and implementing practical and measurable green building design, construction, and operations and maintenance solutions. Utilizing a third-party verification system, buildings can earn a LEED rating if they were designed and built using strategies intended to enhance building performance through environmentally sustainable means such as energy savings, water efficiency, CO2 emissions reduction, improved indoor environmental quality, and stewardship of resources and sensitivity to their impacts.

In order to earn LEED certification, a project must earn credits established by LEED to obtain ratings in the categories of certified, silver, gold, or platinum, which is the highest level of LEED certification. LEED certification has become increasingly popular on college campuses and serves as a means to demonstrate the institution's commitment to environmental sustainability.

The Green Building Certification Institute (GBCI) was established by USGBC to provide a series of exams to allow individuals to become accredited for their knowledge of the LEED rating system. This is recognized through either the LEED Accredited Professional (LEED AP) or LEED Green Associate (LEED GA) designation.

More information about LEED can be found at www.usgbc.org. The LEED rating system guidelines do not presently extend into the landscape around the building. A new initiative is under way called the Sustainable Sites Initiative, which is anticipated to be incorporated into the USGBC rating system as early as 2013.

Sustainable Sites Initiative

The Sustainable Sites Initiative (SITES) is a partnership of the American Society of Landscape Architects, the Lady Bird Johnson Wildflower Center, and the United States Botanic Garden in conjunction with other stakeholder organizations to establish and encourage sustainable practices in landscape design, construction, operation, and maintenance. The guidelines and performance benchmarks developed by this partnership were released in 2009 and are available at www.sustainablesites.org. The SITES guidelines were modeled after LEED and developed to eventually be adopted by the USGBC as part of a future certification process to include a building's exterior landscape. The program is presently in the pilot stage. More than 150 different organizations are participating in the two-year pilot project, which runs from 2010 to 2012.

SITES refers to the term "ecosystem services," which describes the goods and services provided by healthy landscapes and ecosystems. The SITES initiative considers the importance of protecting the natural environment, including flood protection by wetlands or filtration of air and water by vegetation and soils. SITES describes the ecosystem services as providing benefits to humankind and to the ecosystem as a whole that are not typically reflected in our current economic accounting.

While the LEED standards award points for somewhat isolated values, such as reducing irrigation water use, SITES considers the ecosystem as a whole. For example, SITES credits various aspects of soil preservation, soil quality, and soil use, which have a direct and fundamental impact on water use and plant health.

The SITES rating system, which can be viewed at www.sustainablesites.org, outlines the credits and points obtained by reaching the performance benchmarks.

Zero Waste—or Darn Close!

According to the Zero Waste International Alliance, "Zero Waste is a goal to guide people in changing their lifestyles and practices to emulate sustainable natural cycles, where all discarded materials are designed to become resources for others to use.

"Zero Waste means designing and managing products and processes to systematically avoid and eliminate the volume and toxicity of waste and materials, conserve and recover all resources, and not burn or bury them.

Photo by Marc Fournier

UMass Amherst Compost Area

"Implementing Zero Waste" will eliminate all discharges to land, water, or air that are threats to planetary, human, animal, or plant health."

Businesses and communities that achieve over 90 percent diversion of waste from landfills and incinerators are considered to be successful in achieving Zero Waste.

Business Principles

The Planning Group of the Zero Waste International Alliance adopted the following principles on April 5, 2005, to guide and evaluate current and future Zero Waste policies and programs established by businesses. These Zero Waste Business Principles will be the basis for evaluating the commitment of companies to achieve Zero Waste. These ten principles will also enable workers, investors, customers, suppliers, policymakers, and the public to better evaluate the resource efficiency of companies.

1. **Commitment to the triple bottom line** – We ensure that social, environmental, and economic performance standards are met together. We maintain clear accounting and reporting systems and operate with the highest ethical standards for our investors and our customers. We produce annual environmental or sustainability reports that document how we implement these policies.

2. **Use Precautionary Principle** – We apply the precautionary principle before introducing new products and processes, to avoid products and practices that are wasteful or toxic.
3. **Zero Waste to landfill or incineration** – We divert more than 90 percent of the solid wastes we generate from Landfill from all of our facilities. No more than 10 percent of our discards are landfilled. No solid wastes are processed in high temperature facilities to recover energy or materials.
4. **Responsibility: Take back products and packaging** – We take financial and/or physical responsibility for all the products and packaging we produce and/or market under our brand(s), and require our suppliers to do so as well. We support and work with existing reuse, recycling and composting operators to productively use our products and packaging, or arrange for new systems to bring those back to our manufacturing facilities. We include the reuse, repairability, sustainable recycling, or composting of our products as a design criteria for all new products.
5. **Buy reused, recycled & composted** – We use recycled content and compost products in all aspects of our operations, including production facilities, offices, and in the construction of new facilities. We buy reused products where they are available, and make our excess inventory of equipment and products available for reuse by others. We label our products and packaging with the amount of post-consumer recycled content and for papers, we label if chlorine-free and forest-friendly materials are used. Labels are printed with non-toxic inks – no heavy metals are used.
6. **Prevent pollution and reduce waste** – We redesign our supply, production and distribution systems to reduce the use of natural resources and eliminate waste. We prevent pollution and the waste of materials by continual assessment of our systems and revising procedures, policies, and payment policies.
7. **Highest and best use** – We continuously evaluate our markets and direct our discarded products and packaging to recover the highest value according to a defined hierarchy.
8. **Economic incentives for customers, workers, and suppliers** – We encourage our customers, workers, and suppliers to eliminate waste and maximize the reuse, recycling, and composting of discarded materials through economic incentives and a holistic systems analysis. We lease our products to customers and provide

bonuses or other rewards to workers, suppliers, and other stakeholders that eliminate waste. We use financial incentives to encourage our suppliers to adhere to Zero Waste principles.

9. **Products or services sold are not wasteful or toxic** – We evaluate our products and services regularly to determine if they are wasteful or toxic and develop alternatives to eliminate those products which we find are wasteful or toxic. We design products to be easily disassembled to encourage reuse and repair. We design our products to be durable, to last as long as the technology is in practice.
10. **Use non-toxic production, reuse, and recycling processes** – We eliminate the use of hazardous materials in our production, reuse, and recycling processes, particularly persistent bio-accumulative toxics. We eliminate the environmental, health, and safety risks to our employees and the communities in which we operate.

Excerpted from the Zero Waste Definition and Zero Waste Business Principles, www.zwia.org. For examples of businesses that have succeeded in diverting more than 90 percent of their waste from landfills and incinerators, go to www.earthresource.org or www.grrn.org

Zero Waste in Grounds Operations

The following are examples of initiatives in grounds operations that foster Zero Waste:

- Composting leaf, yard, food, and other organic wastes and reusing the compost in the campus landscape. This practice reduces materials sent to landfills or incinerators and reduces the need for fertilizers that are toxic and can contaminate groundwater supplies.
- Purchasing any supplies in bulk, thereby reducing the need for packaging and the volume of waste sent for disposal.
- Practicing integrated pest management (IPM) to reduce the need for toxic pesticides.
- Working with suppliers to require them to take back and reuse pallets or bulk containers used for deliveries.

Photo by Marc Fournier

UMass Amherst Mount Trashmore

- Installing outdoor recycling/trash clusters to recycle paper, cardboard, bottles, and cans, thereby saving valuable natural resources and reducing the volume of trash sent to incinerators and landfills.
- Procuring outdoor site furnishings such as picnic tables, park benches, planters, and recycling containers made with recycled plastic and steel to extend the life of these products and reduce the maintenance needs. These furnishings can also be recycled at the end of their useful life and made into new products.

Zero Waste is a laudable stretch goal. Meeting with your staff to develop zero waste strategies can be both productive and enlightening. You'll find waste and toxics reduction opportunities in places you never thought of before!

Environmental Regulations

It is difficult to say for sure what new regulations will be defining our operations in the future, but it is safe to say that new restrictions on water, pesticides, fertilizers, and petroleum fuels are very possible. When this manual was first published in 2001, climate change, carbon neutrality, zero waste, and sustainability were barely a whisper. But now they are frontline issues directing our operations. The Clean Air Act, the Clean Water Act, the Federal Insecticide, Fungicide, and Rodenticide Act (FIFRA), Resource Conservation and Recovery Act (RCRA), and the Occupational Safety and Health Administration (OSHA) have all influenced our industry for the past 30 to 40

Photo by Marc Fournier

Lasell College Outdoor Recycling Container

years. These acts are continually amended with additional restrictions or guidelines. Listed below are a few examples of recent changes that can affect our operations.

We are all regulated by the National Pollutant Discharge Elimination System (NPDES) administered by the Environmental Protection Agency (EPA) for stormwater management. That program is currently undergoing Proposed National Rulemaking to strengthen the stormwater program, so additional requirements are quite possible.

States are regulated by the Clean Air Act and the National Ambient Air Quality Standards (NAAQS), also administered by the EPA. Federal funds for highway construction and other federal programs are tied to meeting these standards, and states are penalized when they fail to meet them. Increased population in areas subject to stagnant air inversions have led to restricting landscape equipment use during poor air quality days in some states and cities. In 2007, the governor of Arizona banned the use of handheld blowers on state property in the largest counties because of failing air quality.

The states around the Great Lakes and other areas have a number of local bans on fertilizers with phosphorus used for lawn care to reduce algae growth caused by runoff. Michigan has banned the use of fertilizers with phosphorus for residential or commercial lawns after January 2, 2012. Many states have specific stormwater management regulations regarding water quantity retention or quality improvement standards, which are creating new management areas such as bio-retention cells or rain gardens.

As stewards of the landscapes under our care, it is important that we maintain them in a responsible and sustainable way. We need to be aware of potential environmental issues in our areas, including future water shortages, air quality, noise, and light concerns. We must plan ahead for possible water restrictions, including water rationing or use of reclaimed water, when designing new landscapes. We need to consider purchasing new equipment that is quieter, more efficient, uses less fuel, emits fewer pollutants, and uses alternative fuels. We must also keep in close contact with the agency administering FIFRA in our states to make sure we are not depending on products containing chemicals that are banned or being phased out.

And we must endeavor to avoid the use of harmful chemicals in the first place by employing strategies like IPM that manage ornamental plants in landscapes in ways that reduce the potential for pest and disease problems by following a sequence of steps designed to minimize impacts on the environment.

It will be a lot easier to follow new guidelines if you have planned for them in advance and set yourself on a path ahead of the curve.

A wide range of information is available from local, state, regional, and federal agencies, including EPA regional offices. Visit their websites or contact their staffs for innovative ways to make your grounds operations more sustainable!

Photo by Marc Fournier

UMass Amherst Oak Tree Move

Turf in a Sustainable Landscape

Of all the plants in the landscape, turf is the most maligned. It is often used as the example of a water-wasting landscape and one that uses excessive amounts of fertilizer and pesticides. Turf can be an integral part of a sustainable, drought-tolerant, or water-wise landscape if it is designed for a specific use such as athletics, public events, or informal gathering, not just as a filler. Turf also helps reduce heat islands, absorbs carbon dioxide, and sequesters carbon in the soil. In fact, a recent long-term study by researchers at Colorado State University proved that turf grass lawns sequester an additional .44 tons of carbon in the soil every year. Along with good design, proper installation and sustainable maintenance practices are required to make turf part of a sustainable, water-wise landscape.

Design

During the design phase, turf should be used if it adds real value to the landscape and serves a physical need for activities. Areas should be large and designed for efficient irrigation and mowing. Small, narrow, or winding areas of turf are difficult to irrigate without overspraying. Simple shapes are also more efficient to mow and may require less additional trim mowing or string trimming. Site furnishings such as benches or light poles should be on pads to facilitate mowing and avoid string trimming. In some regions it may be best to keep trees out of turf because of their different irrigation

Photo by Marc Fournier

Lasell College East/West Quad Turf

requirements. Mulch or plant ground cover around trees helps reduce weeds and eliminate damage to the trees from mowing and trimming equipment. Slopes should be planted with shrubs or ground cover rather than turf for ease of maintenance, employee safety, and probable water savings.

The design phase is the time to include requirements for topsoil depth, subsoil scarification, irrigation standards, and any concerns about drainage so these specifications are included in the project bid package. This is also the time you may have to justify the additional cost for your requirements and show how they will reduce the long-term maintenance and water costs.

Installation

The quality and depth of topsoil is the most critical factor in creating sustainable landscapes and can only be ensured during installation. Far too often, topsoil is of poor quality and its depth is reduced to cut costs. Six inches or less of topsoil over compacted subsoil is one of the reasons grass grows poorly and requires frequent irrigation and fertilization. Frequent irrigation is what gives turf its bad name. Healthy turf, when given the opportunity, can have deep roots of two feet or more. When it does, it requires less frequent irrigation, is better able to withstand dry periods, and is able to recover quickly after heavy use.

For these reasons it is imperative during construction that the subsoil be well scarified to allow water, air, and root penetration. Install at least 12 inches of high-quality topsoil mixed with compost to provide adequate organic matter. This will allow the soil to have a good mix of air, water, and mineral/organic matter for healthy root growth. Soil should be tested during installation for type and fertility so the proper additives can be incorporated from the onset.

This will also give the maintenance manager a known baseline from which to work. If the turf will be used for athletic events, the composition will need to be different from a lawn that is used for occasional events or light activity. Athletic turf will need to drain quickly after heavy rains to avoid event cancellations, keep the playing surface safe, and regenerate quickly after events to maintain quality for safe play.

The need for adequate topsoil and soil preparation during installations cannot be overstressed. Far too often we spend millions of dollars designing and constructing green buildings, but cut the soil and landscape budget because of cost pressures. The result is a green building loaded with the latest innovations and an unsustainable landscape that does not meet green expectations.

Maintenance

Horticulturally sound maintenance practices are also keys to water-efficient turf. Mow at the highest setting acceptable, as more top growth promotes deeper root growth. Many lawns are cut too short, resulting in stress and water loss. Mow as high as the turf species will allow. The clippings are not visible if the grass is not allowed to get too long between cuttings. Also mow with a mulching deck to leave the clippings on the lawn. Clippings left on the turf quickly break down and reduce the amount of fertilizer needed. Leaves can also be mulched with the mowers and left on the lawn. Light to moderate leaf cover completely disappears after mowing. Regular aerating keeps the soil from becoming compacted in areas that are heavily used. Top dress lawn areas with fine compost after aerating to add organic matter to the soil profile, improving soil fertility and tilth.

Grounds managers should test the soil annually to analyze nutrient levels and compare with established baselines. The goal is to have the right amount of nutrients available for the plants when needed, and not too much so that the nutrients run off or leach through the soil, contaminating surface and ground waters with nitrates or other chemicals. Excessive amounts of nitrogen lead to rapid growth, which then requires more frequent mowing. Organic fertilizers such as compost, dried blood, and bone meal tend to have lower percentages of nutrients, but they bind well in the soil and are not lost as easily to leaching or runoff. They supply a steady, balanced supply of nutrients for the grass to remain healthy but not grow in excessive spurts. The downside is that they are often more expensive and may require more labor to apply.

If your facility is large enough, you can produce your own compost on site. If not, compost may be available from a nearby municipality or commercial producer. It is worth investigating to see if the green waste produced from your facility can be hauled to a local compost producer to be used in making the compost and then purchased for a reduced price. Other organic "waste" products may be available locally that can be incorporated into your turf fertilization plan. Compost, manures, or other additives

Photo by Ellen Newell

Arizona State University Compost Spreader

should all be tested for nutrient and salt analysis, just as commercial fertilizers are tested.

Healthy, dense turf is less susceptible to weeds and disease, requiring fewer applications of herbicides or fungicides. Grounds managers may be able to change long-held negative perceptions about weeds in turf and point out that a few weeds are a good thing because chemicals are not used. Filling in worn areas with sod or overseeding lawns regularly to keep turf dense will go a long way in preventing weeds from getting established.

Overseeding warm season grasses with annual rye in the fall for year-round green lawns is a common practice in the southern regions of the country. This practice may require additional water, especially during the germination phase (depending on region). Warm season grasses such as Bermuda or St. Augustine are grown from spring warm up until fall cool down, with annual rye overseeded for green grass during the colder months. A lot of water and maintenance energy can be saved if the warm season grass is allowed to naturally go dormant in the fall and then green up in the spring. If you are working with a water budget or attempting to be as sustainable as possible, eliminating overseeding can save water, energy from mowing, and dollars spent for seed and labor. This may not be possible with athletic facilities, because healthy growing turf is necessary to keep playing surfaces consistent and safe for players.

Renovations

There are times when turf does earn its reputation for wasteful water use. Removing turf from existing landscapes where it does not fill a real need and was used as a filler is one way to reduce water and maintenance needs. Turf should be analyzed as an option during remodeling or renovation projects. If there is enough time and the area is small enough, the unwanted turf in the area to be redesigned can be covered with plastic or a thick layer of mulch to kill the grass rather than using an herbicide. Also, good-quality turf can be removed with a sod cutter and used to repair damaged or worn areas elsewhere on the site. The new landscape can have a weed mat specified to inhibit any grass growth. If the sod was removed during the redesign, specify new topsoil with organic matter to replace the soil removed with the sod. If mature trees are growing within the turf, it might actually be more sustainable to keep the turf and cover it with mulch to avoid damaging or compromising the trees' roots. Each situation needs to be evaluated, taking into consideration the health and age of the trees versus the amount of water that needs to be conserved on the site.

Water Management in Sustainable Landscapes

Limiting outdoor water use in the landscape is one of the priorities for sustainable landscapes. The western desert regions have been consciously conserving water for years. But with increased population growth, recent droughts, and climate change ramifications, other regions with plenty of water historically are now looking at cutting back on outdoor water use. The Southeast and Mid-Atlantic states have recently experienced dry years with significant droughts. During these times, outdoor watering was often restricted or banned outright. Drought-stressed landscapes are obviously not very attractive and can represent a significant loss in plant life and monetary loss to the landscaping industry while irrigating is restricted. Planning for less traditionally available water in the future while keeping valuable landscapes viable is a challenging but important goal for today's landscape professionals. A number of housing and commercial developments in the West are already operating with water budgets when they use potable water for irrigation. We will see a considerable increase in operations with water budgets in the future, whether due to external restrictions or increased water costs. All new landscape designs need to be planned and installed using xeriscape principles or based on natural precipitation amounts.

When faced with a formal water budget or simply the need to reduce water use, two strategies should be adopted. The first is to make sure the existing irrigation system has been properly designed and installed, and then operated and maintained as efficiently as possible. The second is to look for alternate sources of water.

Irrigation Systems

Grounds managers should examine their entire irrigation system, including the points of connection, pumps, controllers, main and lateral lines, heads, and emitters. Upgrades should be made to antiquated systems to increase irrigation efficiency. Water audits should be taken around the site for baseline information. A simple test to perform is the distribution uniformity audit, which measures how evenly the water is delivered to the area by the irrigation system. To do the audit, a series of uniform catch cans are placed around the site at varying distances from the spray heads. The system is then run for a set time, and the water is measured in each can. Excellent results from a well-designed and -operating system are 80 percent efficiency for rotors and 75 percent efficiency for pop-ups. Those systems with the poorest distribution uniformity audit results should be upgraded first.

Replace controllers with the newest models, which allow for multiple programming and the ability to run cycle and soak programs for slopes, clay soils, or newly seeded areas. A number of centralized control systems use evapotranspiration data to run the site's controllers. Some require simple soil probes (soil moisture tensiometers), while others use an onsite weather station or regional weather information. Shortening the water window, maximizing flow rates, and reducing pump run times are all possible with centralized controllers. Another labor-saving advantage is rain shutoff, which shuts down all controllers during rain events. This system helps conserve water and prevent the negative impression when the public sees irrigation systems running during a storm. These systems can be expensive to install and require varying amounts of training to operate, but when used properly, they can save large amounts of water, labor, and dollars over the long term.

Irrigation mainlines and laterals should all be buried deep enough to avoid freeze breaks or mechanical damage from aerating. Install matched precipitation heads and pressure reducers if needed to meet optimum operating pressure for the chosen heads. Install drip systems where appropriate. Zones should be designed to contain plants with like water needs and uniform sun exposures. The tendency is to design the longest run the flow will allow to save money and get away with a smaller controller. It is better in the long run to have more valves and controllers with additional stations to allow for landscape changes in the future and to ensure that each zone has a uniform water requirement.

For example, a zone that wraps around a building, resulting in southern and eastern exposures, does not have a uniform water requirement. The proper spray head or emitter should be chosen for each site depending on plant type, wind exposure, slope, and so on. They should also be sited to avoid spraying windows, sidewalks, or other nonplant areas, saving water and unnecessary maintenance labor costs. The irrigation industry has done a good job developing new heads that are efficient and have uniform distribution patterns. Install drip or low-volume emitter systems in planting beds whenever possible. With a little research, a grounds manager should be able to find an appropriate product for each site. Staff should be trained on the importance of regular cleaning of filters and flush-outs on low-volume systems.

Irrigation System Maintenance

The best-designed and -installed system is useless if it is not properly and regularly maintained. Irrigation systems need to be checked at least weekly. Respond immediately to reports of broken heads, leaking or stuck valves, or heads out of adjustment. During weekly maintenance checks, manually run systems to check for heads needing adjustments and leaks. Watch to see if there is any runoff or puddling, which indicates that the time should be reduced or set to multiple run times, such as a cycle and soak program. This type of program may also be needed on slopes or areas with low-percolation soils. During maintenance checks, look at the plants in each area to see how they are responding to the amount of water they are receiving. It is important to train the irrigation technicians to look at both the mechanics of the system and plants' responses. Controllers need to be checked weekly to make sure power is still on and programs have not gone to a default mode. Staff will have to modify schedules as seasons, weather conditions, and plant growth change.

Alternate Sources for Irrigation Water

The second strategy is to look for alternative sources of water. The obvious first choice is to look at harvesting rain that falls on roofs, roads, and parking lots, as well as other hardscapes. Stormwater management is now the norm for all new construction and mandated in most instances by the National Pollutant Discharge Elimination System program, so it makes sense to harvest this water for use on the landscape. An inch of rain that falls on a 1,000-square-foot roof equals 623 gallons of water, making harvesting well worth the effort. This can be done by physically collecting water in barrels on a small scale, or piping systems to underground storage tanks or retention ponds. Large sites may want to collect the storm runoff into ponds to be pumped for irrigation when needed. These ponds can also be significant landscape features, adding beauty, habitat, and recreational opportunities.

Depending on the collection system, the water can be used via gravity flow or pumped to where it is needed when irrigation is resumed. The choice of barrels, underground cisterns, or an aboveground holding pond depends on the size of the site, the amount of rainfall per year, and when it rains in relationship to when irrigation is needed. Water can also be directed as it runs off roofs or hardscapes into bio-swales and water gardens using curb cuts for surface flow or underground piping. The design should slow the flow of water and allow it to soak into the landscape, bioretention basins, or rain gardens, rather than rushed into storm drains, creeks, ditches, or dry wells. This strategy also helps keep pollutants from reaching ground and surface waters.

Permeable pavements and hardscapes can also be used to capture rainfall for use in the landscape and avoid runoff as part of stormwater management. Plants and especially trees next to a permeable pavement can benefit from having access to additional soil mass containing water and air. Structural soils and commercially available supports such as Silva Cell or Grass Pave can be used to help stabilize the area around the trees and allow traffic while also keeping water and air available to the plants.

Municipal reclaimed water or greywater from a single site can also be used as alternate sources of irrigation water. Greywater from a single building could include water from sinks, showers, and water fountains that is then piped to a holding tank for treatment and then to the landscape for irrigation. Irrigation systems using grey or reclaimed water should be posted and use purple irrigation markers so the public is aware that the water is not approved for drinking. The quality of reclaimed water varies widely, but it often comes with additional salts. Reclaimed water should be tested regularly so the groundskeepers know what they are using and are able to change their practices accordingly. In some cases plantings may need to be replaced with more salt-tolerant species. Reclaimed water may be less expensive to purchase but may cost more to use due to the filtering and treatment requirements. As fresh water becomes scarcer in certain areas, reclaimed water or stormwater may be the only logical irrigation option.

Plants in a Sustainable Landscape

The careful selection of plant material is critical to the success of a sustainable landscape project. When selecting your plant material, it is important to identify the primary use of the area involved and how much or how little maintenance you plan to provide in the upkeep of the landscape. Selecting the right plant for the site conditions will determine the success of your project. The following factors should be taken into consideration:

- **Area use:** Determine how the area will be used—for example, foot traffic, outdoor eating, recreation, screening or physical barrier.
- **Water requirements:** Plant water requirements must be understood and questions such as the following answered: Will the area be irrigated? What are the drainage and runoff issues? Will there be limitations on supplemental watering? Are there opportunities for rain gardens?
- **Sunlight:** Select plants that meet the specific site sunlight conditions in the spot they will be planted. In an urban environment, 10 feet may be the difference between full sun and full shade.
- **Soil conditions:** The existing soil conditions must be determined by soil testing or a thorough analysis and matched to the specific needs of the plant species. More plants fail because of this issue than any other.
- **Native vs. non-native:** Opinions of using only native plants in the landscape vary widely. Some institutions or individuals insist that since a plant is listed as a native to a particular locale, it must be better adapted than a non-native. However,

scientific evidence proves this is not true, especially since so many of our planting sites are in urban environments, which have disturbed soils and are subject to pressure from auto exhaust, compaction, new pests, and human disturbance. Native or not, be sure any plant is suited to its environment.

- **Arboretums and botanical gardens:** Consider whether the plant will be used as a display, for research or educational opportunities, or to enhance a collection.
- **Sustainable maintenance:** Consider how much pruning will be required and how much tree mess (fruit, leaves, twigs) will need to be collected. Using low-maintenance plants saves time and money and reduces emissions.
- **Safety concerns:** Select plants that will not interfere with signage or lighting or limit visibility.
- **Aesthetic benefits:** Finally, select plants that will support your design goals: accent architecture, create human scale, identify spaces, create views and vistas, provide screening, or the form, color, and texture needed for the design intent.

Grounds managers also need to consider the above when replacing trees in the landscape. Many a good design or usable space has been ruined because of a well-intentioned but poorly selected and placed tree.

Tips for success:

- Use a diverse selection of plant material to minimize your losses in case an insect or disease problem develops.
- Group plant types that have similar culture requirements.
- Consider space, time, and financial factors.
- Do not use invasive plant species (lists for your region can be found through state extension services).
- Remember, Mother Nature will win in the end, so selecting plants that will grow in your existing conditions is a far better choice than trying to modify your conditions to accommodate your plants.

Photo by Marc Fournier

UMass Amherst Planter

Sustainable Outdoor Site Furnishings

A vast quantity of natural resources are consumed in the manufacture of the park benches, picnic tables, planters, cigarette butt containers, recycling bins, trash containers, and other outdoor site furnishings. There are two major ways to reduce the amount of the resources used in these products and the associated greenhouse gas impacts of these purchases.

Products Containing Postconsumer Recycled Materials

There are two major types of recycled materials—preconsumer and postconsumer. Preconsumer recycled materials are generated in manufacturing facilities as scrap and are often reused because they are high value, uniform, located onsite, and meet predetermined specifications. Postconsumer recycled materials are those that are used by society recycled. Some prime examples include newspaper, office paper, cardboard boxes, aluminum cans, steel cans, plastic tubs, and plastic bottles. It is important to reuse these postconsumer recycled materials in order to conserve the imbedded energy originally used to manufacture them. Also, using postconsumer recycled materials to make new products conserves energy, water, and virgin materials. And finally, it significantly reduces the generation of greenhouse gases created in the manufacture of new products made with virgin materials.

Issues with the structural design of some early products have been solved. Many now perform well, are aesthetically pleasing, and reduce maintenance costs thanks to their ability to withstand the effects of the outdoor climate. Although they are sometimes more expensive from an initial cost perspective, they are cost-competitive from a life-cycle cost perspective.

A wide range of outdoor site furnishings made with postconsumer recycled materials, especially plastics, is now available in the marketplace. Anything from outdoor park benches to accessible picnic tables to recycling/trash clusters is being offered. Companies selling these products include Max-R (www.max-r.net), Midpoint International, Inc. (www.midpoint-int.com), and Conversion Products, Inc. (www.conversionproducts.com).

When purchasing these products, be sure to ask the manufacturers about the percentage of postconsumer and preconsumer recycled materials in the product, and search for the highest postconsumer recycled content you can find in a product that is aesthetically pleasing and performs well.

Repurposing

We can give old fence posts, lumber, and other materials a second life by repurposing all or parts of them into planters, edging timbers, and other innovative enhancements to our landscapes. This strategy makes further use of the embedded energy used to make the original products, and also reduces the need for virgin materials, energy, and water (and the resulting greenhouse gas generation) needed to manufacture new products.

Green Roofs

The installation of green roofs is rapidly gaining popularity on college and school campuses for a variety of reasons. In the urban environment, the value of a green roof in capturing and reducing stormwater runoff is increasingly more important, as stormwater runoff carries contaminants into our valuable waterways. A green roof installation can also reduce the heat island effect in the urban environment. In addition, green roofs can provide thermal resistance of the roof, possibly saving costs in cooling the building in the summer months. Green roofs do not always have to be on top of a building; they can be installed over underground portions of a building or underground parking garages. Depending on the design of the building, a green roof installation can be turned into an amenity and increase your usable space by creating accessible rooftop gardens, which might include seating areas or even space to plant herb gardens, edible crops, or native plant species.

When deciding if a green roof will work in your situation, there are many factors to consider, including weight-bearing capacity of roof system, waterproofing and drainage, slope, maintenance, utilities, fire prevention, safety concerns, accessibility, wind, sunlight, climate, growing medium, plants, and use of the space.

It is essential to take into consideration the weight-bearing capacity of the roof. This must be determined by a structural engineer. Whether you are retrofitting an existing building or designing a new building, the load-bearing capacity of the roof structure is critical. In addition, waterproofing and drainage systems must be designed correctly. You must consider the safety aspects of a green roof during all phases of the project, including construction and installation of soil and plants, as well as the safety of the staff maintaining the green roof and adjacent utilities after the green roof is in place. If the roof is designed to be an accessible and usable space, safety railings, walls, or other means must be installed to ensure the safety of users.

There are two basic types of green roof systems—extensive and intensive. Some roofs are designed to be a combination of the two.

An extensive green roof is designed to be lightweight, low maintenance, and require no or very little irrigation. Extensive green roofs are the most common types used on existing buildings, as they can be successful with as little as 3 to 4 inches of growing media. The growing media is specially designed for roof top plantings and can be custom blended for your specific plant needs and climate. For this type of roof, the typical plant choices usually include a variety of sedum species, which are ideally suited to these growing conditions. Sedums species have varied foliage colors and flowers, so interesting tapestry-like designs can make them an attractive choice. Some other plant species may be suitable for this use; consult local growers to determine what works best in your climate.

There are two basic construction methods in extensive green roof construction. The first places the soil mix directly on the waterproof membrane and drainage layers, then plants are planted on the site. The second is the tray system, whereby trays holding the soil media and with fully grown plants are placed on a protection layer over the waterproof membrane. The tray system has the advantage of having established plants at completion of construction and allowing easy access to the sub-roof layer if necessary by removing the trays, as in the event of a roof leak repair.

An intensive green roof system can hold the weight of deeper soil media, which can greatly increase your plant palate and usability of the space. An intensive green roof can include trees, shrubs, perennial plants, and the opportunity to create a real site amenity. The plants you choose will be determined by your climate as well as how much maintenance you want to invest in the care of the plantings. In some cases it is possible to install an intensive green roof on an existing building, but more commonly this style of roof is included in the design of a new building.

There are a number of incentives for green roof installations. Many governments, municipalities, and nonprofit organizations are providing incentives that can help offset the cost of installation. For example, in Washington, D.C., a nonprofit called

DC Greenworks (www.dcgreenworks.org) facilitates the installation of green roofs, assists with obtaining funding support for the project, and even coordinates community and student volunteers to participate in the installation. If you are seeking LEED certification for a building, adding a green roof will enable you to obtain additional credits. Adding a green roof to your building is another way to demonstrate your institution's commitment to environmental sustainability.

Snow and Ice Removal — Sustainable Strategies

Every year, amazing amounts of fuel, lubricants, sand, salt, ice melt, plow blades, and other materials are consumed in snow and ice removal operations, polluting our air and groundwater and damaging our trees and landscape. Some of the negative environmental impacts of these operations are unavoidable because we have to ensure the safety of students, faculty, staff, or customers. But there are many ways to reduce and mitigate the impacts. Below are some tips on making snow and ice removal operations more sustainable.

Green Technology, Fuels, and Lubricants in Snow and Ice Removal

Most of the vehicles and equipment used to remove snow and ice run on gasoline and diesel. There are now a wide range of vehicles and equipment that run on alternative fuels, produce lower emissions, and are more fuel efficient. There are also vegetable-

Photo by Spring Valley Landscape

Magic Minus Zero Spreader

based and recycled lubricants available, as well as other options, and are described in detail in Chapter 2: Green Fuels, Vehicles, and Equipment.

Environmentally Friendly Deicers

Over the past decade or so, a number of environmentally friendly deicers containing proprietary ingredients have been introduced. One example that has been used successfully is called Magic Minus Zero, a proprietary liquid formula of magnesium chloride combined with an agricultural by-product of the distilling process called Ice B' Gone. In 2008, Magic Minus Zero earned the "Designed for the Environment" recognition from the EPA.

With a simple motorized pump and tank system, the deicers are easily applied to bulk rock salt at a rate of approximately 8 gallons per ton to transform this corrosive, potentially destructive, and inefficient material into a highly effective ice-melting product, which is 90 percent less corrosive, safe for concrete, brick, and pets, and environmentally friendly.

In addition to being used to pretreat rock salt, liquid deicers can be applied directly to paved surfaces before a storm to prevent ice and snow from bonding to pavement surfaces and prevent black ice. Many have a working temperature down to –35°F, while regular rock salt is only effective down to 18°F. This is a net 53° gain in working temperature, which is similar to calcium chloride without the adverse corrosive effects.

Unlike plain rock salt or calcium chloride, which are corrosive, environmentally friendly deicers neutralize the corrosive nature of rock salt. They reduce damage to spreaders and other grounds equipment, steel doors, thresholds, carpets, flooring, and concrete.

Using environmentally friendly deicers save saves money, time, and labor. Rock salt applications are reduced by 30 to 50 percent. The need for road sand on pavement is virtually eliminated, saving countless hours of labor and equipment time removing sand from pavement, turf, mulched planting beds, and buildings. The Amherst College Grounds Department reported its outdoor spring cleanup of sand was reduced from three weeks to one and a half days.

Environmentally Friendly Ice Melts

Numerous types of ice melt products combine more environmentally friendly, less corrosive salts like magnesium chloride with environmentally friendly agents like Ice B' Gone. These agents increase the melting effect of the salt, lower its effective operating temperature, and reduce equipment, turf, and concrete damage.

One example is Magic Salt, which contains Ice B' Gone and magnesium chloride. Another example is Greenscapes, which contains Ice Ban 200, magnesium chloride, and a water-soluble green coloring that enables staff to see where they have treated and avoid overtreatment, thereby reducing the amount of ice melt used and reducing costs.

Special thanks to:

John Hancock, Spring Valley Landscape, Inc., Hatfield, MA

Pam Monn & Jen Konieczny, Grounds Management Department, University of Massachusetts, Amherst, MA

Bob Shea, Amherst College Grounds Department, Amherst, MA

Hap Eaton, Highway Department, Deerfield MA

Photo by Marc Fournier

UMass Amherst Oak Tree Move

Photo by Marc Fournier

UMass Amherst Three Bench Planter

Teamwork and Sustainability: A Personal Perspective

By R. Marc Fournier

When I went back to college to obtain my MBA in the mid-1990s, my two concentrations were environmental management and organizational behavior. The education I received in these two areas helped me to build an extremely successful, empowered, team-based Grounds Management Department at UMass Amherst. Staff, students, and faculty learned how to work together, share ideas, and craft innovative solutions to complex problems. We developed solutions together that we would never have been able to create alone.

I remember one day when we were trying to design a pondside seating area. We had been struggling with the design for weeks. One day I brought an eclectic group of staff from the Landscape Services and Construction Services areas together at the site. We were trying to create a seating area with new recycled lumber benches and a planter that would take advantage of the views of the pond, campus buildings, and landscape. We had been focused on a linear approach that would use benches and a rectangular planter to face in one direction or another. During our onsite brainstorming session, one of the team members said "Hey, why don't we build a triangular planter and have three benches face outward from the planter on all sides to highlight all three views?" It was truly one of those "ah-ha!" moments, and a solution I believe we would never have reached had we not created these nonhierarchical, empowered teams. I'll never forget those days. They were the best of my career.

I realize now, years later, that sustainability and teamwork, today's version of what we were doing many years ago, are natural partners. They work well together and complement each other. They are both organic, both based on systems thinking, and both look at a view of the whole.

We need all the creative ideas and energy we can get from our staffs to solve the critical and complex problems caused by climate change now and in the future. I believe team-based management is one critical component of the solution.

I urge you to study the works of Peter Drucker, Tom Peters, Rosabeth Moss Kanter, Tom Kelley, Dan Goleman, Peter Senge, and many others to learn how to tap the wealth of knowledge and enthusiasm of your staff and make sustainability the true mantra of your grounds operations!

CHAPTER 2

Green Fuels, Vehicles, and Equipment

By R. Marc Fournier

Editor's Note: This chapter discusses various options about green technologies and their applications to campus grounds and landscaping. The environmental technologies included are used as examples and illustrations of the applicability of such items in the effective management of grounds operations. It is recognized that there may be alternative technologies available, however, the authors utilized these technologies to support the need for and potential application of environmentally friendly technologies in the grounds setting. Neither the authors nor APPA imply any endorsement of the technologies or equipment discussed, and such discussions are for illustrative and informational purposes only.

Consumer demand for more environmentally friendly grounds equipment is nearly nonexistent. Until now, grounds professionals have focused our environmental efforts mainly on management strategies including reducing pesticide use, IPM, xeriscaping, composting, and organic fertilizer sources, among others.

We must now expand our vision to include how we can reduce the environmental impacts of the equipment we use in our grounds operations. Only a few enlightened educational institutions, municipalities, government agencies, and companies are demanding and purchasing "green" grounds equipment, vehicles, biofuels, and biobased lubricants. Equipment manufacturers and distributors say the present and future regulations, not consumer demand, are driving these changes.

Why no demand? Perhaps environmental protection is not instilled in our culture. Maybe it's the initial higher cost of new "green" technology, the lack of adequate government regulations and incentives, or the lack of a carbon tax to account for the

Photo by Marc Fournier

UMass Amherst Biodiesel Dump Truck

true cost of our operations. Perhaps we still believe that all of our mowers, string trimmers, chain saws, leaf blowers, tractors, backhoes, dump trucks, wood chippers, gasoline, diesel, and lubricants don't make a difference in the big picture.

Yet, in urban areas, this equipment accounts for an appreciable portion of man-made hydrocarbons, which have been proven to cause asthma and other pollution-related health issues. Looking at the big picture, our grounds equipment and vehicles do contribute significantly to climate change. As educational institutions, we must continue to be leaders in developing and testing new technologies that will become the tools of the future that enable us to mitigate our effects on climate change. And it is our duty and responsibility to present and future generations, especially as environmental professionals, to do our part in making incremental positive change wherever we can to reduce environmental impacts large and small.

The good news is, due to existing and future environmental regulations focused on reducing emissions and fuel use, manufacturers have been developing innovative technologies and products that will be useful in grounds operations. This chapter will spotlight technology advances and regulations in three major areas:

- Alternative fuels and biobased lubricants
- Grounds vehicles
- Grounds equipment

Alternative Fuels and Biobased Lubricants

Alternative Fuels: Biodiesel

Biodiesel is a renewable alternative fuel produced domestically from a wide range of vegetable oils and animal fats. It can be produced from preconsumer products (derived directly from plants) or postconsumer "waste" (like used cooking oil—yellow grease, or grease trap grease—brown grease). It is nontoxic and can reduce pollutant emissions compared with petroleum diesel. It also improves engine operation by raising diesel fuel's lubricity and combustion quality. Biodiesel blended with petroleum diesel can be used to fuel diesel vehicles without modifying the vehicles—20 percent biodiesel and 80 percent petroleum diesel (B20) is the most popular blend. B20 or other biodiesel blends are approved for use with various types of diesel-powered equipment without modification. The federal government has recently renewed incentives to make the cost of biodiesel competitive with petroleum diesel. Contact equipment manufacturers to determine if B20 or other biodiesel blends are approved for use in their diesel products.

Alternative Fuels: Compressed Natural Gas (CNG)

Virtually all natural gas consumed in the United States is produced in North America, and, compared with gasoline and diesel engines, natural gas engines can produce lower amounts of some harmful emissions and the greenhouse gas carbon dioxide. The cleaner-burning nature of natural gas may result in reduced maintenance requirements, such as less frequent oil changes and extended engine life. In addition, natural gas does not spoil or clog fuel systems in grounds equipment during seasonal storage, whereas liquid fuels can.

Natural gas must be compressed and stored at high pressure to enable adequate mowing time. This sealed and pressurized fuel-storage system has the advantage of eliminating evaporative emissions and spillage, as well as the potential fuel theft sometimes associated with liquid-fueled grounds equipment. As of August 2010, there were more than 800 CNG fueling stations in the United States, with stations in almost every state. Over the past decade, CNG has been the least expensive U.S. motor fuel.

Alternative Fuels: Propane

Also known as liquefied petroleum gas or LPG and autogas, propane is the most widely available alternative transportation fuel in the United States. As of August 2010, there were 2,503 propane vehicle fueling stations with locations in all 50 states. Most propane consumed in the United States is produced domestically, and, compared with gasoline and diesel engines, propane engines can produce lower amounts of some harmful emissions and carbon dioxide. The cleaner-burning nature of propane may result in reduced maintenance requirements, such as less frequent oil changes and extended engine life. Also, like CNG, propane does not spoil or clog fuel systems in grounds equipment during seasonal storage.

Propane is stored as a liquid under relatively low pressure and becomes a gas at normal pressure (meaning it enters the engine as a gas). The liquid storage gives it a high energy density, so equipment can run a long time on a tank of fuel, while the sealed and pressurized storage has the advantage of eliminating evaporative emissions and spillage as well as potential fuel theft.

There are two options in the propane arena. You can buy original equipment manufacturer (OEM) propane equipment or convert conventional equipment to run on propane. One company, Enviro-Gard, patented the propane technology found on OEM mowers from many manufacturers and also converts gasoline mowers (and other gasoline-powered equipment) to propane. The company's conversion kits range from 6.5 horsepower (HP) to 37 HP. Like OEM products, the conversions are certified by the EPA. Propane mower conversions cost $1,000 to $3,000, including parts and labor. For more information about Enviro-Gard, visit www.onyxsolutions.com.

To find other companies that can perform propane conversions, contact your state's Propane Gas Association or use the Propane Education & Research Council's Find a Propane Retailer tool (www.usepropane.com).

Alternative Fuels: Electricity

Electric power is quiet, requires little maintenance, and produces no tailpipe emissions. And electricity produced from renewable sources such as solar and wind further reduces the environmental impact of equipment powered by electricity. Electric mowers, string trimmers, and other grounds equipment connected to an electricity supply with a cord or powered with rechargeable batteries are popular for residential use, but the rigors of commercial grounds applications have limited their use for this application. However, recent improvements in battery technology have resulted in new products with potential commercial application. Hustler Turf's Zeon—the first all-electric, zero-turn-radius mower—provides up to 80 minutes of continuous mowing time, enough to mow more than an acre. The Ariens AMP Rider provides up to 75 minutes of continuous mowing time (U.S. Department of Energy Clean Cities Guide to Alternative Fuel Commercial Lawn Equipment, September 2010).

Biobased Lubricants

The history of biobased lubricants has been a difficult one. In 2003, biobased hydraulic oils were three times more expensive than their petroleum-based alternatives and provided one-third the service life, and no manufacturers would approve them for use in their equipment. Consumer demand was near zero.

In 2007, they were twice as expensive and provided half the service life, and manufacturers were beginning to accept them. Consumer demand was still anemic.

Today, the cost for biobased lubricants continues to decrease compared with petroleum-based counterparts, quality continues to increase, and the number of products accepted by manufacturers is increasing. Products include tractor oils (a combination of transmission and hydraulic oil used by tractors in golf course facilities), grease (used in dam, marine, and drill rod applications), and chain saw bar and chain lubricant. Visit www.bioblend.com for more information on biobased lubricant options.

Demand is still weak. The only organizations purchasing these products are forward-thinking colleges and universities, private firms such as elevator companies required to use environmentally friendly hydraulic oils, and construction companies doing work in or near environmentally sensitive areas.

Biobased Lubricants: Re-refined Motor Oil

Re-refined motor oil is enjoying a resurgence in popularity. Much of the negative press of 10 years ago has faded away. New re-refineries are being built. Younger technicians are more accepting of these re-refined products, which have been used successfully for years in Europe. And re-refined motor oil is the same price or less expensive than its virgin petroleum-based counterpart.

Used oil is collected from oil change locations across the country and goes through a rigorous quality control process prior to re-refining. Re-refining motor oil reduces the need to tap limited virgin crude resources and allows environmentally conscious organizations to "close the loop" by recycling used motor oil and purchasing re-refined oil.

One example, EcoPower (www.ecopoweroil.com), is a re-refined motor oil produced by Safety-Kleen. It is recycled and twice refined in the world's largest re-refinery, and it exceeds the highest North American standards for motor oil performance in gasoline engines. Safety-Kleen's used oil re-refining process uses up to 85 percent less energy than the process to make stocks out of crude oil. Closing the re-refining loop conserves valuable, nonrenewable resources. It reduces greenhouse gas emissions by more than 80 percent and reduces heavy metals emissions by 99.5 percent.

All major car manufacturers have approved the use of American Petroleum Institute (API) certified re-refined oil such as EcoPower in their vehicles.

Biobased Lubricants: Biobased Motor Oil

Vegetable-based motor oils have been slower to gain acceptance. Green Earth Technologies, manufacturer of environmentally friendly automotive products, produces Ultimate Biodegradable G-OIL SAE 5W-30 Bio-based Full Synthetic Motor Oil, the world's first biobased motor oil to pass the engine test criteria for API SM Certification and be granted the API "Donut" (June 2010). It is being offered by retailers in Hawaii, California, Colorado, Texas, Indiana, Arizona, and Florida. Visit www.getg.com for more information on this alternative.

Biobased Lubricants: Biobased Bar and Chain Oil

STIHL BioPlus™ bar and chain oil is made with a vegetable oil base. This means that the oil is less harmful to humans, animals, micro-organisms, and plants. The oil also offers excellent flow characteristics at low temperatures and has a high flash point. It is available in 1 quart, 1 gallon, 5 gallon, and 55 gallon containers and is rated by the Coordinating European Council to be 93.8 percent biodegradable in only 21 days.

News of Austria's ban on nonbiodegradable chainsaw lubricants spurred Husqvarna, a manufacturer of chain saws and other forest equipment based in

Charlotte, North Carolina, to introduce a sunflower-oil based lubricant called ProForest. Spectrum, an oil blender in Hornsby, Tennessee, formulates and packages the lubricant for Husqvarna.

BioBlend BioLube CBC is a readily biodegradable chain saw bar and chain lubricant. Its excellent lubricity and temperature stability provide smooth mechanical performance and superior antiwear protection, while its added tackiness minimizes sling loss. BioLube CBC is readily biodegradable, and its nontoxic formula protects vegetation, wildlife, and the environment. It is suitable for the lubrication of chain saws and similar wood-cutting equipment in all ecologically sensitive environments. It is offered in two viscosities, ISO 46 (generally preferred in colder conditions) and ISO 100 (generally preferred in warmer conditions).

Grounds Vehicles

Grounds operations use a wide variety of medium- and heavy-duty vehicles, including dump trucks, bucket trucks, construction vehicles, recycling trucks, refuse trucks, and box trucks. These vehicles consume copious amounts of fuels and emit harmful pollutants and greenhouse gasses.

The medium- and heavy-duty vehicle industry is changing rapidly, with fleets adopting alternative fuels and advanced technologies to reduce petroleum use and comply with the 2010 EPA and California Air Resources Board (CARB) emission standards. The U.S. Department of Energy's Clean Cities Program has long maintained its Heavy-Duty Vehicle Search on the Alternative Fuels and Advanced Vehicles Data Center (AFDC) website. This section brings together an overview of alternative fuel power sources, including engines, microturbines, and fuel cells, and hybrid propulsion systems along with chassis compatible with the systems developed by Clean Cities.

Because of the significant amount of pollutants and greenhouse gases emitted by these vehicles, it is critical that we as grounds professionals understand the new technology options that will enable us to mitigate the environmental impacts of our medium- and heavy-duty vehicles.

Regulations: 2010 Heavy-Duty Emissions Standards

The EPA and CARB regulate emissions from engines of medium- and heavy-duty vehicles by weight rather than by models, as in light-duty vehicles. The EPA classifies medium-duty vehicles as those over 8,500 lbs., while the CARB medium-duty classification starts at 14,000 lbs. Emissions fall into two categories:

- Air pollution emissions are smog-forming pollutants emitted by a vehicle. They include particulate matter (PM), nonmethane hydrocarbons (NMHC), and nitrogen oxides (NOx).
- Greenhouse gas (GHG) emissions, primarily carbon dioxide (CO2), contribute to climate change. The EPA has put forth proposals to regulate GHG emissions in passenger cars and light-duty trucks.

According to the EPA, heavy-duty trucks and buses account for about one-third of NOx emissions and one-fourth of PM emissions from all highway traffic, even though they comprise only 2 percent of the total number of vehicles on the highway. The EPA established the following emission limits for medium- and heavy-duty engines manufactured in 2010:

- PM—0.01 g/bhp-hr
- NMHC—0.14 g/bhp-hr
- NOx—0.20 g/bhp-hr

A separate EPA diesel fuel regulation limited the sulfur content in on-highway diesel fuel to 15 parts per million (ppm), down from the previous 500 ppm. Ultralow sulfur diesel fuel was introduced in 2006 as a "technology enabler" to pave the way for advanced, sulfur-intolerant exhaust emission control technologies, such as catalytic diesel particulate filters and NOx catalysts. PM and NMHC are well controlled by these catalytic filtering systems. NOx have been reduced by the use of exhaust gas recirculation (EGR) and selective catalytic reduction (SCR).

- EGR is a NOx emissions reduction process that recirculates a portion of an engine's exhaust gas back to the engine cylinders. This dilutes the mixture of gases and reduces the combustion temperature. Because NOx form primarily when a mixture of nitrogen and oxygen is subjected to high temperature, the lower combustion temperature results in reduced NOx output.
- SCR involves injecting urea into a stream of exhaust gas. The urea, known as diesel exhaust fluid, is combined with engine exhaust in the presence of a catalyst to convert smog-forming NOx into harmless nitrogen and water vapor.

Conversion emission standards for heavy-duty vehicles manufactured before 2010 remain the same as the standards applicable in the year of engine manufacture. Conversion companies must obtain a certificate of compliance for each model year engine family being converted.

Clean Diesel Trucks, Buses, and Fuel: Heavy-Duty Engine and Vehicle Standards and Highway Diesel Fuel Sulfur Control Requirements (Diesel Fuel and Engines)

In 2000, the EPA moved forward on schedule with its rule to make heavy-duty trucks and buses run cleaner by finalizing the Highway Diesel Rule (the "2007 Heavy-Duty Highway Rule") in January 2001.

The final rule requires a 97 percent reduction in the sulfur content of highway diesel fuel, from its 2000 level of 500 ppm to 15 ppm. By addressing diesel fuel and engines together as a single system, this program will provide annual emission reductions equivalent to removing the pollution from more than 90 percent of today's trucks and buses, or about 13 million trucks and buses, when the current heavy-duty vehicle fleet has been completely replaced in 2030. This is the greatest reduction in harmful emissions of soot, or PM, ever achieved from cars and trucks.

To attain these pollution reductions, the sulfur in diesel fuel had to be lowered to enable modern pollution control technology to be effective on these vehicles. The US required a 97 percent reduction in the sulfur content of highway diesel fuel from its 2000 level of 500 ppm (low-sulfur diesel) to 15 ppm (ultra-low sulfur diesel, or ULSD). Refiners began producing the cleaner-burning diesel fuel, ULSD, for use in highway vehicles beginning June 1, 2006.

ULSD enabled advanced pollution control technology for cars, trucks, and buses so that engine manufacturers could meet the 2007 emission standards through a flexible, phased-in approach between 2007 and 2010. ULSD also enabled light-duty passenger vehicle manufacturers to use similar technologies on diesel-powered cars, sport utility vehicles, and light trucks.

Once this rule is fully implemented, the environmental benefits will include annual reductions of 2.6 million tons of smog-causing NOx emissions and 110,000 tons of PM. In the long term, this program will result in more than $70 billion annually in environmental and public health benefits at a cost of $4 billion per year.

Since the standards were finalized in 2001, the EPA has worked with the regulated community and other stakeholders to ensure a smooth transition. Where necessary, they have issued several technical amendments to the regulations to ensure a smooth introduction of the program. In late 2005, the EPA began participating with the Clean Diesel Fuel Alliance, a group of more than 20 industry, government, and consumer organizations that are working together to provide information on the benefits of ULSD and cleaner-burning diesel cars, trucks, and buses.

All new diesel engines are certified to comply with EPA emission standards in place at the time of certification. Retrofit technologies may be added to further reduce emissions from certified engine configurations. The most common retrofit technologies are devices for engine exhaust after-treatment. These devices are installed in the exhaust system to reduce emissions and should not impact engine or vehicle operation.

Examples of retrofit devices include diesel particulate filters and diesel oxidation catalysts. Some engines are equipped with after-treatment technologies as part of their originally certified emission control system, and may not be eligible for retrofit. Retrofit technologies may also include crankcase emission control devices, engine component upgrades, or other modifications that reduce emissions.

Retrofit technologies are evaluated by EPA's National Clean Diesel Campaign and CARB, and each program maintains verified technology lists. For more information on this program, visit www.epa.gov and www.clean-diesel.org.

Photo by Steve Russell, Massachusetts Dept. of Energy Resources

National Lumber Hybrid Chassis

Alternative Fuel and Advanced Medium- and Heavy-Duty Vehicles

Multiple-Stage Construction of Medium and Heavy-Duty Vehicles

Vocational, heavy-duty trucks are typically manufactured in multiple stages. An incomplete vehicle or chassis cab is progressively upfitted with specialized equipment according to the specific tasks that the vehicle will perform and then certified as a complete vehicle by a final-stage manufacturer before delivery to the end user. The incomplete vehicle may be modified, or "manufactured," by multiple intermediate-stage manufacturers before going to the final-stage manufacturer, or may only require a single manufacturing operation by the final-stage manufacturer. The process performed on the incomplete vehicle by intermediate- or final-stage manufacturers depends on the end-use application and the associated specialized equipment requirements, which may include installing equipment such as refuse-packing bodies, paint-striping systems, snowplows, or aerial platform boom truck bodies, or modifying the chassis (e.g., moving or adding axles or modifying the length of the frame).

Owing to the vast array of possible final vehicle configurations and to increase overall flexibility of the manufacturing process, alternative fuel storage systems (e.g., CNG, LNG, or propane) may be installed by intermediate- or final-stage manufacturers rather than by the incomplete chassis OEM. This may add steps to the manufacturing process but it also allows greater design flexibility. This installation is typically transparent to the vehicle purchaser and is consistent with the multistage manufacturing approach utilized within the market segment. The intermediate- and final-stage manufacturers are typically coordinated by the vehicle dealer, final-stage manufacturer, or equipment manufacturer, depending on the established purchasing arrangements, which may be unique for each type of vehicle purchased or for each fleet.

Four major systems must be integrated into each heavy-duty vocational truck:

1. **Chassis:** For alternative fuel applications, chassis configurations are selected based on end-use requirements in the same way that conventionally fueled chassis cabs are, except in cases where additional frame length or increased gross vehicle weight ratio is required to accommodate a larger and/or heavier fuel storage system. Chassis are available in conventional and cab-over-axle configurations based on manufacturers' decisions about the best design that will accommodate alternative fuel engines.

2. **Engine:** Chassis are available with OEM engines or gasoline or diesel engines that may be converted to operate on alternative fuel by installing an emissions-certified conversion system. Alternative fuel engines are designed to operate on CNG, LNG, or propane. They can be dedicated to operate full time on alternative fuel, bi-fuel to run on either alternative fuel or gasoline, or dual-fuel to run on alternative fuel and use diesel for ignition assist. Advanced hybrid vehicles combine gasoline or diesel operation with battery power that reduces petroleum consumption when operating on electric power.
3. **Fuel System:** CNG, LNG, and propane are stored in tanks onboard a vehicle. These cylindrical tanks are heavier than gasoline or diesel tanks and less flexible in shape, making them more challenging to package on the vehicle. This can result in less volume or weight capacity for these alternative fuel vehicles compared with a conventional fuel system vehicle. Specialty equipment manufacturers have recognized the challenges associated with packaging alternative fuel storage systems and have developed products that seamlessly integrate the alternative fuel system into their product or body structure. Thoughtful design innovations, including rooftop, back of cab, and frame-mounted options, can overcome these drawbacks. In other cases, utility body manufacturers have integrated the fuel system into the body equipment to minimize any reductions in fuel storage capacity.

Photo by Steve Russell, Massachusetts Dept. of Energy Resources

Waste Management Propane Trash Truck

4. **Specialty Equipment Upfitting:** The final step is upfitting the chassis with the equipment necessary to do the job, such as bucket lifts, recycling bodies, refuse packers, and utility bodies.

Alternative Fuel Power Sources (Including Engines, Fuel Cells, and Microturbines)

Natural Gas Engines: Current-production natural gas engines are designed to operate solely on natural gas (dedicated), on either natural gas or gasoline (bi-fuel), or on a combination of natural gas and diesel fuel (dual-fuel). Dedicated and bi-fuel natural gas engines are spark-ignited, and dual-fuel engines utilize a minimal amount of diesel for pilot ignition in compression ignition combustion. Natural gas is stored onboard the vehicle as either CNG or LNG. CNG is more common and has a longer history of use in vehicular applications, but LNG is gaining popularity in heavy-duty applications that require maximum fuel capacity and extended driving range. CNG is stored at pressures of 3,000 to 3,600 lbs. per square inch in specially designed and constructed cylinders onboard the vehicle. LNG is cooled to a cryogenic temperature of approximately –260°F and stored as a liquid onboard the vehicle in double-wall, vacuum-insulated storage tanks. Vehicles that operate on LNG are typically heavy duty and require more range than CNG can provide.

Natural gas is a clean-burning alternative fuel that offers a number of advantages to users. It is clear, noncorrosive, and odorless, though an odorant is commonly added. Compared with conventional diesel vehicles, natural gas vehicles (NGVs) can produce significantly lower amounts of emissions, including NOx, PM, and CO2. Additionally, natural gas is generally less expensive than diesel or gasoline.

Propane Engines: Propane—also known as liquefied petroleum gas, LPG, or autogas— is a by-product of crude oil refining and natural gas processing. Propane is a gas at room temperature and is stored onboard a vehicle in a tank pressurized to around 150 lbs. per square inch.

Propane vehicles operate much like gasoline vehicles with spark-ignited engines. The two types of propane fuel-injection systems are vapor and liquid injection. In a vapor-injection system, liquid propane is controlled by a regulator or vaporizer, which converts the liquid to vapor, which is then drawn into the combustion chamber. In a liquid-injection system, fuel is delivered to the combustion chamber in liquid form.

Compared with conventional gasoline vehicles, propane vehicles can produce lower amounts of CO and CO2.

Battery Electrics: A battery-electric vehicle operates solely on the power provided by a battery pack that is recharged by being plugged into the local power grid. Batteries may be lead acid, nickel metal hydride, or lithium ion. Electric vehicles powered by rechargeable batteries offer a number of aesthetic benefits. There is reduced noise owing to the lack of an internal combustion engine (ICE), no gear changes, and fewer moving parts. The vehicles themselves generate zero NOx, PM, and CO emissions, although the associated electricity-generating facility does produce emissions.

Fuel Cells: Fuel cells produce electricity through a chemical reaction— typically between hydrogen and oxygen—with water and heat as by-products. In a fuel cell vehicle, the electricity is used to power a motor that drives the vehicle's wheels.

In addition to producing zero harmful tailpipe emissions, hydrogen fuel cells are attractive for transportation applications for two main reasons. First, hydrogen can be produced from various sustainable and domestic resources. Second, fuel cells are more efficient than conventional ICEs, converting roughly 50 percent of the hydrogen's energy into electricity. Hydrogen storage is one of the major barriers to use of fuel cell vehicles. Hydrogen has a low energy density. To give fuel cell vehicles an adequate driving range, hydrogen must be stored onboard the vehicles as a very high-pressure gas, a cryogenic liquid, or in another medium (e.g., methanol, ethanol, or natural gas) from which hydrogen is extracted.

Microturbines: A microturbine acts as an auxiliary power unit in series hybrid vehicles. The microturbine charges the batteries, which in turn power the electric motor that drives the wheels of the vehicle. The microturbine can be fueled with natural gas, waste methane, biodiesel, diesel, or propane. Hybrid buses with microturbines operate in New York City; Baltimore; Charlotte, North Carolina; and in several large cities in Europe.

Engines Certified for Biodiesel: Biodiesel or biodiesel blends are used by heavy-duty vehicle operators to reduce petroleum consumption and pollutant emissions. Biodiesel is a domestic, renewable fuel for diesel engines, which must meet the specifications of ASTM D6751. Biodiesel is derived from vegetable oils, animal by-products, or biomass conversion, but it is not the same as raw vegetable oil. Rather, it is produced by a chemical process that removes the glycerin from the oil.

B5 (5 percent biodiesel, 95 percent petroleum diesel) is frequently used in heavy-duty diesel vehicles. Engine manufacturers may also certify their engines for use with B20 (20 percent biodiesel, 80 percent petroleum diesel). Significant reductions of PM, CO, and hydrocarbon emissions can be achieved with B20 blends. Minor impacts on peak torque and fuel economy are related to the lower energy density of biodiesel fuels, but thermal efficiency is unchanged. The National Renewable Energy Laboratory's Biodiesel Handling and Use Guide is an excellent source of information about biodiesel transportation fuel (www.afdc.energy.gov).

Conversion Engines: Fleets that own numerous older diesel trucks may decide to have them converted to operate on alternative fuel. Conversions of heavy-duty vehicles involve replacing or rebuilding the engine and adding fuel tanks.

Manufacturers are now packaging alternative fuel engines and power trains to be a direct replacement for their diesel counterparts. A Cummins Westport CNG engine, for example, is configured to mount in a chassis just like a diesel engine, and an Allison parallel hybrid transmission can mount in the same space as a standard automatic transmission. Companies that perform alternative fuel conversions are certified by the EPA or CARB to convert specific make and model year engines.

Hybrid Propulsion Systems by Design

Hybrid vehicles rely on two or more sources to produce, store, and deliver power. In hybrid electric vehicles, these two sources are a conventional ICE and electricity. In hydraulic hybrids, they are the conventional engine and a hydraulic pump/motor with a hydraulic energy storage system.

Photo by Patrick Bartole, New Jersey City University

New Jersey City University 2005 Ford Escape Hybrid

Hybrid configurations use a combination of energy sources, including a power source paired with an electric motor and batteries. These configurations are attractive for specific drive cycle applications, including stop-and-start delivery vans and trucks, refuse collection, transit buses, utility bucket trucks, and warehouse tractors. Each of these applications involves engine stops and starts, extended idling, and frequent braking.

Parallel Hybrid System: Parallel hybrid systems have both an ICE and an electric motor connected directly to the transmission. Most designs combine a large electrical generator and a motor into one unit, replacing both the conventional starter motor and the alternator. To store energy, a hybrid uses a large battery pack with a higher voltage than the normal automotive 12 volts.

Parallel hybrids can be further categorized depending on how balanced the different portions are at providing motive power. The ICE may be the dominant portion (the electric motor turns on only when a boost is needed), or vice versa. Others can run with just the electric system operating.

Series Hybrid System: In series or serial hybrids, the ICE drives an electric generator instead of directly driving the wheels. The generator can either charge the batteries or power an electric motor that moves the vehicle. When large amounts of power are required, the motor draws electricity from both the batteries and the generator. Series hybrids can also be fitted with an ultracapacitor or a flywheel to store regenerative braking energy, which can improve efficiency by minimizing the losses in the battery. Because a series hybrid lacks a mechanical link between the ICE and the wheels, the engine can run at a constant and efficient rate, even as the vehicle changes speed.

Parallel Hydraulic Hybrid System (Launch Assist): The hydraulic launch assist system uses a hydraulic pump and motor and hydraulic storage tanks to supplement the conventional vehicle power train. During braking, the vehicle's kinetic energy drives the pump/motor as a pump, transferring hydraulic fluid from the low-pressure reservoir to a high-pressure accumulator. The fluid compresses nitrogen gas in the accumulator and pressurizes the system. The regenerative braking captures about 70 percent of the kinetic energy produced during braking. During acceleration, fluid in the high-pressure accumulator is metered out to drive the pump/motor as a motor. The system propels the vehicle by transmitting torque to the driveshaft.

Series Hydraulic Hybrid System: In a series hydraulic hybrid system, the conventional transmission and driveline are replaced by the hydraulic hybrid power train, and energy is transferred from the engine to the drive wheels through fluid power. The vehicle uses hydraulic pump/motors and hydraulic storage tanks to recover and store energy, similar to what is done with electric motors and batteries in hybrid electric vehicles. The system is suited to vehicles that operate in stop-and-go duty cycles, including heavy-duty refuse hauling. The engine operates at its "sweet spot" of fuel consumption facilitated by the continuously variable transmission functionality of the series hydraulic hybrid system and by regenerative braking.

Hybrid Propulsion Systems by Fuel

Diesel Hybrids: Diesel electric hybrids are powered by both a diesel engine and an electric motor. The diesel engine generates electricity for the electric motor. The electric motor derives its power from an alternator or generator that is coupled with an energy storage device such as a set of batteries or supercapacitors.

Medium-duty vehicles that stop and start often are well suited for this technology, which captures regenerative braking energy to power the electric motor. Hybrid vehicles produce zero emissions when running on electricity and reduce fuel use at the same time. The diesel engine's high torque combined with hybrid technology make this technology an excellent combination for medium- and heavy-duty vehicles.

Photo by Steve Russell, Massachusetts Dept. of Energy Resources

M2e Electric Diesel Hybrid

Photo by Marc Fournier

Cambridge Landscape Hybrid Bucket Truck

CNG Hybrids: A CNG hybrid system features a CNG-powered engine, an electric generator, inverters, two motors, and a battery pack. The electric motor derives its power from an alternator or generator that is coupled with an energy storage device, such as a set of batteries or supercapacitors.

Because natural gas is mostly methane, NGVs have much lower NMHC emissions than gasoline vehicles but higher emissions of methane. Because the fuel system is closed, there are no evaporative emissions, and refueling emissions are negligible. Cold-start emissions from NGVs are also low, because cold-start enrichment is not required; this reduces both volatile organic compound and CO emissions.

Fuel Cell Hybrids: Fuel cell hybrids operate much like other hybrid electric vehicles but with fuel cells producing electricity that charges the batteries, and a motor that converts electricity from the batteries into mechanical energy that drives the wheels. The efficiency of fuel cell hybrids can be increased through use of advanced technologies such as regenerative braking, which captures and stores energy that would otherwise be lost during braking.

For more detailed information and an overview of individual medium- and heavy-duty vehicles listed by application, please refer to the U.S. Department of Energy document titled *Clean Cities' Guide to Alternative Fuel and Advanced Medium- and Heavy-Duty Vehicles,* September 2010.

For the most up-to-date heavy-duty vehicle information, visit the AFDC website at www.afdc.energy.gov.

Case Study: Innovative Cambridge Landscape Co. Hybrid Bucket Truck

Cambridge Landscape Co. in Cambridge, Massachusetts, has taken two major steps in greening its fleet. It has purchased two hybrid bucket trucks. Called Utility Bucket Lift by Navistar, these trucks are truly impressive.

Sixty-five and 75-foot Terex aerial booms are mounted on Navistar chassis. What is very different is the propulsion system for the hydraulic circuit of for the aerial boom. The technology is referred to as Mild-Parallel Hybrid with Electric Power Take-Off system, or a diesel electric hybrid.

Two 170-volt lithium ion, Power Electronic Carrier, hybrid batteries power a 60 HP electric motor through a DC to AC inverter. To keep the wheelbase short, Cambridge Landscape worked with the manufacturer to mount the lithium ion batteries near the base of the boom. The electric motor turns the main shaft of an automated manual gearbox, which turns a countershaft, which drives a traditional power take-off (PTO).

Normally, diesel trucks have to idle constantly while running the PTO, which powers the hydraulic circuit for the aerial boom. In trucks equipped with Eaton Mild-Parallel Hybrid technology, the truck idles for about 5 minutes or until the hybrid batteries are fully charged, and then it shuts down. The hybrid batteries then power the aerial boom until they run out of electrical charge, at which time the truck automatically restarts and recharges the hybrid batteries. The key is that the truck does not have to run the whole time. It idles for approximately 21 minutes to provide an hour's worth of aerial boom run time. Cambridge Landscape Co. staff report fuel savings of nearly 50 percent, and emissions are also reduced by that factor.

The total cost for the trucks outfitted with hybrid technology ranged between $210,000 and $225,000. Cambridge Landscape applied for and received grants from the EPA and the Northeast States for Coordinated Air Use Management for approximately $40,000 of the $57,000 incremental cost above a nonhybrid bucket truck.

It is to be hoped that we will see more of these environmental/financial successes in the near future. Innovative technology like this along with companies willing to invest in the future will lead the way in greening our grounds operations!

Grounds Equipment

Regulations Related to Powered Grounds Equipment

Numerous federal, state, and local regulations now govern the use of vehicles and powered large, small, riding, and handheld equipment used in our grounds operations. These regulations relate to the use of dump trucks, loaders, tractors, chippers, mowers, trimmers, chain saws, leaf blowers and vacuums, and stump grinders, among many others. The section focuses on the major federal regulations governing grounds vehicles and equipment. Contact your state and local environmental agencies for more information on their regulations.

Small Spark-Ignition Engine Rule

In 1990, Congress asked the EPA to look for sources of air pollution that were not generated by cars, trucks, and large industrial facilities. The research covered nonroad mobile sources, including recreational vehicles, farm and construction equipment, boats, locomotives, and lawn and garden power equipment. Subsequently, the EPA has been developing emission standards for virtually all types of nonroad equipment.

As part of that effort, the EPA is implementing a regulation that establishes emission standards for small spark-ignition engines of 25 HP (19 kW) or less. These engines are predominantly used in lawn and garden power equipment and in some farm, construction, and utility equipment.

Until recently, small engines of this type were not regulated at all except in California. According to EPA estimates, in many large urban areas, pre-1997 lawn and garden equipment accounts for as much as 5 percent of the total manmade hydrocarbons that contribute to ozone formation, which causes pollution-related health problems for urban residents.

Small engines used in power equipment emit a variety of pollutants. These include hydrocarbons (HC) and NOx, which lead to the production of ground-level ozone, the principal component of smog. Ozone can impair human lung functions and inhibit plant growth. In addition, NOx contributes to the production of acid rain. These engines also produce CO, a colorless, odorless, and poisonous gas that results from incomplete fuel combustion. Infants and people with heart disease or respiratory problems are especially susceptible to CO poisoning.

The regulation, commonly called Phase 1 of the small spark-ignition engine rule, sets allowable exhaust levels for HC, CO, and NOx from engines of 25 HP or less. The rule applies to all small engines produced after September 1, 1997, as well as to some produced earlier. Allowable emission levels vary depending on engine size, use, and age. Compared with their unregulated counterparts, the EPA estimates that engines complying with the new emission standards will emit on average more than one-third fewer hydrocarbons.

Before an engine manufacturer can sell a regulated engine model in the United States it must obtain a certificate of conformity from EPA. The manufacturer must label each certified engine to indicate compliance with the small spark-ignition engine rule. The language may read "this engine conforms to Phase 1 U.S. EPA regulations for small non-road engines" or indicate compliance with both EPA and California regulations. Emission labels will be found on the engine, or if the engine label is obscured, on the piece of equipment itself.

According to EPA analysis, the small engine regulation will increase the cost of equipment by an average of $5 to $7 per unit, but durability will improve and fuel efficiency will increase for most small engines. These improvements in fuel efficiency and durability will result in lower operating costs over the life of the equipment and will probably offset the initial increase in cost.

In the final small spark-ignition engine rule announced by the EPA in September 2008, some changes to the initial rule were adopted for small non-road engines, including the following:

- HC+NOx exhaust emission standards of 10 g/kWh for Class I engines starting in the 2012 model year and 8 g/kWh for Class II engines starting in the 2011 model year. Manufacturers are expected to meet these standards by improving fuel systems and engine combustion, and in some cases by adding catalysts. These standards are consistent with the requirements recently adopted by CARB. US EPA did not adopt new exhaust emission standards for handheld equipment.
- New evaporative emission standards for both handheld and non-handheld equipment. The new standards include requirements to control fuel tank permeation, fuel line permeation, and diffusion emissions. When fuel works its way through plastic fuel tanks and rubber hoses, the outer surfaces of these materials are exposed to ambient air and the gasoline molecules are emitted

directly into the air, contributing to air pollution. Control of running losses is also required for non-handheld engines.

When fully implemented, the new standards will result in a 35 percent reduction in HC+NOx emissions from new engines' exhaust and will reduce evaporative emissions by 45 percent.

For more information, visit www.epa.gov, or see the EPA publications titled *Small Spark-Ignition Engine Rule Questions & Answers US EPA August 1998,* and *Small Spark-Ignition Engine Final Rule Overview US EPA September 2008.*

Small Spark-Ignition Engine Technology Advances

To comply with the Small Spark-Ignition Engine Rule, many companies have been developing innovative ways to reduce emissions and fuel consumption while maintaining equipment performance, durability, and cost. This has been a significant challenge. The following section provides an overview of some of the most prominent advances.

Strato-Charged® Engines

In 1998, Zenoah (now owned by Husqvarna) introduced the Strato-Charged® engine, designed with advanced technology that reduces impact on the environment through efficient engine design, increased fuel economy, and reduced emissions. The Strato-Charged® two-stroke engine does the following:

- Achieves up to 20 percent more fuel efficiency than standard two-stroke engines
- Produces low emissions that meet regulations without the need for a heated, heavy catalytic converter
- Requires no valve adjustments, oil changes, or daily oil reservoir level checks
- Generates 15 to 20 percent more horsepower than a typical four-stroke or four-stroke hybrid engine of the same engine displacement size

Zenoah's Strato-Charged® two-stroke engines operate at maximum efficiency with just three moving parts. By comparison, four-stroke or four-stroke hybrid engines contain as many as 30 moving parts. Zenoah Strato-Charged® two-stroke engines are 20 to 25 percent lighter than four-strokes or four-stroke hybrids of the same engine size, resulting in less operator fatigue. The Strato-Charged engine has been honored for technology that allows it to meet clean air regulations without the need for a heavy, hot catalytic converter. The stratified charge engine is a type of internal-combustion engine that runs on gasoline. The name refers to the layering of the charge inside the cylinder. The stratified charge engine is designed to reduce the emissions from the engine cylinder without the use of exhaust gas recirculation systems, also known as EGR or catalytic converters.

Husqvarna and RedMax use this technology in some of their equipment. Zenoah products that include the patented Strato-Charged® engine technology have a "Z" in the model number. For more information, visit www.zenoah.net.

Shindaiwa C4 and Hybrid 4® Engine Technologies™

Landscaping equipment has traditionally been powered by the two-stroke engine because of its excellent power-to-weight ratio and multiposition capability. Shindaiwa C4 Technology®, a unique cross between two-stroke and four-stroke engines, combines the best of both technologies: light weight, excellent torque, and great throttle response, with all-day, all-position operation. It also includes eco-friendly exhaust gas emissions, low noise, and better fuel economy.

First developed in the 1980s, the two-stroke/four-stroke hybrid engine uses proprietary technology that has many mechanical advantages over its two-stroke cousin.

Shindaiwa's C4 Technology® (Compression-Charged Clean Combustion) uses patented technology controlled by Shindaiwa. Shindaiwa's engineers have successfully isolated half of the twin cylinder hybrid technology and miniaturized it for optimum performance and weight. Shindaiwa C4 Technology® combines the best features of the two-stroke engine (compactness, power-to-weight ratio, minimum-moving parts) and the four-stroke engine (precise metering of combustion gases). For more information, visit www.shindaiwa.com.

Hybrid 4® engine technology is available in 18 Shindaiwa models in three engine sizes: 24.5cc, 34cc, and 79.7cc, and among the following product categories: blowers (both handheld and backpack), brush cutters, edgers, hedge trimmers (both standard and shafted/articulating), Multi-Tool™, PowerBroom®, trimmers, and water pumps. For more information, visit www.hybrid4engine.com.

STIHL 4-MIX® Engine

The STIHL 4-MIX® engine combines the advantages of two-stroke and four-stroke engines in a single unit. Unlike conventional four-stroke engines, which require separate systems for the fuel supply and engine lubrication, the new STIHL 4-MIX® engine is fueled with the new 50:1 4-MIX® fuel mixture. Since it is lubricated by the fuel mixture, the STIHL 4-MIX® engine dispenses with such parts as the oil pump, oil tank, and oil pan. This makes the STIHL 4-MIX® engine a real featherweight. Lubrication by the fuel mixture also makes time-consuming service work—such as regular adjustment of the valve clearance, oil checks, oil changes and disposal of the waste oil—unnecessary. The valve adjustment just needs to be checked after the first 139 hours of operation.

Because the fuel burns with fewer residues, emissions from the STIHL 4-MIX® engine are already more than 25 percent lower than the stringent ceiling imposed by European Union regulations in 2007.

The 4-MIX® engine offers 5 percent more horsepower, 17 percent more torque, and 15 percent less vibration than its two-stroke counterpart and less noise. The 4-MIX® engine is used in STIHL brush cutters, hedge trimmers, pole pruners, and the KombiSystem. For more information, visit www.stihl.com

Alternative Fuel Mowers

Lawn mowing contributes significantly to the nation's petroleum consumption and pollutant emissions. Mowers consume 1.2 billion gallons of gasoline annually, about 1 percent of U.S. motor gasoline consumption. Commercial mowing accounts for 35 percent of this total and is the highest-intensity use. Large property owners and mowing companies cut lawns, sports fields, golf courses, parks, roadsides, and other grassy areas. In addition to gasoline, commercial mowing consumes more than 100 million gallons of diesel annually.

Powering commercial lawn service equipment with alternative fuels is an effective way to reduce petroleum use. A single commercial lawnmower can annually use as much gasoline or diesel fuel as a commercial work truck. Alternative fuels can also reduce pollutant emissions compared with conventional fuels. Numerous biodiesel, compressed natural gas, electric, and propane mowers are now available to help keep

Photo by Ellen Newell

Arizona State University Propane Mower

the grass green and the nation clean. Many manufacturers, including Ariens, Hustler, Dixie Chopper, Husqvarna, Scag, and others, offer alternative fuel powered mowers.

For more information on mowers powered by alternative fuels, see the U.S. Department of Energy Clean Cities *Guide to Alternative Fuel Commercial Lawn Equipment,* September 2010.

Other Innovative Green Grounds Equipment

There are many examples of innovative grounds equipment powered by alternative fuels. Here are a few.

Husqvarna Automower® Solar Hybrid Mower

Husqvarna's Automower® Solar Hybrid, is the world's first fully electric automatic lawn mower that is partly powered by the sun. The product uses considerably less energy than any conventional mower because, in addition to a charging station, it comes with a large integrated solar panel. When daylight is available, the solar cells enable the mower to extend its cutting periods before it needs recharging. That means a cut lawn in a shorter time, lower power consumption, and an extended battery life. It is suitable for lawns up to 2,200 square meters, depending on light conditions.

STIHL Lithium Ion Hedge Trimmer

The STIHL HAS 65 Lithium Ion Hedge Trimmer is powered by sophisticated 36 volt lithium ion battery technology.

Photo courtesy of STIHL

STIHL Lithium Ion Hedge Trimmer

Lehr Eco Trimmer ST025DC

Propane string trimmers are new to the market. The Lehr trimmer was introduced in spring 2009. It's as powerful as a gas trimmer, you don't have to buy and store gasoline, and propane is less polluting than gasoline. However, you do have the ongoing cost of 1-pound propane canisters (estimated at $2 to $5 each), which can't be refilled (but can be recycled) and give you only two hours of run time each. The ST025DC has a detachable curved shaft and weighs 15 lbs. with the propane canister.

Husqvarna TB 1000 Battery-Powered Cultivator

The Husqvarna TB 1000 Battery-Powered Cultivator is the world's first battery-powered cultivator. It is lightweight, quiet, effective, and easy to operate. This versatile gardening tool can also be equipped with accessories for ridging, edging and dethatching.

Special thanks to:

Ed Burke and Kevin O'Leary, Dennis K. Burke, Inc., Chelsea, MA

Stephen B. Russell, Mass Clean Cities, Massachusetts Department of Energy Resources, Boston MA

Tom Perron, Boyden & Perron, Amherst, MA

Jim Kelley, Cambridge Landscape Co., Inc., Cambridge, MA

Mike Pateneaude, Applications Specialist, Northeast STIHL, Shelton, CT

Josh Lepage, Sales Manager – Product Integration, Navistar Inc., Warrenville, IL

Karl Heinz and Dave Sarkisian, Cleaves Co., Inc., Needham, MA

George Mellick, Shelter Tree Inc., North Attleboro, MA

Mike Devine, Richey & Clapper, Inc., Sudbury, MA

CHAPTER 3

Designing a Successful Grounds Maintenance Organization: The Broadcast and Zone Approach

By Fred Gratto

Imagine that you are sitting on a bench on a college campus on a summer day. You see bikers glide by, hear a carillon in the distance, and notice the cheery chatter of students talking in a nearby courtyard. The patio in front of you is clean, a big sycamore tree offers shade, and you're impressed by the handsome brick walls. The fragrance of jasmine on a nearby fence is pretty sweet, and the kaleidoscope of colors provided by a mass of flowers is impossible to miss. So is the vibrant turf all around. The area is free of litter, sidewalks are neatly edged, and gurgling water cascades off a nearby sculpture. You're impressed because the campus landscape is just as nice as the building architecture you see at a glance. The setting is really special and it makes you feel good. You're thinking this is just what a college campus should look like. Looks simple enough. But you're not fooled. You know that a lot of planning and hard work is needed to create a safe and beautiful campus, and you know how difficult it is to keep it looking well maintained. Often, one of the toughest challenges is controlling where people go. We're facilities folks, so we can't just allow students and everybody else to walk or bike or drive or park wherever they want to. We are concerned about movement around campus, leisure behavior, and the optimum use of open space. There has to be some organization, a comprehensive plan, and features in the campus landscape that result in a theme of crowd control. Without these, there are no rules, and the campus can look frayed and worn, just like the new blue jeans students wear these days.

What Students Want

Just like everybody else on this planet, students want good, dependable, timely, service. It's obvious that they prefer a relationship with their campus similar to the ones they have with their supermarket, department store, favorite restaurant, insurance company, and bank. They want what they want when they want it. "Students increasingly are bringing to higher education exactly the same consumer expectations they have for every other commercial establishment with which they deal. Their focus is on convenience, quality, service, and cost" (Levine & Cureton, 1998, p. 12).

Think about what you want from your bank, for example. You probably want an automated teller machine on every corner, a parking space right next to it, and no extra fees. Likewise, students want convenience. For instance, students usually don't want to have to walk very far to their next class, although they might jog for miles to get some exercise. Shortcuts are a common problem. "Many colleges and universities do not define pedestrian routes clearly. When this is the case, students often create their own routes across campus grounds" (Brandon & Spruch, 2008, p. 361). When students are at liberty to take the shortest route possible, they can create paths or damage landscaping. There are lots of ways to manage foot traffic and guide people. Posts and rope, stone walls, shrubs, fences, benches, railings, and bike racks work well. Another effective way to intercept paths, redirect people, and control where bikers go is to build brick seat walls. In addition to helping people stay on sidewalks, they make other significant contributions because they provide seating, define spaces, protect landscaping, and add to the aesthetic appeal of other brick features on campus. Brick curbs are positive features as well. Even those just one brick high do an effective job of guiding people. It's amazing what just a little elevation and a subtle hint can do to determine where people walk.

What the University Wants

Universities want a lot of things, such as high-quality students and academic programs, excellent faculty, supportive alumni, a great football team, a beautiful campus, and a good reputation. They also want students to learn. "Colleges and universities establish conditions to attract, satisfy, and retain students for purposes of challenging them to develop qualities of the educated person, including a capacity for complex critical reasoning, communication, leadership, a sense of identity and purpose, an appreciation for difference, and a commitment to lifelong learning" (Strange & Banning, 2001, p. 2). We typically think of learning as taking place in classrooms, but research has confirmed that students establish relationships and learn from each other on campus in environments outside the classroom. Settings such as courtyards, patios, or a grassy knoll can contribute to the learning experience. A brick plaza, for example, can be a quaint space that provides seating, an opportunity to linger and meet with friends and, one day, memories of special days at one's alma mater. Because college students spend more time out of class than in class, it is important to provide settings that encourage social interaction. "In fact, when asked what they learned in college, graduates frequently mention that participation in activities outside of class increased their confidence, competence, and self-assurance" (Marchese, 1990, p. 5). Bonds formed in college help students reconsider what they believe, encourage them to consider the perspectives of others, and incline them to evaluate their own priorities in life. "They amplify, dampen, or distort the force of the curriculum, instruction, codes of conduct, and institutional norms. They can trump the best teacher's ace and stalemate the most thoughtful dean. Relationships are labs for learning to communicate, empathize, argue, and reflect. Encounters with others who have diverse backgrounds and strongly held opinions create the context for increased tolerance and integrity" (Chickering & Reisser, 1993, p. 392).

Students need places on campus to spend time with each other, as do faculty, staff, visitors, alumni, and all the rest of us. Arranging environments is a powerful technique used to influence human behavior. This is why college campuses need to build and maintain places and spaces where people can get together without much effort. We need places that encourage people to slow down and sit a while, rather than just hurriedly pass from one place to another. But there has to be a good reason for them to do this. One reason might be an inviting brick patio or courtyard that provides seating and encloses a space to help people feel safe and comfortable. High-quality lawns and open spaces are also magnets for people to get together. It is pretty gratifying to transform a sandy, boring space that people used to just walk across into an invigorating place that is an attractive destination for conversation, entertainment, reading, or just relaxing. By way of creative designs and effective maintenance, we can capture the potential of a setting and reclaim a worn-out space. When you see people reading, talking, studying, sipping coffee, or just enjoying the moment in a beautiful place that they never noticed before, you'll know that your efforts have been successful.

What You Want

You want to accomplish something that matters, something that makes a difference, right? It's no fun for the grounds crew to maintain an area that looks bad when they get there and just as bad when they leave. Mowing and weed-eating sandy, dirty lawns that barely hang on because they are so walked out is not very productive. Turf is terrific. Few aspects of a campus environment are prettier than lush green grass, nicely mowed and edged. But it takes an effective maintenance program to care for lawns and, of course, other landscape features such as shrubs, flowers, trees, bike racks, benches, tables, patios, and irrigation systems. It is critical to get the maintenance of campus grounds and everything in and on them to an acceptable, sustainable level. This is what you want, because the appearance of a college or university impacts a lot of things, such as faculty and student recruiting, funding levels, and reputation.

Impact of Grounds Maintenance

Grounds maintenance is both an art and a science. It is an art because vision, imagination, and talent are required to design and implement a landscape plan. It is a science because plants and people, cars and trucks, mowers and bicycles, and other features on campus have specific needs. Therefore, we need to design and build roads, service areas, seating, patios, sidewalks, lighting, detention ponds, walls, berms, athletic fields, and a dozen other features in the landscape, keeping in mind those who use the facilities and those who have the tall task of taking care of them. While doing this, one of our goals is to have a beautiful campus. As important as this is, it is trumped by the need to provide positive outdoor environments, places where people feel safe and comfortable because they really are. Safety is first. Everything else is secondary.

Grounds management is a combination of physical and social planning that evolved from civil engineering, urban planning, park administration, and landscape architecture. Just the right amounts of several ingredients are necessary to prepare a campus environment that meets the needs of all of the people all of the time. Some of the critical factors are color: plenty of it to catch lots of attention; sense of scale: the awareness that outdoor places and spaces are in just the right proportion, neither too big nor too small, so that people feel cozy and comfortable in them; and line: in nature, there are few straight lines. There are curves and undulations, as we notice with clouds, hills, rivers, and other features in our natural world. Straight lines have their function, but curved walks and roads are nicer to look at than those that are as straight as a bowling alley.

They are more intriguing as well, because they hold our attention longer since we cannot see past them and don't know what is just around the next curve. Another critical factor is texture: the surfaces people walk on, drive on, sit on, touch, and come into contact with need to be designed with people in mind. Plants, of course, also have a texture of their own, which is a design concern because some plants have soft leaves and present no problem if someone brushes up against them. Others have prickly leaves or thorns that allow them to be used to direct pedestrian traffic. Durability is an especially important design concern. It doesn't matter how pretty things are if they won't stand up to the incredible amount of use and traffic on a typical campus. Form is another design factor. Just like people, plants and trees have different shapes. They grow to specific heights, sizes, and shapes. Also, some plants like cold weather and some do not. Some plants like a lot of sunshine and some do not. Therefore, plant selection is a critical matter because trees and shrubs need to be compatible with the setting—not too big, too small, too wide, or inclined to grow so fast that they are a recurring challenge, needing to be pruned frequently. Knowing these design concerns and a host of other factors and knowing how to lead people are all critical to successful grounds maintenance.

Knowledge and Leadership Are Keys to Success

Industrial America grew up in a work environment that is nearly obsolete today. At its foundation was functional specialization that pegged workers into narrowly defined roles that required arms and backs but no brains. This approach created a chasm between the supervisor and the worker that stymied cooperation and initiative. Now, we realize that the best approach to accomplishing objectives involves empowering people to make decisions, which allows them to use their skills and abilities to help leaders manage organizations. No matter how much we invest in sophisticated new technology and shiny leadership theories, we will never be at our best, truly competitive and great at meeting customer needs, until we make better use of our most important resource: people. This involves a lot of things. One essential perspective is treating workers with respect, listening to their ideas, and getting them involved in solving problems.

All the vision in the world and a commanding voice would not enable anyone to steer a ship from the flagpole. A closer relationship is required. Supervisors need to stay involved with their employees, just as coaches do in sports. Employee morale increases when leaders view workers more as equal partners than silent followers.

Productivity can also be increased through supervisory leadership. The world of sports has plenty of stories about average teams that accomplished mighty feats because of the inspiration provided by leadership. Effective leaders can change direction, provide input, and improve results, and people will be glad they did. Legendary college basketball coach John Wooden saw it this way: "A coach is someone who can give correction without causing resentment." This is necessary in facilities organizations as well, because motivating and inspiring are still jobs without a finish line. A long time ago, Andrew Carnegie, the famous American industrialist, observed, "The average person puts only 25 percent of his energy and ability into his work. The world takes off its hat to those who put in more than 50 percent of their capacity and stands on its head for those few-and-far-between souls who devote 100 percent."

Grounds maintenance is conspicuous work. Doing it well requires preparation and organization, whether repairing a road, finishing concrete, scattering salt on icy steps, landscaping a new building, trimming trees, or refurbishing a bus stop. Our jobs are especially difficult because they take place under the watchful eyes of the public, many of whom are weekend gardeners and think they know the best way to do things. Few people, however, have a sustained interest in the art of managing people and directing resources to ensure that a campus is maintained safely and attractively. But grounds managers do, and they find ways to be helpful and get things accomplished. Effective leaders know and appreciate those who do the work of the organization. "In the world according to great managers, the employee is the star. The manager is the agent" (Buckingham & Coffman, 1999, p. 230). Genuine cooperation results when supervisors encourage employees to identify and solve problems. Supervision through cooperation and empowerment requires a fair exchange of responsibilities and benefits so that all can share the fruits of sustained efforts. There are probably several ways to organize departments and do this, but three are most commonly used.

Zone Maintenance

Most people take care of things better if they own them. For example, people who rent a house may not be too concerned about the impact that pets might have on carpet. Perhaps they move pictures often and are not bothered by all the holes in the walls, because the home is not theirs. Likewise, drivers of renta1 cars might not be as careful as they are with their own vehicles. Squeezing into a tight parking space is no problem. The ding in the door from the other guy might not be such a big concern. Another observation is that people litter in public spaces, but they probably would not throw trash on the ground in their own yards.

People tend to care more about things if they are personally responsible for them. For example, a grounds worker who operates the same mower every day will likely take better care of it. The tires are equally inflated. The blades are changed as needed and the moving parts get greased every day. The condition of a piece of equipment can often reveal the level of attention to detail and tell supervisors a lot about the work habits of the operator. On the other hand, the problem of poorly maintained equipment can develop if mowers or dump trucks, for example, are operated by different people every day. No one knows who scraped the fender, lost the fire extinguisher, or forgot to check the oil.

As with equipment, a supervisor and crew with responsibility for a specific campus area can nurture a sense of ownership and foster teamwork. Often, people are more interested in their jobs if they have their own areas to take care of. They take pride in improvements made over time and feel good about their contributions. They notice changes from one day to the next, are mindful of unfinished details that must be attended to, and pitch in to help one another. A zone approach to deployment of personnel can also encourage friendly competition.

People like to be the best. They like to win. Certainly, doing as well as or better than peers is important to many of us. Unlike some kinds of work, landscape maintenance is not abstract. Our work is conspicuous, and we can see what has been accomplished at the end of the day. Noticing which landscaped areas look better than others is easy. Peer pressure can be a positive factor if it raises the level of interest and pride that people have in their work. If productivity is increased and the level of grounds maintenance improves, good things are happening.

We are in the service business, and the general public, campus employees, students, and faculty are our customers. It's important for our customers to see us occasionally, and zone maintenance allows this to happen more frequently since the same people are usually in the same areas every day. As a consequence, we can create a favorable impression for our organization when a customer approaches a lead worker or supervisor with a question or request and finds someone who can provide accurate information or make a decision. The level of customer satisfaction increases when an individual's concern is regarded as important enough to be acted on quickly.

Another positive aspect of zone maintenance is that workers often see the same people every day. As people come to campus in the morning or go about their business throughout the day, they often have routines. They usually arrive to work at the same time each day; probably park in the same location; walk, bike, or jog the same routes; and work in the same building. These situations allow grounds maintenance personnel to have occasional contact with people and develop relationships. This is important because the opportunity to establish rapport, show an interest in the needs of others, and provide timely service is a good situation worth nurturing.

A zone approach to maintenance of campus grounds assigns a specific supervisor and a specific crew to a particular area, and they perform all the necessary tasks in it. Therefore, it is important to develop expertise in several skills so that individuals are qualified to do any job on any team, such as the mowing crew, irrigation crew, tree crew, pruning crew, or horticultural team. When employees have the skills necessary to perform many different tasks, the whole organization benefits because people can solve any problem, meet any challenge, and fill any void—and they know it. Confidence and can-do attitudes are the logical outcome. This fosters a sense of ownership, ensures continuity, increases job satisfaction, facilitates supervision of jobs, and allows people to demonstrate a sustained commitment toward making the campus a better place. So, providing opportunities and training that increase abilities and create jacks-of-all-trades is good for individuals and the organizations in which they work, especially when zone maintenance is the preferred way to organize the workforce.

The zone approach also offers some potential challenges as well. There may be a tendency for people to create boundaries and the possibility that staff members will reach beyond the beneficial friendly competition and create silos or lose a sense of teamwork with the larger grounds organization. Multiple crews may require additional equipment to accommodate their competing schedules, as weather and horticultural requirements often mean everyone will want to use the same piece of equipment at the same time. New groundskeepers in the zone-based organization may require more training to become proficient in their positions. Consequently, the zone approach is more frequently used on campuses that cover larger geographic areas and have larger staff and more equipment resources.

Broadcast Maintenance

Having the same crew responsible for the same area of campus every day is also an effective approach to grounds maintenance. The resulting routines and familiarity are good. But so is variety. Doing the same tasks at the same location every day can get physically and mentally tiring. It's refreshing to see and do other things and take on different opportunities and challenges. Too much of the same thing saps energy, dulls attitudes, lowers productivity, and causes a drain on the brain. This is true because, over time, we adapt to the sights, sounds, and smells that constantly surround us.

Eventually awareness fades, and the constants in our environment become much less noticeable. For example, enter an air-conditioned building on a sultry summer day and a refreshing breeze of cool air greets you. But, within 10 seconds or 10 strides down the hallway, you probably don't notice it anymore. The same thing happens with beaches, mountains, sunrises, pay raises, fancy cars, life in general and, unfortunately, with people. We get too used to things. I teach an undergraduate class each semester, and I recently asked one of my students how the university could serve them better. A young lady replied, "Surprise us. We're just in our routines every day and we need something different to get interested in; everybody does."

In the world of facilities management, surprises are generally not something we want. Nonetheless, a change of pace is good, and a broadcast approach to grounds maintenance can provide this somewhat by providing work settings that differ daily or change several times throughout a workweek. For this reason and others, a broadcast approach to campus maintenance works well, because people work in different areas of campus each day. This is helpful because we all like a little difference in our days, whether at work or at home.

A broadcast approach uses teams. For example, the mowing team performs all the mowing in a discrete area and then moves on to another one. The pruning team, irrigation team, and other teams function in this manner also. There is an advantage in having crews of specifically trained people move about campus and do all of a certain type of work. It is common for a mowing team, herbicide crew, or tree crew to handle all needs of these types, rather than have separate crews for each area. This broadcast approach avoids duplication, efficiently uses labor and equipment resources, nurtures cooperation, and allows personnel to respond to problems in a timely manner. Training time for replacement employees is minimal, and people can become highly specialized and effective in their jobs.

The broadcast approach has its potential challenges as well. Once the task becomes too routine, attention wanders and the quality of work tends to slip. For the same reasons, monotony is a real challenge, and employees' job satisfaction can diminish over time. While people may take ownership of their task or individual effort, there is less ownership for the appearance of the whole area and less pride in their job, their institution, and potentially themselves.

A Combined Approach

Another approach to organizing campus grounds maintenance is a combination of assignments in which crews have responsibility for specific areas, yet their efforts are augmented by crews of specialists that move about campus. This approach allows a unified workforce to handle peak demands, such as mowing during the rainy season or snow removal during winter months. The appropriate approach to maintenance for any campus and the best methods to be used will vary from one geographical location to another. Also, amount of rainfall, exposure to the sun, soil condition, topography, climate, intended and unintended uses, expectations, and resources all help determine maintenance priorities and regimens. Matching the best maintenance approach to landscaped sites is the essence of effective grounds management.

Summary

The most important component of any service organization is people. This is especially true of grounds management, because effective maintenance is highly dependent on good supervision and knowledgeable people. The grounds management function, therefore, must have personnel who are competent and committed. They must fully understand the scope of their duties and responsibilities and know the mission of the entire organization. People can do things better when they have opportunities to do the many different and important tasks necessary to maintain campus grounds. We need people who have seen the big picture.

People require less supervision as they become more capable and more self-sufficient, more responsible, more confident, and better able to contribute to the mission. A happy consequence of being more proficient and having more qualifications is that employees are more motivated and qualified for other job opportunities. In the long run, this is good for people and good for the organization, because when there are increased chances for upward mobility, people are more hopeful, more motivated, and more productive.

Work performance is usually the result of two factors: commitment and competence. Motivation results in commitment, and committed employees are always in demand. Competent employees are the result of experience, knowledge, and opportunity. More opportunities are usually better. One of the greatest shortcomings of supervisors in all types of situations is a failure to recognize the capabilities and potential of others. People are like 10-speed bicycles. We all have more gears than we ever use. We are capable of so much more than what our current jobs require of us. Challenging workers beyond the normal call of duty allows them to develop as they acquire new experiences. This contributes to the culture of an organization in which continuous improvement has been identified as a goal.

References

Buckingham, M., and C. Coffman. 1999. *First, Break All The Rules.* Simon & Schuster, New York, NY.

Brandon, R., and A. Spruch. 2008. Inspired Landscapes. *American School and University,* November.

Chickering, A., and L. Reisser. 1993. *Education and Identity.* San Francisco: Jossey-Bass Publishers.

Levine, A., and J. Cureton. 1998. Collegiate Life: An Obituary. *Change* 30, no. 30 (May/June).

Marchese, T. 1990. A New Conversation about Undergraduate Teaching: An Interview with Professor Richard J. Light, Convener of the Harvard Assessment Seminars. *AAHE Bulletin 42,* no. 9: 3–8.

Strange, C., and J. Banning. 2001. *Educating by Design.* San Francisco: Jossey-Bass.

CHAPTER 4

Landscape Inventory and Measurement

By Gerald Dobbs

"How many people do you need?"

Facility managers have all heard that question before. In grounds management, the answer involves defining the level of expectations and the frequency of service, but it starts with "How much and what is it?" Therefore, measuring and inventorying the campus is essential to making staffing and management decisions.

Landscape management is actually a form of asset management. If trees, athletic fields, sidewalks, parking lots, flower beds, benches, and lawns are seen as facility assets, it becomes clearer that managers must measure and quantify what they are maintaining. Only when the landscape assets have been measured and quantified (inventoried) can a landscape manager develop a year-round maintenance plan that effectively uses available resources—labor, materials, and finances.

Global Positioning Systems

Until recently, managers had two methods to inventory landscape assets. They could perform a field survey, actually measuring and counting on the site, a time-consuming process. Or they could use maps and a planimeter, a measuring device that is used to trace the boundary of the area being measured on a map. Once traced, the planimeter number displayed on the dial wheel is used in a mathematical formula to calculate the size of the area being measured. This is a time-consuming, tedious, yet accurate process to calculate area. However, individual site assets such as trees still need to be individually inventoried and manually located on the site maps.

In the latter part of the 20th century, 24 global positioning system (GPS) satellites were put into orbit. These satellites, maintained by the United States government, create a free, space-based, global navigation system that provides reliable location information anywhere there is an unobstructed line of sight from the ground to four or more satellites.

On a handheld GPS receiver, such as those produced by Trimble, Garmin, or Leica, radio signals coming in from those satellites are tracked and the user can "lock in" the location at any given point and information about any asset within a given area. The receiver also allows an operator to type in the name of an asset and record any other pertinent information. For instance, you can plot the corners of a flower bed, or the location and current condition of a white oak tree with a 23-inch diameter.

Geographic Information Systems

The data collected in this GPS receiver can be downloaded into an office computer with compatible geographic information system (GIS) software (essentially a data-based program that can correlate and integrate data with maps), so the information collected in the field can be translated and seen electronically as a computer-aided design (CAD) map. Asset information collected in the field can also be placed into individualized layer maps dedicated to a specific asset such as turf, trees, or irrigation systems. Several layer maps dedicated to specific assets can be created so that one or more assets can be viewed and studied at one time. For example, you could view both the turf and trees, but not the irrigation system, or any combination of assets. With the correct geographic data-based program, such as Pathfinder or MUNSYS, queries can be made to locate a particular asset using category-type identifiers such as the asset name, location, or identification number.

As an example, Michigan State University Physical Plant used MUNSYS in conjunction with AutoCAD software to collect all spatial data from the maps and translate the data into useful information for management purposes. To date, Michigan State University has used this system to measure, map, and quantify all the site features on campus, including trees, shrub beds, turf areas, wood lots, naturalized areas, roads, sidewalks, parking lots, and loading docks (see Figure 4.1).

Figure 4.1: Customer Funding Source Areas — Michigan State University

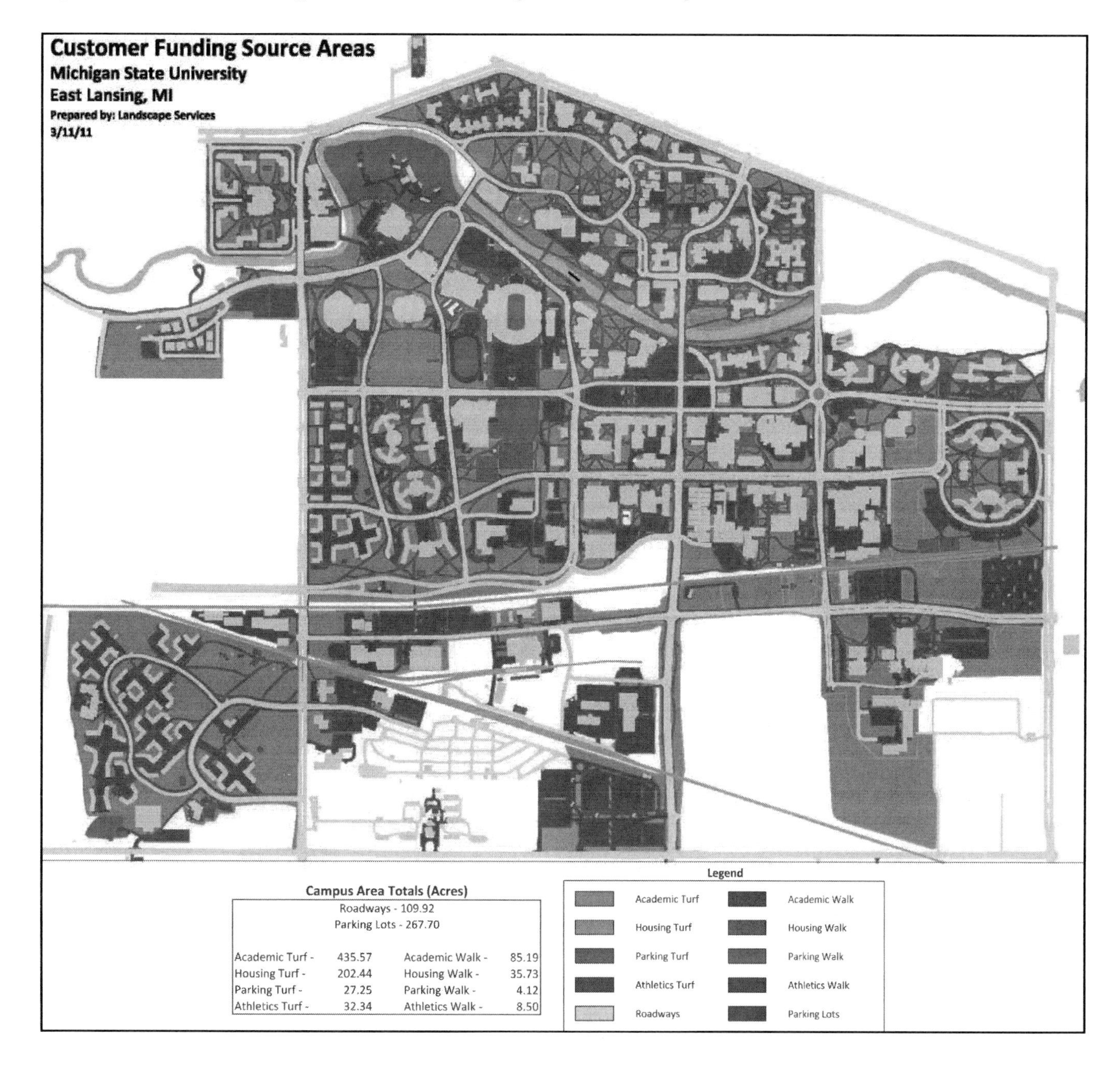

A landscape manager can gather spatial information such as quantities, location, area size, age, plant size, types, and treatments of assets within the green spaces. Areas can be further sorted by secondary factors such as funding source (see Figure 4.2). This provides the basic information necessary to make such management decisions as budgeting and work scheduling or to calculate staffing needs, supply purchases, and equipment requirements.

Figure 4.2: Landscape Services Overhead Breakdown by Funding Source

Funding Source	Area (acres)	Sidewalks	Lawn Panels	Road Area	Parking Lot Area
Academic	540.07	83.03	362.03	95.01	0.00
Housing	247.32	34.82	212.50	0.00	0.00
Parking	242.21	4.14	20.09	0.00	217.97
Contracts	106.56	0.00	69.90	0.00	0.00
Athletic	30.88	1.00	29.88	0.00	0.00
Totals:	1167.04	123.00	694.41	95.01	217.97

Contracts	Area (acres)
Ag Expo	27.9073
Corporate Research	34.9928
Observatory	3.7157
Henry Center	9.8213
Dobie Road	0.9294
Pavilion	29.1941
Total:	106.5606

Application and Management Decisions

When the special data and quantities are combined with factors like the age and life expectancy of those same assets, the manager can calculate when and how much funding will be necessary for renewal and replacement of landscape assets.

Now that we have measured and quantified our landscape, we are one step closer to answering our basic question, "How many people do you need?" The answer can vary from site to site, from campus to campus, and from region to region. An acre that is heavily landscaped with formal flower beds, fountains, and topiaries will require a vastly different landscape maintenance plan with different labor and material needs than an acre that is park-like, with lawn panels and large trees. Once the landscape area is mapped, measured, and quantified, and the levels of service to be provided to those areas determined, the manager can begin to calculate the staffing resources that are needed, as demonstrated in Chapter 5. It also becomes much easier to determine the types of employee positions (or skills) and the associated labor costs needed to maintain the landscape to the customer's satisfaction.

If the manager is maintaining several acres with large specimen trees, the landscape maintenance plan may require hiring one or two arborists. If several acres of lawn areas are being maintained, two groundskeepers may be needed to mow and maintain the turf areas. Or, if several acres of parking lots, sidewalks, and roadways are being maintained, equipment operators may be needed to run street sweepers or paving machines. Mapping the different types of landscape areas and measuring the quantities of the assets in those areas can help a manager accurately estimate the labor cost to maintain those sites.

The data can also be helpful in calculating what types of supplies and services are needed to maintain the landscape. Although the actual needs will vary from site to site, quantities and costs of materials such as fertilizers, mulch, and lawn chemicals can be easily calculated using the measures and quantities. If the landscape plan requires a specialized service that is outside the normal scope or ability of the staff, such as tree work or maintenance of street lights, measuring, mapping, and quantifying those assets will help the manager to estimate, bid, and contract their maintenance.

Finally, the manager needs to know what types and how many pieces of equipment are needed to maintain the landscape area. Determining both the size of the area to be maintained and the quantity of the assets to be maintained is invaluable in determining the type and amount of equipment required because each type of asset demands different levels and frequencies of maintenance. Managers of landscape areas can use the asset information coupled with operational rates of equipment that manufacturers provide to determine what type and how many units of equipment are needed to do the job effectively and efficiently.

New GPS and mapping technologies also provide the ability to track a GPS receiver and measure its movements through the day. This can provide the quantities for determining actual versus theoretical productivity on a real-time basis and gives the landscape manager strong, reliable data for deciding how to provide the most cost-effective and efficient service possible.

Measuring and quantifying your landscape assets is critical to efficient and effective management, determining resource needs, and planning for capital renewal and replacement. Using GPS and GIS systems makes this portion of the landscape manager's job a little easier and a lot more accurate.

CHAPTER 5

Grounds Staffing Guidelines

By Thomas Flood, Robert A. Getz, John Lawter, and John Burns

In the ten years since *Operational Guidelines for Grounds Management* was first published, it has provided a one-of-a-kind guide to grounds managers throughout North America. However, one common misconception persists, that this guide will tell every user the correct staffing requirements for their institution.

This guide is not—and cannot be—the final authority in answering the question, "How large should my grounds staff be?" In fact, no guideline could possibly cover the climate differences between Michigan and New Mexico, the horticultural variations from Seattle to Savannah, or the nuances of urban versus rural environments, or large institutions versus small institutions.

Unlike the maintenance of mechanical equipment such as chillers, which can be distilled down to degree days and operating hours, the maintenance of grounds is an individual thing. Yes, we can broadly define the level of service, but what that looks like in the arid southwest is quite different from the temperate rain forest of the northwest. Location also affects things you may never think of such as weed and pest control requirements, mulching and edging expenses, and irrigation needs.

And the variables continue to compound. The number of students on campus affects the volume of litter; and the species of grass and turf maintenance practices determine mowing frequency, school policies regarding use, the extent of sports activities, and so on.

Finally, unlike mechanical equipment or routine processes such as carpet cleaning, the landscape is a living system, subject to extremes of weather, disease, and storms.

Each year, APPA conducts a survey of hundreds of colleges, universities, and schools as part of its Facilities Performance Indicators (FPI) program. A component of the FPI program collects data in the areas of grounds and landscape management. As with any benchmarking program, the collection of such data evolves over time, especially as participants redefine and clarify the data collection process.

One aspect of the benchmarking process is to assist grounds managers to determine the number of full-time equivalent employees (FTEs) needed to maintain grounds operations based on a variety of variables that include the level of maintenance reported, school size, and APPA region. Such data can be an invaluable tool to determine potential staffing levels at educational institutions, but it is critical that this data be used correctly. Because of these innumerable variations in grounds management and reporting as enumerated below, the FPI data does not, and cannot, provide a universal benchmark of grounds staffing that can be applied to all schools. However, the FPI does provide an invaluable resource for schools to compare data with peer institutions that share common variables such as region, climate, size use, horticulture, and grounds management programs.

In an effort to answer this recurrent staffing question, the author undertook a five-year analysis of FPI data. The collected responses were evaluated to determine the number of Grounds FTE (full-time equivalent employees) per acre, maintained in three traceable variables: maintenance level reported, school size, and APPA region. In only the most recent data year did the increase in reported maintenance level correspond to a decrease in the numbers of acres maintained by FTE. In all other years, and with all other variables, there was no correlation between maintenance level, region, or school size and the number of employees required to maintain the grounds.

In conversations with grounds professionals at dozens of schools, the respondents reported having many different suborganizations in their departments. For example, they may have solid waste and recycling removal, a motor pool or vehicle repair shop, moving and setup activities, or masonry operations to name a few. Informal evidence indicates that these FTEs are not being removed when reporting to the FPI, further exacerbating the problem.

We recognize that there are innumerable benchmarking variables that affect not only grounds operations, but also maintenance and custodial operations. Over the past several years grounds professionals have worked diligently to identify meaningful variables, and these have been integrated and refined into APPA's FPI survey and report.

The APPA FPI program provides critical information for grounds managers that will assist organization to benchmark their operations both regionally and nationally. We encourage institutions to be accurate in reporting their data and stay be involved in future data collection efforts at http://appa.org/research/FPI/index.cfm.

Does the fact that many institutions have variables outside of any benchmarking effort detract from benchmarking programs? The answer is a definitive "No." The key is to understand the process and the variables involved, select comparable institutions, and examine the data carefully to make sure you are comparing apples to apples.

This guideline is just that. The types of equipment and scenarios listed are finite, and there are many others to examine. However, it is a great beginning and a great resource to create a working management guideline for your individual institution. Following the staffing guideline, you will find three case studies, all of which have been developed using these similar parameters and all of which provide accurate, evidence-based information for making sound management decisions.

Fortunately, the days of comparing grounds operations at peer institutions on an FTE per gross square footage (GSF) of building basis are over, but be aware that Acres/FTE may or may not be a better standard. Determining your own management practices and staffing comparisons is well worth the time and effort.

Staffing Guidelines

By Robert A. Getz

Providing guidelines for calculating the staffing requirements for a particular grounds area is based on two essential factors. First is the type of area that must be maintained and the tasks associated with that maintenance. Second is the amount of care to be provided, or the level of attention to be paid, to the grounds area. This section presents a series of matrices that integrate these two factors, facilitating determination of the staffing requirements for a particular type of grounds area. The Levels of Attention are described first, followed by matrices presenting tasks for grounds areas ranging from flower beds to football fields.

These matrices are designed to illustrate that each maintenance task may be accomplished with greater or lesser levels of attention. Higher levels of attention will require more staffing. The matrices are the building blocks of the grounds staffing guidelines. This chapter provides a detailed explanation of how the matrices can be used to determine required staffing levels.

Levels of Attention

The Level of Attention is the amount of time dedicated to a maintenance task. The following six sections detail what is expected at each Level of Attention. These levels were developed in part from the National Recreation and Park Association's *Park Maintenance Standards,* in which they are referred to as "modes." They provide a word picture of what one would expect to see when encountering each of the types of spaces. Level 1 is reserved for a special, high-visibility area that requires maintenance levels beyond the norm. Level 2 is the norm one expects to see on a regular, recurring basis. This Level of Attention is the standard desired.

Levels 3 and 4 are lower than the norm and result from insufficient staff or funding. For whatever reason, sufficient staff is not available to accomplish the care and maintenance required for the landscaped material and the standard (Level 2) is not maintained.

Level 5 is one step before land is allowed to return to its original state. Level 6 is the point at which the land is allowed to return to its natural state and is not included in the matrices.

Level 1

State-of-the-art maintenance applied to a high-quality diverse landscape. Associated with high-traffic urban areas, such as public squares, government grounds, or college, university, or school campuses.

TURF CARE. Grass height maintained according to species and variety of grass. Mowed at least once every five working days but may be as often as once every three working days. Aeration as required but not less than four times per year. Reseeding or sodding as needed. Weed control to be practiced so that no more than 1 percent of the surface has weeds present.

FERTILIZER. Adequate fertilization applied to plant species according to their optimum requirements. Application rates and times should ensure an even supply of nutrients for the entire year. Nitrogen, phosphorus, and potassium percentages should follow local recommendations. Trees, shrubs, and flowers should be fertilized according to their individual requirements for optimum growth. Unusually long or short growing seasons may modify the chart slightly.

IRRIGATION. Sprinkler irrigated – electric automatic commonly used. Some manual systems could be considered adequate under plentiful rainfall circumstances and with adequate staffing. Frequency of use follows rainfall, temperature, season length, and demand of plant material.

LITTER CONTROL. Minimum of once per day, seven days per week. Extremely high visitation may increase frequency. Receptacles should be plentiful enough to hold all trash usually generated between servicing without overflowing.

PRUNING. Frequency dictated primarily by species and variety of trees and shrubs. Length of growing season and design concept also a controlling factor, i.e., clipped vs. natural-style hedges. Timing scheduled to coincide with low demand periods or to take advantage of special growing characteristics.

DISEASE AND INSECT CONTROL. At this maintenance level, the controlling object is to avoid public awareness of any problem. It is anticipated at Level 1 that problems will either be prevented or observed at an early state and corrected immediately.

SNOW REMOVAL. Snow removal starts the same day that accumulations reach .5 inches. At no time will snow be permitted to cover transportation or parking surfaces longer than noon of the day after the snow stops. Application of snow-melting compound and/or gravel is appropriate to reduce the danger of injury due to falls.

SURFACES. Sweeping, cleaning, and washing of surfaces should be done so that at no time does an accumulation of sand, dirt, or leaves distract from the looks or safety of the area.

REPAIRS. All repairs to all elements of the design should be done immediately when problems are discovered, providing that replacement parts and technicians are available to accomplish the job. When disruption of the public might be major or the repair is not critical, repairs may be postponed to a time period that is least disruptive.

INSPECTIONS. A staff member should conduct inspection daily.

FLORAL PLANTINGS. Normally, extensive or unusual floral plantings are part of the design. These may include ground-level beds, planters, or hanging baskets. Often, multiple plantings are scheduled, usually for at least two blooming cycles per year. Some designs may call for a more frequent rotation of bloom. Maximum care, including watering, fertilizing, disease control, disbudding, and weeding, is necessary. Weeding flowers and shrubs is done a minimum of once per week. The desired standard is essentially weed free.

Level 2

High level of maintenance. Associated with well-developed public areas, malls, government grounds, or college, university, or school campuses. Recommended level for most organizations.

TURF CARE. Grass should be cut once every five working days. Aeration is carried out as required but not less than two times per year. Reseeding or sodding must be done when bare spots are present. Weed control is practiced when weeds present a visible problem or when weeds represent 5 percent of the turf surface. Some pre-emergent herbicide products may be used at this level.

FERTILIZER. Adequate fertilizer level to ensure that all plant materials are healthy and growing vigorously. Amounts depend on species, length of growing season, soils, and rainfall. Rates should correspond to at least the lowest recommended rates. Distribution should ensure an even supply of nutrients for the entire year. Nitrogen, phosphorus, and potassium percentages should follow local recommendations. Trees, shrubs, and flowers should receive fertilizer levels to ensure optimum growth.

IRRIGATION. Sprinkler irrigated – electric automatic commonly used. Some manual systems could be considered adequate under plentiful rainfall circumstances and with adequate staffing. Frequency of use follows rainfall, temperature, season length, and demand of plant material.

LITTER CONTROL. Minimum of once per day, five days per week. Offsite movement of trash depends on size of containers and use by the public. High use may dictate more frequent cleaning.

PRUNING. Usually done at least once per season unless species planted dictate more frequent attention. Sculpted hedges or high-growth species may dictate a more frequent requirement than most trees and shrubs in natural-growth plantings.

DISEASE AND INSECT CONTROL. Usually carried out when disease or insects are inflicting noticeable damage, reducing vigor of plant material, or whenever the situation could be considered a bother to the public. Some preventive measures may be used, such as systemic chemical treatments. Cultural prevention of disease problems can reduce time spent in this category. Some minor problems may be tolerated at this level.

SNOW REMOVAL. Snow removed by noon of the day after the snowfall. Gravel or snowmelt may be used to reduce ice accumulation.

SURFACES. Should be cleaned, repaired, repainted, or replaced when their appearances have noticeably deteriorated.

REPAIRS. Should be done whenever safety, function, or appearance is in question.

INSPECTIONS. Inspection should be conducted by a staff member at least once a day whenever regular staff is scheduled.

FLORAL PLANTINGS. Normally no more complex than two rotations of blooming plants per year. Care cycle is a minimum of once per week, but watering may be more frequent. Health and vigor dictate cycle of fertilization and disease control. Beds are essentially kept free of weeds.

Level 3

Moderate-level maintenance. Associated with locations that have moderate to low levels of development or visitation, or with operations that (because of budget restrictions) cannot afford a high level of maintenance.

TURF CARE. Grass cut once every ten working days. Normally not aerated unless turf quality indicates a need or in anticipation of application of fertilizer. Reseeding or sodding only when major bare spots appear. Weed control measures normally applied when 50 percent of small areas—or 15 percent of the general turf—is infested with weeds.

FERTILIZER. Applied only when turf vigor seems to be low. Low-level application once per year. Suggested application rate is one-half the level recommended.

IRRIGATION. Dependent on climate. Locations that receive more than 25 inches of rainfall a year usually rely on natural rainfall with the possible addition of portable irrigation during periods of drought. Dry climates that receive less than 25 inches of rainfall usually have some form of supplemental irrigation. When irrigation is automatic, a demand schedule is programmed. When manual servicing is required, the normal schedule would be two to three times per week.

LITTER CONTROL. Minimum service of two to three times per week. High use may dictate higher levels during the warm season.

PRUNING. When required for health or reasonable appearance. With most tree and shrub species, pruning would be performed once every two to three years.

DISEASE AND INSECT CONTROL. Done only to address epidemics or serious complaints. Control measures may be put into effect when the health or survival of the plant material is threatened or when public comfort is an issue.

SNOW REMOVAL. Snow removal is generally based on local law requirements and is usually accomplished by the day following snowfall. Some crosswalks or surfaces may not be cleared at all.

SURFACES. Cleaned on a complaint basis. Repaired or replaced as budget allows.

REPAIRS. Should be done whenever safety, function, or appearance is in question.

INSPECTIONS. Inspections are conducted once per week.

FLORAL PLANTINGS. Only perennials or flowering trees or shrubs.

LEVEL 4

Moderately low-level maintenance. Associated with locations affected by budget restrictions, and thereby cannot afford a high level of maintenance.

TURF CARE. Low-frequency mowing scheduled based on species. Low-growing grasses may not be mowed. High grasses may receive periodic mowing. Weed control limited to legal requirements for noxious weeds.

FERTILIZER. Not fertilized.

IRRIGATION. No irrigation.

LITTER CONTROL. Once per week or less.

PRUNING. No regular trimming. Safety or damage from weather may dictate actual work schedule.

DISEASE AND INSECT CONTROL. None except when the problem is epidemic and the conditions threaten resources or the public.

SNOW REMOVAL. Snow removal based on local law requirements and generally accomplished by the day following snowfall. Some crosswalks or surfaces may not be cleared at all.

SURFACES. Replaced or repaired when safety is a concern and when budget is available.

REPAIRS. Should be done whenever safety, function, or appearance is in question.

INSPECTIONS. Inspections are conducted once a month.

FLORAL PLANTINGS. None. May have wildflowers, perennials, flowering trees, or shrubs in place.

Level 5

Minimum-level maintenance. Associated with locations suffering from severe budget restrictions.

TURF CARE. Low-frequency mowing scheduled based on species. Low-growing grasses may not be mowed; high grasses may receive periodic mowing. Weed control limited to legal requirements for noxious weeds.

FERTILIZER. Not fertilized.

IRRIGATION. No irrigation.

LITTER CONTROL. On demand or complaint basis.

PRUNING. No pruning unless safety is involved.

DISEASE AND INSECT CONTROL. No control expect in epidemic or safety situations.

SNOW REMOVAL. Snow removal done based on local law requirements but generally accomplished by the day following snowfall. Some crosswalks or surfaces may not be cleared.

SURFACES. Serviced only when safety is a consideration.

REPAIRS. Should be done whenever safety or function is in question.

INSPECTIONS. Inspections are conducted once a month.

FLORAL PLANTINGS. None. May have wildflowers, perennials, flowering trees, or shrubs in place.

Level 6

Natural area that is not developed.

TURF CARE. Not mowed. Weed control only if legal requirements demand.

FERTILIZER. Not fertilized.

IRRIGATION. No irrigation.

LITTER CONTROL. On demand or complaint basis.

PRUNING. No pruning unless safety is involved.

DISEASE AND INSECT CONTROL. No control except in epidemic or safety situations.

SNOW REMOVAL. Only as necessary.

SURFACES. Serviced only when safety is a consideration.

REPAIRS. Should be executed whenever safety or function is in question.

INSPECTIONS. Inspections are conducted once a month.

FLORAL PLANTINGS. None.

An Explanation of the Matrices

The matrices that follow represent only some of the types of grounds that exist at our campuses, municipalities, and other organizations. Further areas may be considered for future editions of this publication.

The Sample Staffing Matrix in Figure 5.1 serves as an example to illustrate how grounds staffing calculations are made. The dimensions of the flower bed—10'x100'=1,000 square ft.—were arbitrarily determined. It is shown in Figure 5.2 as a ten-ft.-wide space along the side of a building.

The space may not actually exist anywhere in reality, but it is a dimension that may be readily visualized as a representative space for multiple locations. It may also be quantified by time studies to provide a measuring stick against which specific grounds may be compared. The size of the flower bed can also be easily understood and described by an administrator, supervisor, board member, or other authority, thus facilitating explanation of how final staffing levels have been determined.

Across the top of the matrix, Levels of Attention are noted as 1, 2, 3, 4, and 5. These levels indicate how much attention will be allotted to the flower bed. Level 1 is the highest level of attention, and is normally restricted to prominent local entities such as administrative offices, newly donated buildings, a location frequented by visitors, or another point of interest.

Level 2 is the norm. The attention at this level is what would normally be regarded as day-to-day service. Levels 3 and 4 show a decline in service resulting from cuts in staff as a result of restructuring, downsizing, budget cuts, or leveling.

Finally, Level 5 might more properly be called the Level of Inattention. It is the point at which the next step would be to plow the bed under and seed for grass.

Figure 5.1: Sample Staffing Matrix

10' x 100' = 1,000 Square Feet

	Levels of Attention				
Maintenance Tasks	1	2	3	4	5
Spring Preparation	0.03	0.03	0.03	0.04	0.04
200 Minutes	6.0	6.0	6.0	8.0	8.0
Spring Planting	0.03	0.03	0.03	0.04	0.04
600 Minutes	18.0	18.0	18.0	24.0	24.0
Weed – No Mulch	1.5	1.0			
60 Minutes	90.0	60.0			
Cultivate – No Mulch	1.5	1.0			
30 Minutes	45.0	30.0			
Fall Planting	0.03	0.03	0.03		
300 Minutes	9.0	9.0	9.0		
Fall Clean Up	0.03	0.03	0.03	0.04	0.04
400 Minutes	12.0	12.0	12.0	16.0	16.0
Bulb Planting	0.03	0.03	0.03	0.04	
600 Minutes	18.0	18.0	18.0	24.0	
Pre-Emergent Control	0.03	0.03	0.03	0.04	0.04
5 Minutes	0.2	0.2	0.2	0.2	0.2
Totals					
Minutes/Week	229.1	176.4	101.5	85.8	55.4
/60 Minutes	3.82	2.94	1.69	1.43	0.92
/6 Hours/Day	0.64	0.49	0.28	0.24	0.15
/5 Days/Week	0.13	0.10	0.06	0.05	0.03
Square Feet/Person	7,692	10,000	16,667	20,000	33,333

In the Maintenance Tasks column, a series of tasks required to maintain a flower bed is listed. Under each task, a time is listed based on the Professional Grounds Management Society's publication entitled *Grounds Maintenance Estimating Guidelines*. The specified time is a measure of how long it takes to accomplish the given task once in this 1,000-square-foot flower bed. For example, spring preparation of the flower bed requires 200 minutes. According to the column under Level 1, that time is multiplied by the adjustment factor of 0.03.

What is the rationale of the operation described above? Because the task will be performed only once in the entire 30 week season, the analysis can be broken down as follows:

200 minutes x 0.03 = 6 minutes per week

If the growing season is only 25 weeks, as shown in Level 4, the adjustment factor becomes 0.04, with the following result:

200 minutes x 0.04 = 8 minutes per week

Reading further down the Maintenance Task column, to a task that is performed more frequently, we can see the task labeled Weed-No Mulch. Under Level 2, the adjustment factor of 1.00 indicates that this activity is performed weekly. Thus, a 60-minute task is calculated as:

60 minutes x 1.00 = 60 minutes per week

The adjustment factors account for the time required to accomplish each task, based on the Level of Attention. After all the adjustments are made, each Level of Attention column is totaled. For the Level 2 column, the minutes per week total is 176.4.

This calculation means that one person will require 176.4 minutes on average each week for 30 weeks to accomplish all the tasks normally associated with the 1,000-square-foot flower bed at Level of Attention 2. Dividing that total by 60 minutes converts the minutes to hours, or 2.94 hours per week.

Dividing that total by 6 production hours in each workday converts the hours to 0.49 person/days. Dividing the total by 5 days in a week results in the staffing level required on a weekly basis to accomplish these tasks, or a level of 0.10 for the flower bed example at Level of Attention 2.

The next step is to convert that number into a square footage assignment for one person, using the following formula:

Y square feet / one person = 1,000 square feet / 0.10 person

Y = (1,000 square feet / 0.10 person) x one person

Y = 10,000 square feet per person

In other words, one person may be hired to care for 10,000 square feet of flower beds to meet the criteria noted at Level 2.

The procedure works for each of the other columns; the Level of Attention determines how much square footage an individual can care for. In the Level 5 column, one person is assigned to care for 33,333 square feet of flower beds, or 33 flower beds at 1,000 square feet each.

Ask those to whom you report to measure their flower gardens at home. Let's assume they come up with one that is about equal to this example of 1,000 square feet. Do your supervisors honestly believe that they could plant, maintain, and clean up more than 33 such flower beds without any assistance? That scenario is a true picture of Level 5 flower bed maintenance. Those flower beds would be only marginally above being turned over for grassy areas.

Figures 5.2 through 5.7 illustrate the staffing requirements at each of the five Levels of Attention for a baseball/softball field, a shrub area, a football/soccer field, an open turf area, and turf on the main grounds. These tables may be used to calculate staffing levels for a variety of grounds maintenance areas.

Figure 5.2: Flower Bed

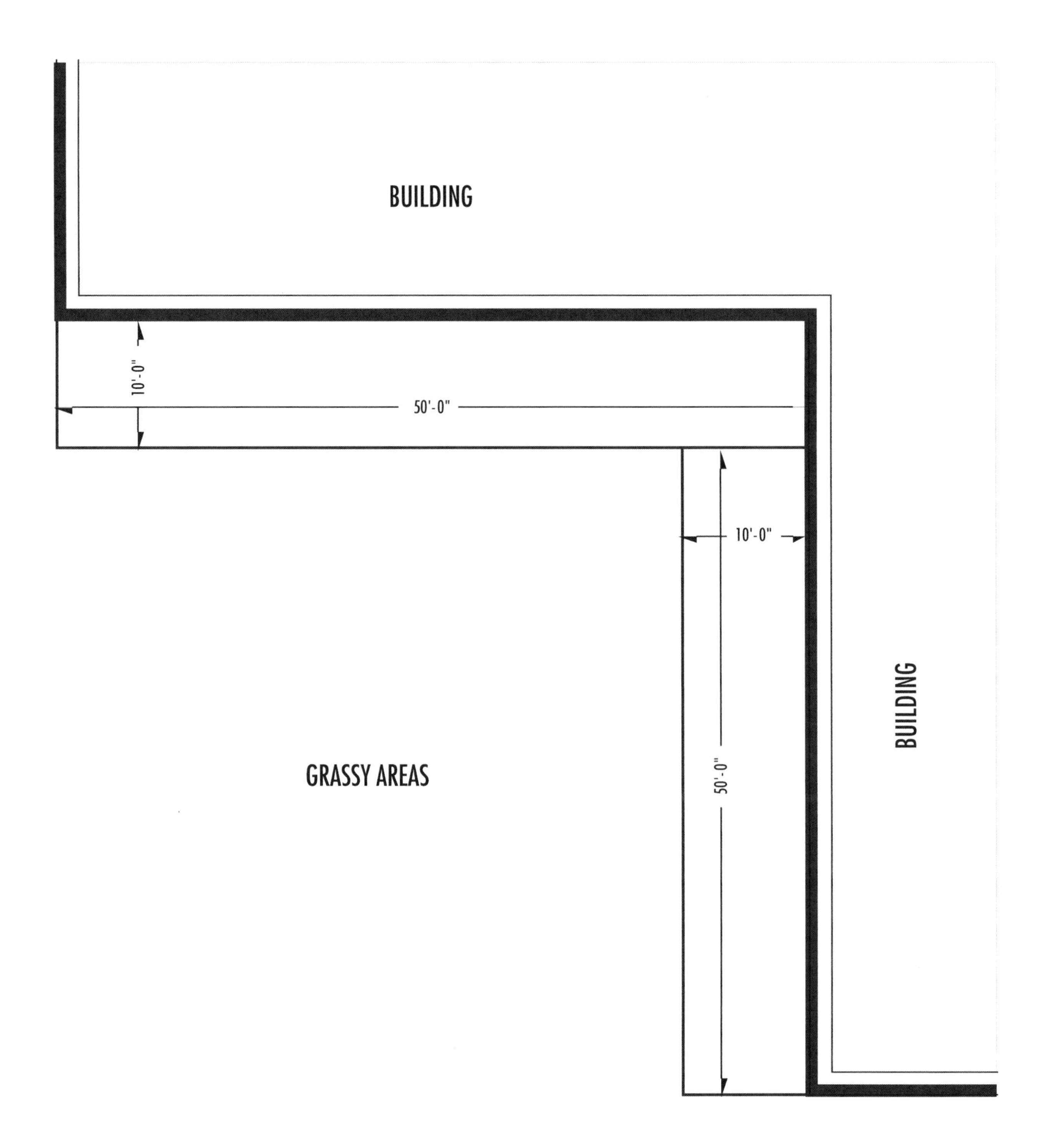

Figure 5.2A: Flower Bed Staffing Matrix[1]

10' x 100' = 1,000 Square Feet

	Levels of Attention				
Maintenance Tasks	1	2	3	4	5
Spring Preparation	0.03[2]	0.03	0.03	0.04[3]	0.04
200 Minutes	6.0	6.0	6.0	8.0	8.0
Spring Planting	0.03	0.03	0.03	0.04	0.04
600 Minutes	18.0	18.0	18.0	24.0	24.0
Weed – No Mulch	1.5[4]	1.0			
60 Minutes	90.0	60.0			
Cultivate – No Mulch	1.5	1.0			
30 Minutes	45.0	30.0			
Mulch			0.03	0.04	0.04
30 Minutes			0.9	1.2	1.2
Weed with Mulch			1.0	0.5	0.25
20 Minutes			20.0	10.0	5.0
Spray	0.17	0.17	0.1	0.12	0.04
10 Minutes	1.7	1.7	1.0	1.2	0.4
Fertilize	0.13	0.1	0.07	0.08	0.04
5 Minutes	0.7	0.5	0.4	0.4	0.2
Police by Hand	1.5	1.0			
15 Minutes	22.5	15			
Police by Vacuum			1.0	0.08	0.04
10 Minutes			10.0	0.8	0.4
Fall Preparation	0.03	0.03	0.03		
200 Minutes	6.0	6.0	6.0		
Fall Planting	0.03	0.03	0.03		
300 Minutes	9.0	9.0	9.0		
Fall Clean Up	0.03	0.03	0.03	0.04	0.04
400 Minutes	12.0	12.0	12.0	16.0	16.0
Bulb Planting	0.03	0.03	0.03	0.04[5]	
600 Minutes	18.0	18.0	18.0	24.0	
Pre-Emergent Control	0.03	0.03	0.03	0.04	0.04
5 Minutes	0.2	0.2	0.2	0.2	0.2
TOTALS					
Minutes/Week	229.1	176.4	101.5	85.8	55.4
/60 Minutes	3.82	2.94	1.69	1.43	0.92
/6 Hours/Day	0.64	0.49	0.28	0.24	0.15
/5 Days/Week	0.13	0.10	0.06	0.05	0.03
Square Feet/Person	7,692	10,000	16,667	20,000	33,333

Notes:

1. If three plantings are planned (spring, fall, and bulbs), the growing season will be assumed to be 30 weeks from the first planting. If one or two plantings are planned (spring and bulbs), the growing season will be assumed to be 25 weeks. These assumptions are used in determining the adjustment factor described in note 2. If the growing season is longer or shorter, the matrix may be altered to allow for that situation.
2. This simple mathematical procedure is used to set a weekly multiplier. For example, for a task that is performed once a week, the adjustment factor is 1.00. For a biweekly assignment, the adjustment factor becomes 0.50. For once a season, divide the number 1 by the number of weeks in the season. Once in a 30-week period is one (1) divided by 30, which results in an adjustment factor of 0.03. The adjustment factor for once in 25 weeks is one (1) divided by 25, which is equal to 0.04. Activity frequency determines the adjustment factor:

Activity Frequency	Adjustment Factor
1.5 times per week	1.5
1 time per week	1.0
Biweekly	0.5
Monthly	0.25

The adjustment factor for infrequent activities must take length of season into account:

Activity Frequency	Adjustment Factor for 30-Week Season	Adjustment Factor for 25-Week Season
5 times per season	5/30 = 0.17	5/25 = 0.20
4 times per season	4/30 = 0.13	4/25 = 0.16
3 times per season	3/30 = 0.10	3/25 = 0.12
2 times per season	2/30 = 0.07	2/25 = 0.08
1 time per season	1/30 = 0.03	1/25 = 0.04

3. Between the third and fourth levels of attention, the fall planting is eliminated. The growing season is thereby reduced from 30 weeks to 25 weeks. In some instances, this shortened growing season will not show a corresponding reduction in the weekly requirements, but overall staff requirements will be reduced. Such

a reduction in staffing requirements results in a saving in total dollars spent for grounds operations.

4. No mulch is used at Level 1 or Level 2. Mulch will be added at Level 3. If you prefer to add mulch at all 5 levels, adjust your matrix accordingly.
5. Bulb planting is eliminated at Level 5.

Figure 5.3: Baseball/Softball Field

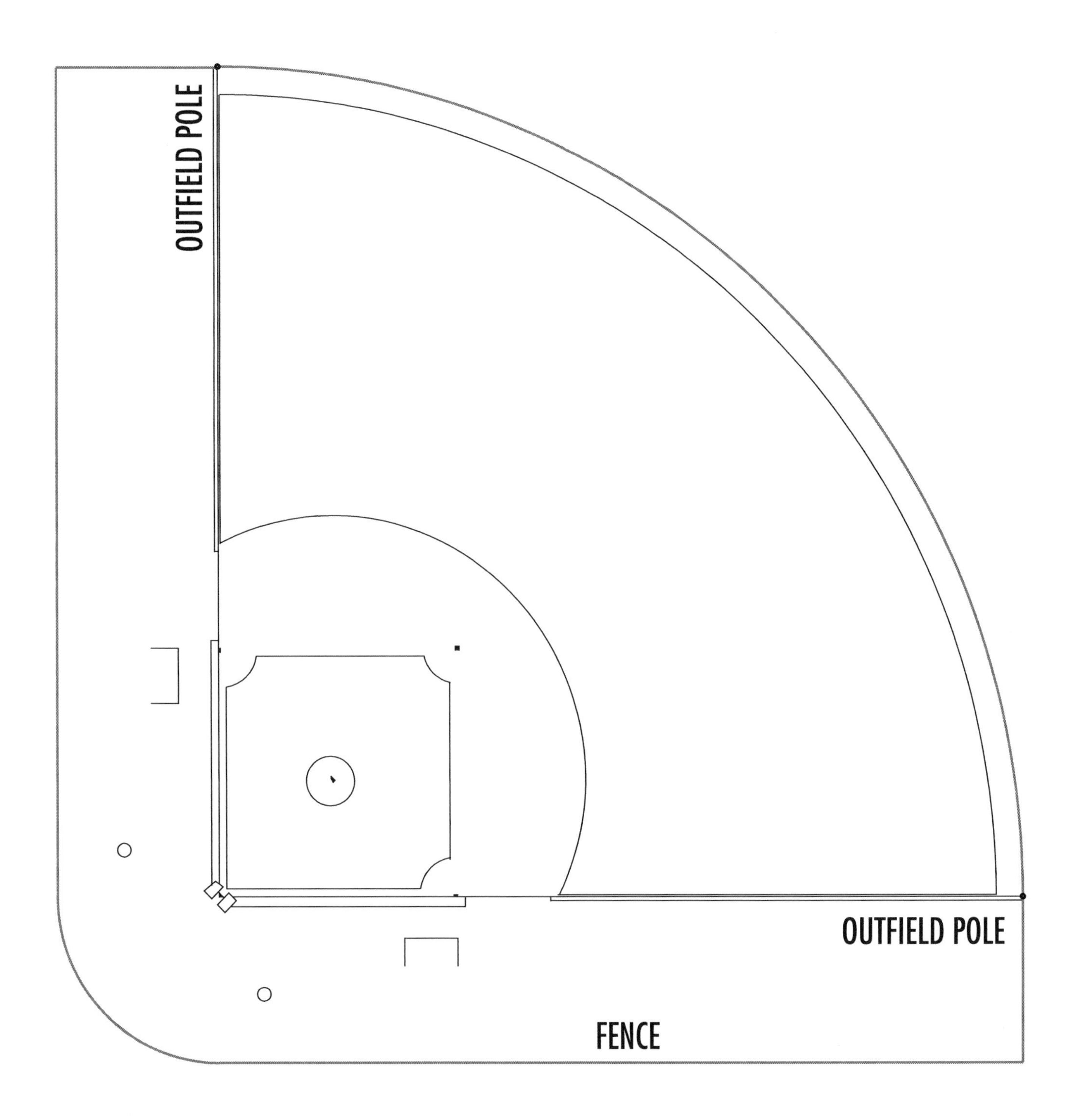

Figure 5.3A: Baseball/Softball Field Staffing Matrix

Field plus Surrounding Area or 1 Acre; 30-Week Season

	Levels of Attention				
Maintenance Tasks	1	2	3	4	5
Mow Field – 30" Riding	1.50	1.00	1.00	0.50	0.50
Mower* – 120 Minutes	180.0	120.0	120.0	60.0	60.0
Seeding*	0.07	0.03			
180 Minutes	12.6	5.40			
Drag Field*	5.00	3.00	1.50	1.00	0.50
45 Minutes	225.0	135.0	67.5	45.00	22.5
Line Field and Rake*	5.00	3.00	1.50	1.00	0.50
75 Minutes	375.0	225.0	112.5	75.0	37.5
Clean Fields/Surrounding Areas*	1.50	1.00	0.50	0.25	
120 Minutes	180.0	120.0	60.0	30.0	
Repair, Regrade, and Reconstruct*	0.07	0.03	0.03		
480 Minutes	33.6	14.4	14.4		
Fertilize*	0.07	0.03	0.03		
60 Minutes	4.20	1.80	1.80		
TOTALS					
Minutes/Week	1010.4	621.6	376.2	210.0	120.0
/60 Minutes	16.84	10.36	6.27	3.5	2.00
/6 Hours/Day	2.807	1.727	1.045	0.583	0.3333
/5 Days/Week	0.5614	0.3454	0.209	0.1166	0.0666
Acres/Person	1.78	2.90	4.78	8.58	15.02

The adjustment factors are:

Activity Frequency	Adjustment Factor
1.5 Times per week	1.5
1 time per week	1.0
Biweekly	0.5
Monthly	0.25

5 times per season	5/30 = 0.17
4 times per season	4/30 = 0.13
3 times per season	3/30 = 0.10
2 times per season	2/30 = 0.07
1 time per season	1/30 = 0.03

* Park Maintenance Computation

Figure 5.4: Shrub Area

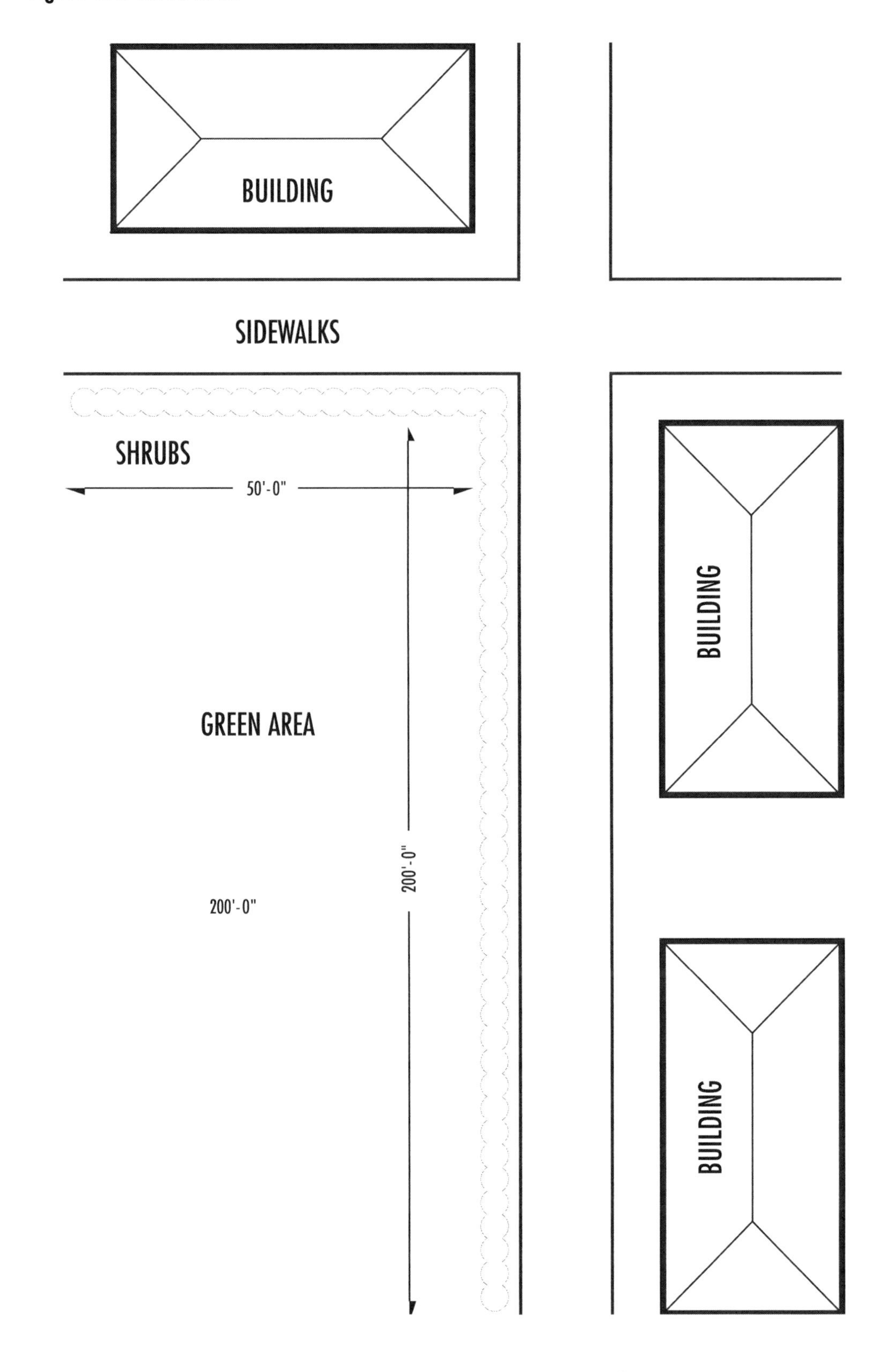

Figure 5.4A: Shrub Area Staffing Matrix

4' x 250' = 1,000 Square Feet; 30-Week Season

	Levels of Attention				
Maintenance Tasks	1	2	3	4	5
Weed – Hand Hoe	1.00	0.50			
60 Minutes	60.0	30.0			
Mulch Bark (Hand Apply)[1]			1.001	1.00	
30 Minutes			30.0	30.0	
Weed – Spray after Mulch			0.07	0.0	
10 Minutes			0.70	0.30	
Police – Hand Pickup	1.50	1.00			
15 Minutes	22.50	15.0			
Police – Vacuum			1.00	0.50	0.50
7 Minutes			7.00	3.50	3.50
Prune	0.1	0.07			
60 Minutes	6.00	4.20			
Fertilize (Broadcast)	0.07	0.03			
5 Minutes	0.35	0.15			
TOTALS					
Minutes/Week	89.20	49.50	37.70	33.80	3.50
/60 Minutes	1.49	0.83	0.63	0.56	0.06
/6 Hours/Day	0.25	0.14	0.1	0.09	0.01
/5 Days/Week	0.05	0.03	0.02	0.019	0.0019
Square Feet/Person	20,000	33,333	50,000	52,632	526,316

The adjustment factors are:

Activity Frequency	Adjustment Factor
1.5 Times per week	1.5
1 time per week	1.0
Biweekly	0.5
Monthly	0.25

5 times per season	5/30 = 0.17
4 times per season	4/30 = 0.13
3 times per season	3/30 = 0.10
2 times per season	2/30 = 0.07
1 time per season	1/30 = 0.03

Note:

1. There is no mulch at Levels 1 or 2. Mulch will be added at Level 3. If you prefer to add mulch at all 5 levels, adjust your matrix accordingly.

Figure 5.5: Football/Soccer Field

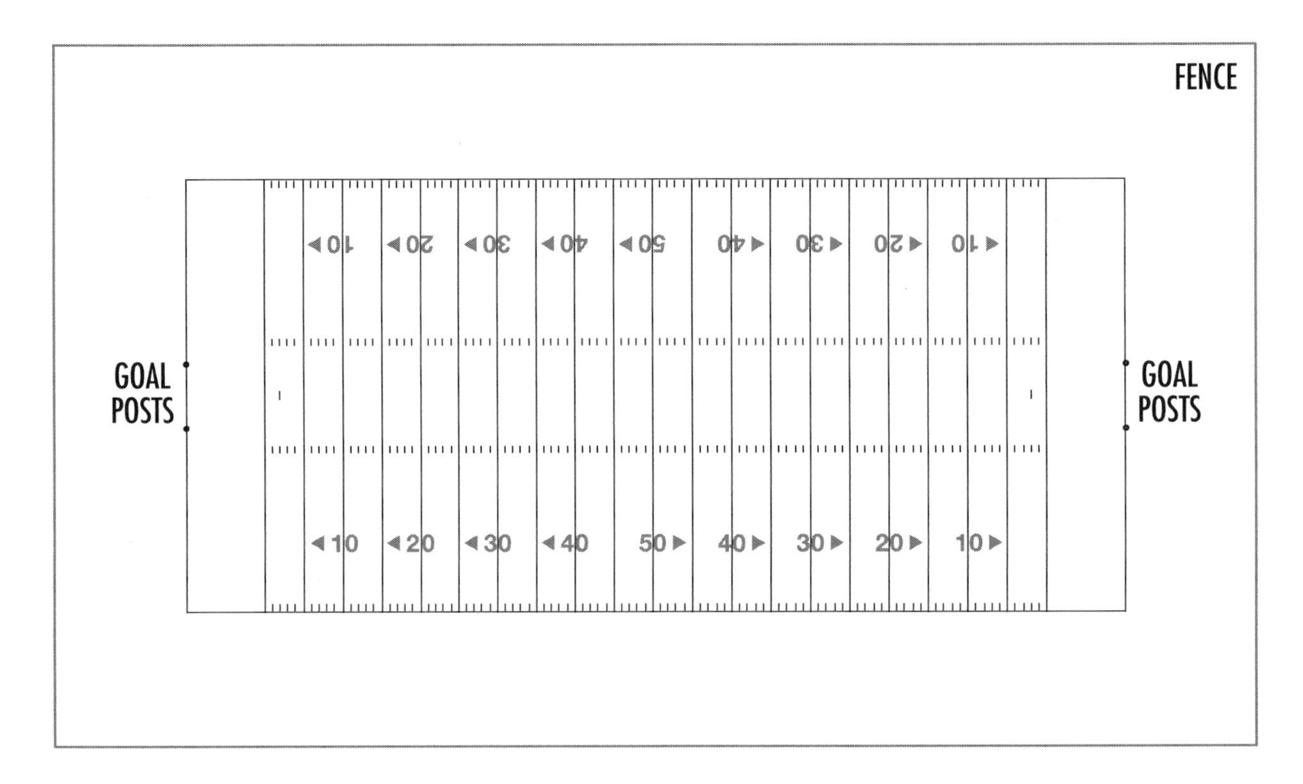

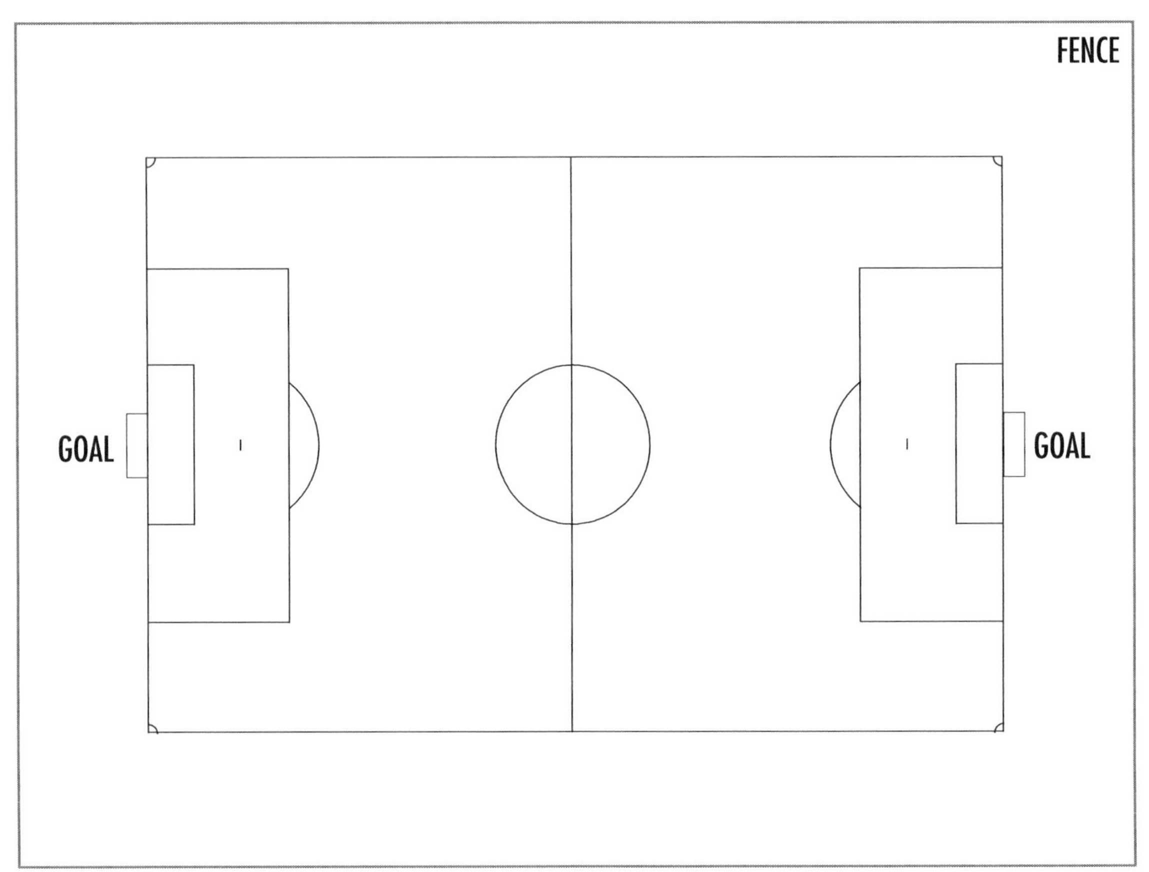

Figure 5.5A: Football/Soccer Field Staffing Matrix

100' x 300' = 30,000 Square Feet plus Surrounding Area or 1 Acre; 30-Week Season

	Levels of Attention				
Maintenance Tasks	1	2	3	4	5
Mow Field – 30" Riding	1.50	1.00	1.00	0.50	0.50
120 Minutes	180.0	120.0	120.0	60.0	60.0
Seeding*	0.07	0.03			
180 Minutes	12.6	5.4			
Clean Fields/Surrounding Areas*	1.50	1.00	0.50	0.25	
120 Minutes	180.0	120.0	60.0	30.0	
Line Field*	1.50	1.00	0.50	0.25	0.25
150 Minutes	225.0	150.0	75.5	37.5	37.5
Repair, Regrade, and Reconstruct*	0.07	0.03	0.03		
480 Minutes	33.6	14.4	14.4		
Goal Post Repair, Replace, Install, or Remove*	0.03	0.03	0.03	0.03	0.03
960 Minutes	28.8	28.8	28.8	28.8	28.8
Fertilize*	0.07	0.03	0.03		
60 Minutes	4.20	1.80	1.80		
TOTALS					
Minutes/Week	664.2	440.4	300.5	156.3	126.3
/60 Minutes	11.07	7.34	5.01	2.605	2.105
/6 Hours/Day	1.845	1.223	0.835	0.434	0.35081
/5 Days/Week	0.369	0.2446	0.167	0.0868	0.07
Acres/Person	2.71	4.09	5.99	11.52	14.29

The adjustment factors are:

Activity Frequency	Adjustment Factor
1.5 Times per week	1.5
1 time per week	1.0
Biweekly	0.5
Monthly	0.25

5 times per season	5/30 = 0.17
4 times per season	4/30 = 0.13
3 times per season	3/30 = 0.10
2 times per season	2/30 = 0.07
1 time per season	1/30 = 0.03

*Park Maintenance Computation

Figure 5.6: Turf Maintenance – Open Area

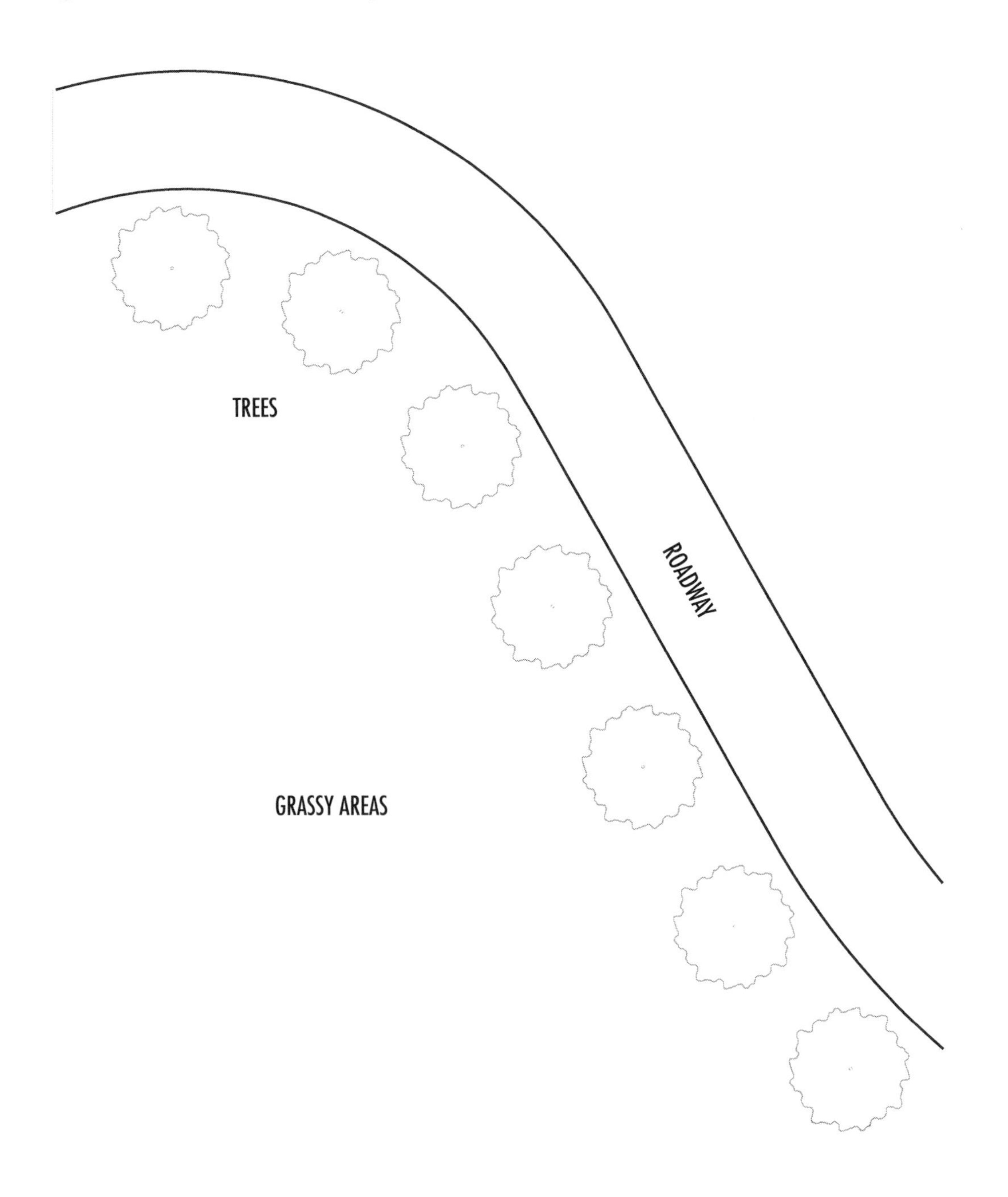

Figure 5.6A: Turf Maintenance – Open Area Staffing Matrix; 1 Acre; 30-Week Season

Maintenance Tasks	Levels of Attention				
	1	2	3	4	5
Mow – 72" Power Ride		1.00	1.00	0.50	
5–7 Gang Reel	1.50	1.00	1.00	1.00	0.50
36 Minutes	54.0	36.0	36.0	18.0	18.0
Fertilize	0.07	0.07	0.03	0.03	
131 Minutes	9.17	9.17	3.93	3.93	
Weed Control*	0.07	0.07	0.03	0.03	
132 Minutes	9.24	9.24	3.96	3.96	
Overseed*	0.03	0.03	0.03		
48 Minutes	1.44	1.44	1.44		
Aerate*	0.10	0.10	0.07	0.03	
120 Minutes	12.0	12.0	8.40	3.60	
TOTALS					
Minutes/Week	85.85	67.85	53.73	29.49	18.0
/60 Minutes	1.43	1.13	0.90	0.49	0.30
/6 Hours/Day	0.24	0.19	0.15	0.08	0.05
/5 Days/Week	0.05	0.04	0.03	0.02	0.01
Acres/Person/Week	20.00	25.00	33.33	50.00	100.0

The adjustment factors are:

Activity Frequency	Adjustment Factor
1.5 Times per week	1.5
1 time per week	1.0
Biweekly	0.5
Monthly	0.25

5 times per season	5/30 = 0.17
4 times per season	4/30 = 0.13
3 times per season	3/30 = 0.10
2 times per season	2/30 = 0.07
1 time per season	1/30 = 0.03

*Park Maintenance Computation

Figure 5.7: Turf Maintenance – Main Grounds

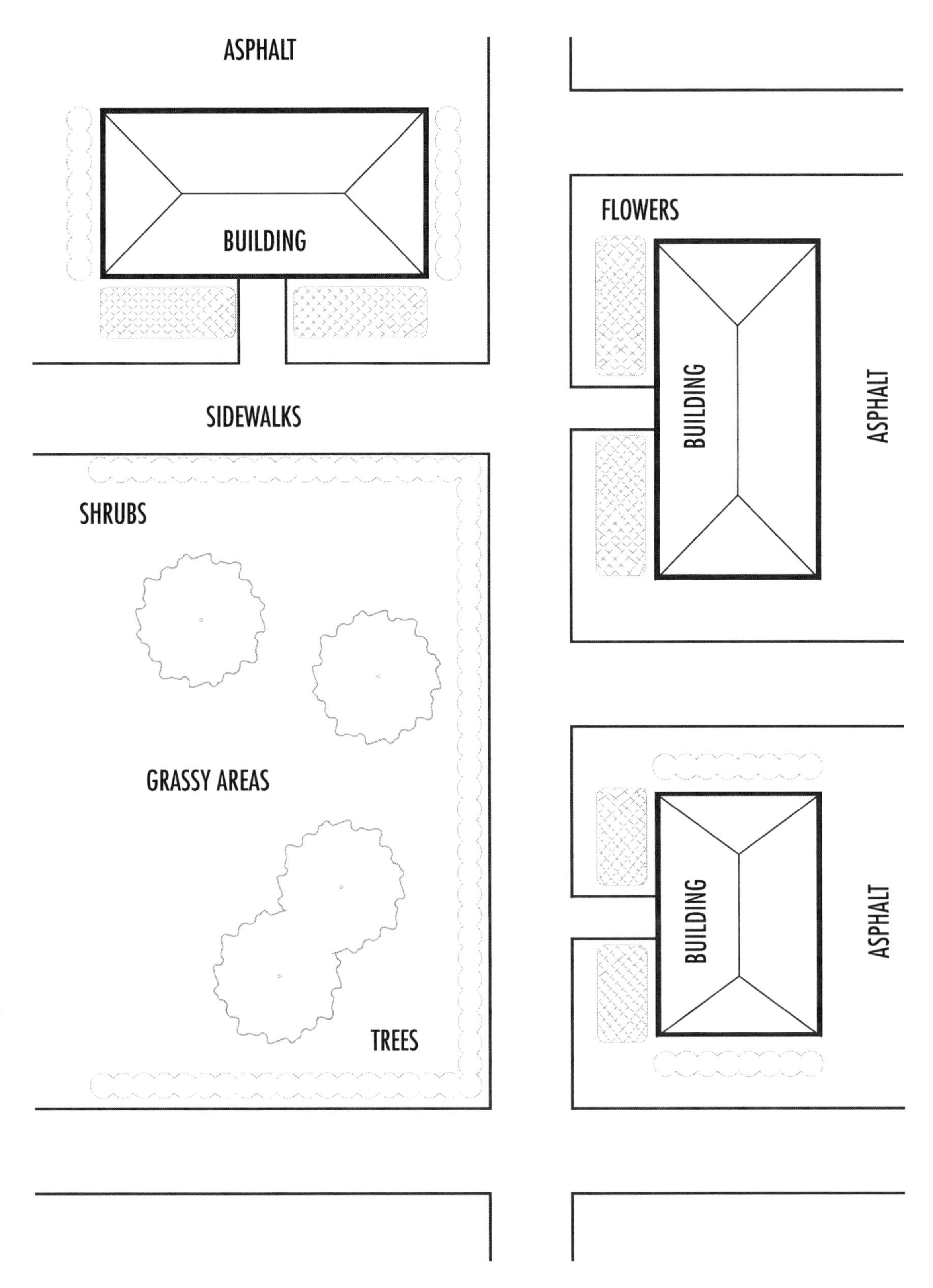

Figure 5.7A: Turf Maintenance – Main Grounds Staffing Matrix

1,000 Square Feet

Maintenance Tasks	Levels of Attention				
	1	2	3	4	5
Mow – 21" Power/Self	1.50	1.00	1.00	0.50	0.50
6 Minutes	9.00	6.00	6.00	3.00	3.00
Fertilizer	0.13	0.07	0.07	0.03	
3 Minutes	0.39	0.21	0.21	0.09	
PTO Broadcast	0.13	0.07	0.07	0.03	
.25 Minutes	0.03	0.02	0.02	0.01	
Crabgrass Control	0.07	0.03	0.03		
15 Minutes	1.05	0.45	0.45		
Weed Control – 15" Boom	0.13	0.07	0.07	0.03	
8 Minutes	1.04	0.56	0.56	0.24	
Sweep - 30" Power Rake	0.20	0.10	0.07	0.03	
2 Minutes	0.40	0.20	0.14	0.06	
Edge, Trim, And Clean Walks – Gas-Powered Edger	1.50	1.00	0.50	0.25	
5 Minutes	7.50	5.00	2.50	1.25	
Shrubs	0.50	0.33	0.17	0.10	
10 Minutes	5.00	3.3	1.70	1.00	
Trim around Raised Objects – String Edger/100 Feet	1.50	1.00	0.50	0.25	
1 Minute	1.50	1.00	0.50	0.25	
Vacuum – 30" Billy Goat	0.20	0.10	0.07	0.03	
10 Minutes	2.00	1.00	0.70	0.30	
Overseed	0.07	0.03	0.03		
30 Minutes	2.10	0.90	0.90		
Aerate	0.20	0.10	0.07	0.03	
30 Minutes	6.00	3.00	2.10	0.90	
TOTALS					
Minutes/Week	36.01	21.64	15.78	7.10	3.00
/60 Minutes	0.60	0.36	0.26	0.12	0.05
/6 Hours/Day	0.10	0.06	0.04	0.02	0.008
/5 Days/Week	0.02	0.01	0.009	0.004	0.0017
Square Feet/Person	50,000	100,000	111,111	250,000	588,235
Acres/Person	1.15	2.30	2.55	5.74	13.5

The adjustment factors are:

Activity Frequency	Adjustment Factor
1.5 times per week	1.5
1 time per week	1.0
Biweekly	0.5
Monthly	0.25

The adjustment factor for infrequent activities must take length of season into account:

Activity Frequency	Adjustment Factor for 30-Week Season	Adjustment Factor for 25-Week Season
6 times per season	6/30 = 0.20	6/25 = 0.24
5 times per season	5/30 = 0.17	5/25 = 0.20
4 times per season	4/30 = 0.13	4/25 = 0.16
3 times per season	3/30 = 0.10	3/25 = 0.12
2 times per season	2/30 = 0.07	2/25 = 0.08
1 time per season	1/30 = 0.03	1/25 = 0.04

What-If Scenarios

The following scenarios illustrate how to use the grounds maintenance matrices. These are only two examples; you can develop an individual calculation based on your own specific situation.

Scenario 1

What if you were in your office one day and your supervisor stopped by to let you know that management was planning to create a special flower presentation at the circle in front of the administrative building. In addition, a second flower presentation is planned for the open area between the park and the bell tower. The full displays are being made possible by the generous contributions of a local family that wants a fitting memorial for their recently deceased father. In laying out these two gardens, you calculate the square footage before consulting your *Operational Guidelines* book to determine the proper staffing.

You compute the circle at 18,435 square feet. The open area is about the size of a football field (325' x 130'), or 42,250 square feet. Looking at the *Operational Guidelines* book you figure that your staffing will be budgeted at current Level 3, which is the same level as the rest of the site. Confirming that the tasks and frequencies match your standards, you add the square footages together, as follows:

18,435 square feet + 42,250 square feet = 60,685 square feet

Going to the matrix for flower beds, you determine that the allowance in square feet per person for Level 3 is 16,667. You divide that number into the square footage to be supported to determine the number of people required to maintain these plantings at Level 3:

60,685 square feet / 16,667 = staffing at 3.6

When you inform your supervisor that you plan to support these new plantings at your current level of coverage, you are told, "We don't want these gardens to look like the rest of the site. This is a special effort, and we want to put our best foot forward. Compute the support at the second or high-level maintenance."

Going back to the manual, you note that 10,000 square feet per person is recommended for Level 2 maintenance, which you divide into the total square footage to determine staffing at the higher level:

60,685 square feet / 10,000 = staffing at 6.1

Scenario 2

What if you were walking the athletic fields when your supervisor told you that maintenance for the fields would soon be outsourced? The outsourcing was to be scheduled for the spring of the next year to allow you to review your needs and determine cutbacks at the end of the snow season. The site has four fields—one each for football, soccer, softball, and baseball. Knowing that the fields are maintained at Level 2, you consult the matrices for each type of field in the *Operational Guidelines* to determine the number of people required to maintain each field:

Football Field: 1 acre / 4.09 acres per person = staffing at 0.24

Soccer Field: 1 acre / 4.09 acres per person = staffing at 0.24

Softball Field: 1 acre / 2.90 acres per person = staffing at 0.34

Baseball Field: 1 acre / 2.90 acres per person = staffing at 0.34

Totaling these staff computations, you determine that staffing of 1.6 is required to do the work that will be outsourced, or one staff member will have to be laid off or reassigned.

Case Study I: Grounds Staffing at the University of Michigan

By John Lawter

The Grounds Department at the University of Michigan maintains 801 acres of land on the Ann Arbor campus. In September 1997, the University of Michigan Grounds Department began a process of developing a model on which to base the staffing and budgets for landscape maintenance of the campus. The objectives of the project were as follows:

- Evaluate our current work responsibilities and compare these to the mission of the department.
- Develop maintenance standards and department-wide priority areas.
- Develop an inventory of the physical campus.
- Combine the maintenance standards and the physical inventory with industry-accepted time standards to determine how many labor hours are needed and where they should be focused.
- Structure the department labor force to reflect the maintenance needs of the campus landscape.

1. Evaluate our current work responsibilities and compare these to the mission of the department.

The team working on the project determined and evaluated all of the different work responsibilities that the department had at the time. These responsibilities were then compared to the core mission of the department. This evaluation allowed us to focus on the types of work that were critical to the success of the department and were seen as important by our customers. It also allowed us to see work that was not part of our core mission. This work was phased out over time—or the responsibility was moved to a department that could better perform the work. By evaluating our work, we were able to better focus the resources of the department on tasks directly related to the maintenance of the campus landscape.

2. Develop maintenance standards and department-wide priority areas.

At the beginning of the process, the department had no defined maintenance standards. The result was inconsistency in the way the campus was being maintained from area to area. We also knew that some areas of campus were seen as more critical to the image of the campus than others, and we needed to be able to address this in our maintenance planning. The solution was a three-level priority system. The following describes each of the priority designations.

Priority One

These are the most visible areas of the campus. In Priority One areas, maintenance is done at the highest levels possible. Priority One areas are designed with a richer palette of plants, with more complex arrangements. The goal in Priority One areas is a consistently outstanding appearance. This is comparable to APPA Level 1.

Priority Two

These are the general areas of the campuses. In Priority Two areas, maintenance is done at average levels. Priority Two areas are designed with a simpler palette and arrangement of plants. Priority Two areas are intended to be clean, simple, and tasteful in appearance. This level is comparable to APPA Level 3.

Priority Three

These are the campus' open spaces, service areas, or natural areas. In Priority Three areas maintenance is done at lower levels. Priority Three areas are designed with a simple palette of plants or no plants at all with very simple arrangements. Priority Three areas have the goal of being functional, simple, or natural in appearance. This level is comparable to APPA Level 5.

The level of maintenance is determined by how many times a maintenance task is performed each month. This is known as a frequency. For example, Priority One lawns have a higher frequency of mowing than Priority Two.

Once maintenance levels and priorities are determined, the campus inventory can begin.

3. Develop an inventory of the physical campus.

In order to accurately plan the campus maintenance, it was necessary to determine the physical land uses of the campus. All areas that are maintained by the Grounds Department were mapped and the square footage of each land use was determined. We currently track 13 different land uses, including turf, planting beds, concrete, and specialty paving. The land uses are tracked both by zone and by level of maintenance priority it has been given.

4. Combine the maintenance standards and the physical inventory with industry accepted time standards to determine the labor hours needed and where the focus of labor should be.

The maintenance standards provide us with the frequency of maintenance, and the inventory provides us with the amount of each land use that needs to be maintained. The final variable in the equation is industry time standards. We chose to use time standards that were developed by the Professional Grounds Management Society (PGMS).

PGMS developed standards concerning the average time it should take to perform specific landscape maintenance tasks. When all of these are multiplied the result is the number of labor hours that it should take on average to perform one frequency of a maintenance task. Once this figure is determined we can determine costs and staffing levels.

The excerpts below are from the spreadsheet examples.

Priority, time standards, and frequencies

Horticultural Crew Work: Perennial Beds																	
					Frequency by Month												
Activities Involved	Qty	Unit	Min. per 1000 SF or LF	Time to complete activity once (hr.)	July	Aug.	Sept.	Oct.	Nov.	Dec.	Jan.	Feb.	Mar.	Apr.	May	June	Freq. per year
Perennial Beds-Hand Weed/Police																	
Priority One Zone	9723	SF	90	14.6	2	2	1	0	0	0	0	0	0	1	2	2	10
Priority Two Zone	12967	SF	90	19.5	2	2	1	0	0	0	0	0	0	0	2	2	9
Priority Three Zone	4598	SF	90	6.9	1	1	0	0	0	0	0	0	0	0	1	1	4

Labor hours needed

Horticultural Crew Work: Perennial Beds													
	Time Distribution by Month in Hours												Total Hours per year
Activities Involved	July	Aug.	Sept.	Oct.	Nov.	Dec.	Jan.	Feb.	Mar.	Apr.	May	June	
Perennial Beds-Hand Weed/Police													
Priority One Zone	29.2	29.2	14.6	0	0	0	0	0	0	14.6	29.2	29.2	146
Priority Two Zone	39	39	19.5	0	0	0	0	0	0	0	39	39	175.5
Priority Three Zone	6.9	6.9	0	0	0	0	0	0	0	0	6.9	6.9	27.6
Total	**75.1**	**75.1**	**34.1**	**0**	**0**	**0**	**0**	**0**	**0**	**14.6**	**75.1**	**75.1**	**349.1**

Annual costs

Horticultural Crew Work: Perennial Beds													
	Cost Distribution by Month												Total Cost per year
Activities Involved	July	Aug.	Sept.	Oct.	Nov.	Dec.	Jan.	Feb.	Mar.	Apr.	May	June	
Perennial Beds-Hand Weed/Police													
Priority One Zone	$ 916	$ 890	$ 536	–	–	–	–	–	–	$ 533	$ 902	$ 897	$ 4,674
Priority Two Zone	$ 1,224	$ 1,189	$ 716	–	–	–	–	–	–	–	$ 1,205	$ 1,198	$ 5,532
Priority Three Zone	$ 217	$ 210	–	–	–	–	–	–	–	–	$ 213	$ 212	$ 852
Total	**$ 2,357**	**$ 2,289**	**$ 1,252**	–	–	–	–	–	–	**$ 533**	**$ 2,320**	**$ 2,308**	**$ 11,058**

The information from these spreadsheets is put together for each of our specialty crews, who use it to execute the necessary maintenance tasks. Staffing levels are determined by the number of labor hours needed. The number of staff is determined using the formula that follows: Each FTE will work 1,560 labor hours per year. This figure accounts for leave/vacation, holidays, breaks, and the like. The excerpt below shows the staffing levels for each specialty crew for one zone of campus.

Estimated Staff Needed by Month for Each Maintenance Category												
Activity	July	Aug.	Sept.	Oct.	Nov.	Dec.	Jan.	Feb.	Mar.	Apr.	May	June
Perennial Beds-Hand Weed/Police												
Horticulture	3.7	4.1	2.3	2.9	2.6	1.2	1.1	1.1	1.4	2.6	3.6	3.9
Turf	0.1	0.4	1.8	0.9	0.9	0	0	0	0	0.4	2	0.7
Irrigation	0.4	0.4	0.4	0.4	0.2	0	0	0	0	0.2	0.4	0.4
Mow/HS	2	2.4	2.2	3.5	2.7	0.4	0	0	0.1	1.1	2.4	2.4
Forestry	0.3	0.4	0.2	0.1	0.4	0.5	1.7	0.5	0.6	0.2	0.6	0.3
Snow Removal	0	0	0	0	0.4	3.1	3	3.1	1.6	0.3	0	0
Total	**6.5**	**7.7**	**6.9**	**7.8**	**7.2**	**5.2**	**5.8**	**4.7**	**3.7**	**4.8**	**9**	**7.7**

5. Structure the department labor force to reflect the maintenance needs of the campus landscape.

The various specialty crews are staffed based on the labor hours provided in the spreadsheet. When multiple crews are needed to perform the same specialty, such as horticulture, every effort is made to structure the crews to have the same labor hours. This provides equity among the crews and fosters a sense of fairness. The department is currently staffed according to what the spreadsheet has determined. Staffing is reviewed each year to determine whether any changes are needed. Individual crew information is rolled into departmental summaries.

Conclusion

Managing the staffing needs and budgets using the data collected from the spreadsheets has proved to be extremely valuable, particularly when trying to identify service changes or reductions. It has allowed us to accurately target areas for reduction that will cause the least impact the overall campus appearance, function, and safety. Having factual information has made explaining how the campus is maintained much easier to customers, upper administration, and staff. The campus inventory is updated yearly to help us reflect the changing campus in our staffing and budgets. The information provided by the spreadsheet also allows us to provide landscape maintenance estimates or service level agreements with customer pay properties on campus.

Case Study II: Grounds Staffing at the University of Texas at Austin

By John Burns

In 2002, the Landscape Services Branch of the Facilities Services Department at the University of Texas at Austin undertook the task of evaluating our whole operation. We started with an internal review—or a type of soul searching—to determine our strengths and weaknesses. This case study will focus on one weakness we identified, our existing method of determining our staffing needs for campus maintenance.

Our staffing was based on how we had done things in the past. The system had worked, so we never bothered to analyze the number of staff in each area of campus. Our crews worked in a zone type of maintenance, with each crew having a crew leader and the number of crew members based on past precedents. During our internal review, we concluded that we needed to base our staffing on facts rather than the reflex response "That's the way we have always done it."

The first step in determining how many full-time employees (FTEs) were needed to maintain the campus was to measure our landscape assets. Our lack of a true inventory was also a weakness, so we were able to address both weaknesses with this one activity. We completed an inventory of assets using several attributes: rider-mowed turf, push-mowed turf, shrub beds, annual beds, and hardscape.

The second step was to determine the maintenance levels and frequency of every task performed for each landscape asset. We used the maintenance descriptions from the first edition of *Operational Guidelines for Ground Management.*

We quickly realized that we were not going to match any of the service levels exactly; we therefore had to determine which service levels we most closely matched. Following the inventory, we correlated each landscape asset as closely as possible with the published service levels, a process which resulted in the following breakdown:

Level 1 3.25 Acres (See Service Level descriptions earlier in this chapter.)

Level 2 153.15 Acres

Level 3 121.1 Acres

Level 4 5 Acres

In order to more easily calculate FTE requirements for specific tasks, we developed a spreadsheet using information from the first edition of PGMS's *Operational Guidelines for Grounds Management* and from *Grounds Maintenance Estimating Guidelines,* 8th Edition.

We entered each landscape, asset measurement, maintenance level, and description into the first sheet of the spreadsheet.

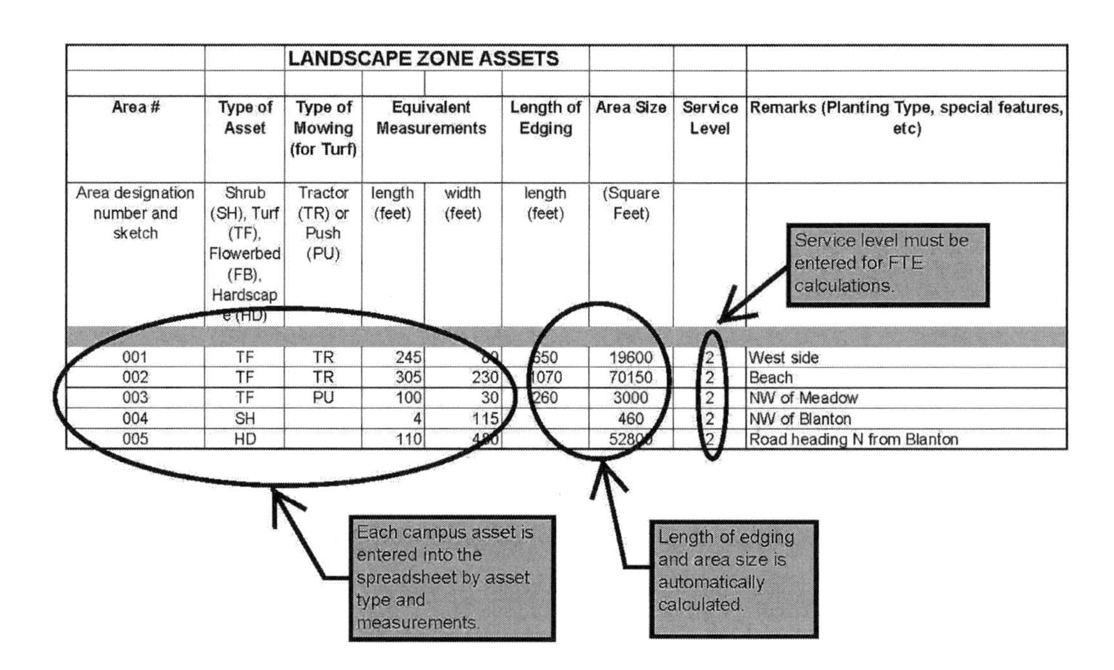

		LANDSCAPE ZONE ASSETS						
Area #	**Type of Asset**	**Type of Mowing (for Turf)**	**Equivalent Measurements**		**Length of Edging**	**Area Size**	**Service Level**	**Remarks (Planting Type, special features, etc)**
Area designation number and sketch	Shrub (SH), Turf (TF), Flowerbed (FB), Hardscape (HD)	Tractor (TR) or Push (PU)	length (feet)	width (feet)	length (feet)	(Square Feet)		
001	TF	TR	245	80	650	19600	2	West side
002	TF	TR	305	230	1070	70150	2	Beach
003	TF	PU	100	30	260	3000	2	NW of Meadow
004	SH		4	115		460	2	NW of Blanton
005	HD		110	480		52800	2	Road heading N from Blanton

Following the initial entries the spreadsheet calculates the FTE requirements for each asset. Total average minutes per week are calculated by multiplying the (adjustment factor) X (time required per 1,000 square feet) [this could also be acres or linear feet] by the total number of square feet.

Turf Maintenance Analysis				**Zone**	**Building Name**							
Total Zone Inventory :												
Turf (tractor)	116,825	SF or	2.68	Acres								
Turf (push mow)	8,000	SF or	0.18	Acres								
Edging	3,650	LF										
String Edge	365	LF										
Growing Year	42	Weeks										
Productive Hrs per workday	5											
					SVC LVL 1		**SVC LVL 2**		**SVC LVL 3**		**SVC LVL 4**	
Task	**Unit**	**Freq.**	**Period**	**Rate**	**Adjust Factor**	**Totals (avg min/week)**	**Adjust Factor**	**Totals (avg min/week)**	**Adjust Factor**	**Totals (avg min/week)**	**Adjust Factor**	**Totals (avg min/week)**
Mow - 72" Power	Acre	1	Weekly	36	1.500	144.824	1.000	96.550	0.500	48.275	0.500	48.275
Mow - 21' Push	SF	1	Weekly	6	1.500	72.000	1.000	48.000	0.500	24.000	0.500	24.000
Edge/Trim, Gas trimmer	LF	1	Weekly	25	1.500	136.875	1.000	91.250	0.500	45.625	0.250	22.813
String Edger	LF	1	Weekly	10	1.500	5.475	1.000	3.650	0.500	1.825	0.250	0.913

To calculate this number multiply the [adjustment factor] X [time required per 1,000 sq. ft.] X [square feet of asset divided by 1,000 sq. ft.]= number of minutes per week required for this task.

To calculate this number multiply the [adjustment factor] X [time required per 1,000 linear ft.] X [linear feet of the asset]= number of minutes per week required for this task.

Identifying the length of the growing season is extremely important to determining the number of weeks per year each task must be performed. Another important factor is productive hours or the number of hours each employee is actually available to accomplish the tasks. We removed travel time, training hours, breaks, and leave time from the total employee hours to determine the average productive time for employees.

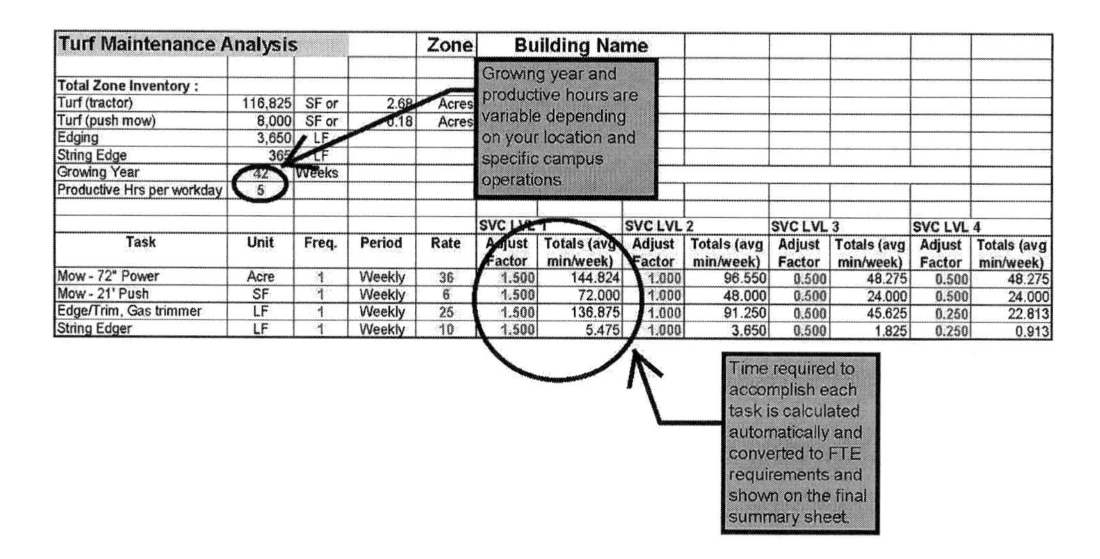

Turf Maintenance Analysis				Zone	Building Name
Total Zone Inventory :					
Turf (tractor)	116,825	SF or	2.68	Acres	
Turf (push mow)	8,000	SF or	0.18	Acres	
Edging	3,650	LF			
String Edge	365	LF			
Growing Year	42	Weeks			
Productive Hrs per workday	5				

Task	Unit	Freq.	Period	Rate	SVC LVL 1 Adjust Factor	SVC LVL 1 Totals (avg min/week)	SVC LVL 2 Adjust Factor	SVC LVL 2 Totals (avg min/week)	SVC LVL 3 Adjust Factor	SVC LVL 3 Totals (avg min/week)	SVC LVL 4 Adjust Factor	SVC LVL 4 Totals (avg min/week)
Mow - 72" Power	Acre	1	Weekly	36	1.500	144.824	1.000	96.550	0.500	48.275	0.500	48.275
Mow - 21' Push	SF	1	Weekly	6	1.500	72.000	1.000	48.000	0.500	24.000	0.500	24.000
Edge/Trim, Gas trimmer	LF	1	Weekly	25	1.500	136.875	1.000	91.250	0.500	45.625	0.250	22.813
String Edger	LF	1	Weekly	10	1.500	5.475	1.000	3.650	0.500	1.825	0.250	0.913

The final summary page of the spreadsheet provides extremely useful management tools. Included on this sheet are the total asset areas for the maintenance zone and FTE requirements for that zone. In the example shown, one employee (1.04 FTE) would be required to maintain the total 8.99 acres of landscape assets.

LANDSCAPE ZONE ASSET INVENTORY AND MANPOWER ANALYSIS					
		update as of :		24-Jun-08	
Zone	Building Name				
Zone Staff:					
Total Zone Size:	391,515	SF or	8.99	Acres of Landscape assets	
Total Asset Inventory for Zone:					% of Total Area
Turf (tractor)	116,825	SF or	2.68	Acres	29.84%
Turf (push mow)	8,000	SF or	0.18	Acres	2.04%
Shrubs	13,130	SF or	0.30	Acres	3.35%
Hardscape	253,560	SF or	5.82	Acres	64.76%
Edging	3,650	LF			
String Edge	365	LF			

If Service Levels as designated in zone asset column:

Manpower Analysis:	SVC LEVEL 1	SVC LEVEL 2	SVC LEVEL 3	SVC LEVEL 4	Total Manpower Req'd
Turf	0.00	0.42	0.00	0.00	0.42
Shrub	0.03	0.22	0.00	0.00	0.25
Hardscape	0.09	0.28	0.00	0.00	0.37
Total	0.12	0.92	0.00	0.00	1.04

Asset totals

Total FTE requirements

In addition to creating the individual spreadsheets for each maintenance zone, we also linked all these sheets to one comprehensive spreadsheet to provide a campus-wide snapshot of all asset areas and their FTE requirements. This is a management tool that is used to calculate FTE requirements for positions that cover the entire campus area, and would not be tied to an individual maintenance zone.

In summary, the data we have collected are a vital management tool we can use to distribute staffing and funds as equitably and effectively as possible. In the years since this review was completed and the results implemented, it has been surprising how many times this information has helped in making important decisions. Budget cuts are never easy, but we are now able to make decisions based on concrete information. Also, we can provide an understanding of the consequences of specific cuts instead of stepping back and saying, "I think we could cut here or there." It is also an important tool when determining staffing requirements for new building landscapes as they are constructed.

Case Study III: Grounds Staffing at the XYZ University

By Thomas Flood

The Grounds staffing guidelines can also be customized to meet the exact types and sizes of equipment used on a site, as well as the exact landscape management program. The data created for use in the staffing calculations can also be used to create a data set for materials consumption as well.

The following are two sets of spreadsheets (Fescue Turf Maintenance Main Areas and Annual Flower Maintenance) that were created for a specific organization and customized to their site-specific landscape management plan. However, many other spreadsheets were created that addressed the following: Bermuda grass turf maintenance, low maintenance turf areas, and tree and shrub maintenance.

While the functionality is not obvious on the printed page, the linking of the cells can be deduced by some careful evaluation. The shaded cells are the only variables that the manager needs to fill in. Once created, the sheets allow the manager an infinite number of "what-if" scenarios, by shifting the areas maintained under high, medium-high, medium or low maintenance uses as defined (roughly Levels 1-4 in the staffing guidelines).

Figure 5.8 is the labor calculation sheet for fescue turf in main campus areas. With four given size pieces of mowing equipment the actual time taken to mow an acre is calculated for each. The total time per year also factors in the frequency of mowing, and the number of weeks per year that turf is actively growing and mowed. Other turf maintenance activities such as fertilizing, weed control, aerating, and irrigation are similarly factored to calculate the total number of labor hours per year. Those hours are all multiplied by a cell containing the average staff hourly wage rate, $15.00 per hour in this example.

Figure 5.8: Turf Maintenance – Labor (XYZ Case Study)

Turf Maintenance - Main Areas										1 year = 40 weeks							
		Levels of Maintenance												Frequency/year			
	LABOR	High		Medium/high		Medium		Low		Total	Total				Med/		
Labor	min/Ac		#Ac.		#Ac.		#Ac.		#Ac.	min/wk	hrs/yr	$15	Labor $/yr	High	high	Med	Low
Mow & trim														40	30	20	10
21" push	165.00	165.00	2.00	123.75		82.50		41.25									
		330.00		0.00		0.00		0.00		330.00	220.00		$3,300.00				
48" rider	70.00	70.00	27.00	52.50	20.00	35.00		17.50									
		1890.00		1050.00		0.00		0.00		2940.00	1960.00		$29,400.00				
72" rider	36.00	36.00		27.00		18.00	33.00	9.00									
		0.00		0.00		594.00		0.00		594.00	396.00		$5,940.00				
16' batwing	13.00	13.00		9.75		6.50		3.25	15.0								
		0.00		0.00		0.00		48.75		48.75	32.50		$487.50				
Fertilize – PTO	15.00	1.13		0.75	30.00	0.38	3.00							3	2	1	0
	15.00	0.00		22.50		1.13				23.63	15.75		$236.25				
– push	130.00	9.75	29.00	6.50	20.00	3.25											
	15.00	282.75		130.00		0.00				412.75	275.17		$4,127.50				
Weed Control	130.00	9.75	29.00	6.50	20.00	3.25								3	2	1	0
		282.75		130.00		0.00				412.75	275.17		$4,127.50				
Overseed	48.00	1.20	30.00	1.20		0.00								1	1	0	0
		36.00		0.00						36.00	24.00		$360.00				
Irrigate	60.00	10.50	29.00	4.50	20.00	0.00								7	3	0	0
		304.50		90.00		0.00				394.50	263.00		$3,945.00				
Aerate	120.00	6.00	15.00	3.00		0.00								2	1	0	0
		90.00		0.00						90.00	60.00		$900.00				
Edge walks	45.00	45.00		22.50		11.25								40	20	10	0
		0.00		0.00		0.00				0.00	0.00		$0.00				
Blow/Vac leaves	70.00	8.75		5.25		1.75								5	3	1	0
(additional labor)		0.00		0.00		0.00				0.00	0.00		$0.00				
						TOTAL					1341.58		$20,123.75				

Figure 5.9 is an extension of Figure 5.8, calculating the materials used and their costs. For example the fuel consumption rate of each piece of equipment is multiplied by the annual hours of equipment operation to calculate the fuel, and the fuel cost per gallon is then applied for the cost estimate. Similarly, annual irrigation water consumption is determined by estimating the annual number of inches of water to be applied and the area irrigated.

Figure 5.9: Turf Maintenance – Materials (XYZ Case Study)

Turf Maintenance - Main Areas										
		Levels of Maintenance								
		High		Medium/high		Medium		Low		
MATERIALS			#Ac.		#Ac.		#Ac.		#Ac.	Total min/wk
Mow										
21" push	165.00	165.00	2.00	123.75	0.00	82.50	0.00	41.25	0.0	
		330.00		0.00		0.00		0.00		330.00
48" rider	70.00	70.00	27.00	52.50	20.00	35.00	0.00	17.50	0.0	
		1890.00		1050.00		0.00		0.00		2940.00
72" rider	36.00	36.00	0.00	24.00	0.00	18.00	33.00	9.00	0.0	
		0.00		0.00		594.00		0.00		594.00
16' batwing	13.00	13.00	0.00	9.75	0.00	6.50	0.00	3.25	0.0	
		0.00		0.00		0.00		0.00		0.00
Fertilize	130.00	9.75	29.00	6.50	50.00	3.25	3.00			
		282.75		325.00		9.75				617.50
# Nitrogen	1#/1000sf	3784.50		4350.00		130.50				
Weed Control	130.00	9.75	29.00	6.50	20.00	3.25				
		282.75		130.00		0.00				412.75
gls/pesticide	.5 gals/ac	43.50		10.00		0.00				
Overseed	48.00	1.20	30.00	0.00	0.00	0.00				
		36.00		0.00						36.00
# seed		90.00		0.00						
Irrigate	60.00	10.50	29.00	4.50	20.00	0.00	0.00			
		304.50		90.00						394.50
Gls water	9"/yr	7,087,259		4,887,765						
Aerate	120.00	6.00	15.00	3.00	0.00	0.00	0.00			
		90.00		0.00						90.00
Edge walks	45.00	22.50	0.00	11.25	0.00	2.25	0.00			
		0.00		0.00		0.00				0.00
Blow/Vac leaves	70.00	8.75	0.00	5.25	0.00	1.75	0.00			
		0.00		0.00		0.00				0.00
										TOTALS

Total hrs/yr	fuel G/hr	gal fuel/yr	# Nitrogen	Gal Water	# seed	Gal/pest	Mat'l Cost	Frequency/year			
								High	Med/ high	Med	Low
							$6,525.50	40	30	20	10
	0.5										
220.00		110						fuel cost =		$2.50	
	1										
1960.00		1960									
	1.2										
396.00		475									
	2										
32.50		65									
	0.5							3	2	1	0
411.67		206	Organic option = $5 / #			$66,120	$514.58				
			8265.00				$12,397.50				
	0.5							3	2	1	0
275.17		138					$343.96				
						53.50	$2,407.50				
	1							1	0	0	0
24.00		24					$60.00				
					90.00		$90.00				
	0							7	3	0	0
263.00		0					$-	Inches water per yr =		9	
				11,975,024			$11,975.02	Water cost/gl =		0.001	
	1							2	1	0	0
60.00		60					$150.00				
	0.3							20	10	2	0
0.00		0					$–				
	0.5							5	3	1	0
0.00		0					$–				
		3038	8265	11975024	90	66174	$34,464.06				

Figures 5.10 and 5.11 display the similar estimation for staffing needs and material costs for annual flowers. In this simpler spreadsheet, the only variables entered are the areas of annual flowers, the frequency (numbers of annual plantings), the labor rate and the water cost. In all of these the other costs are estimated as an average of actual products used.

Figure 5.10: Annual Flower Maintenance – Labor (XYZ Case Study)

Annual Flower Maintenance											
1 year = 26 weeks											
		Levels of Maintenance								Frequency	
	LABOR	High		Medium							
LABOR	min/ 1000 sf		# 1000sf		#1000 sf	Total min/wk	Total hrs/yr	$15	Labor $/yr	High	Med
Preparation	200	15.38	21.50	7.69						2	1
		330.77		0.00		330.77	143.33		$2,150.00		
Planting	600	46.15		23.08						2	1
		992.31		0.00		992.31	430.00		$6,450.00		
Mulching	30	2.31		1.15						2	1
		49.62		0.00		49.62	21.50		$322.50		
Weeding – hand	60	23.08		11.54						10	5
		496.15		0.00		496.15	215.00		$3,225.00		
Watering	20	40.00		20.00						52	26
		860.00		0.00		860.00	372.67		$5,590.00		
Fertilizing	10	3.08		1.54						8	4
		66.15		0.00		66.15	28.67		$430.00		
Spraying (Pest & pre-em)	15	2.88		1.73						5	3
		62.02		0.00		62.02	26.88		$403.13		
Clean-up	200	15.38		7.69						2	1
		330.77		0.00		330.77	143.33		$2,150.00		
						Totals	1381.38		$20,720.63		

Figure 5.11: Annual Flower Maintenance – Materials (XYZ Case Study)

Annual Flower Maintenance																		
		Levels of Maintenance														Frequency/year		
		High		Medium														
MATERIALS	LABOR min/1000 sf		# 1000sf		#1000 sf	Total min/ wk	Total hrs/yr	fuel G/hr	gal fuel/yr	# Nitrogen	Gal Water	Flowers	Comp/ Mulch	Gal/ pest	Mat'l Cost	High	Med	
Preparation	200	15.38	21.50	7.69	0.00			0.25								2	1	
		330.77		0.00		330.77	143.33		35.83						$89.58	Fuel =	$2.50	
yds compost	18 cu yds	774.00		0.00									774		$7,740.00			
Planting	600	46.15		23.08				0.1								2	1	
		992.31		0.00		992.31	430.00		43.00						$107.50			
# flowers	1800	77400.00		0.00								77400.00			$30,960.00			
Mulching	30	2.31		1.15				0.25								2	1	
		49.62		0.00		49.62	21.50		5.38						$13.44			
yds bark nuggets	18 cu yds	774.00		0.00									774.0		$7,740.00			
Weeding – hand	60	23.08		11.54				0.1								10	5	
		496.15		0.00		496.15	215.00		21.50						$53.75			
Watering	20	11.54		7.69				0.1								15	10	inches
		248.08		0.00		248.08	107.50		10.75						$26.88	Water cost =		0.001
Gals		201025		0							201025				$201.03			
Fertilizing	10	3.08		1.54				0.1								8	4	
		66.15		0.00		66.15	28.67		2.87						$7.17			
# Nitrogen	.5#N/1000sf	86.00		0.00						86					$344.00			
Spraying (Pest & pre-em)	15	2.88		1.73				0.25								5	3	
		62.02		0.00		62.02	26.88		6.72						$16.80			
Gal pesticide	.25 gal/1000sf	26.88		0.00										26.88	$1,209.38			
Clean-up	200	15.38		7.69				0.2								2	1	
		330.77		0.00		330.77	143.33		28.67						$71.67			
						Totals	1116.21		154.71						$48,581.18			

This methodology allows the grounds manager to create a customized staffing guideline that takes into consideration the local climate and growing conditions, the exact type of landscape maintenance plan, the level of maintenance, the specific fleet of equipment used, and local specifics such as material costs, the amount of snow removal, litter collection, and custom services such as a motor pool, masonry, or labor shop. Once established, the guideline provides a simple way to examine what potential changes in management activities would do to the staffing and material requirements, and conversely, how the level of service or frequency of activities in different areas could affect the total staffing or budget requirements.

CHAPTER 6

Contracting Options

By Stephanie DeStefano

Limited resources, higher expectations, a growing commitment to sustainability, Leadership in Energy and Environmental Design (LEED®) certifications, and reduced staff are just a few of the major challenges facing landscape and facility managers today. Meeting these challenges successfully requires examining all options, including outsourcing operations. How do you decide if outsourcing is the right approach to managing your grounds operations? This complex question can be answered only after a careful evaluation of your unique needs and goals. Managers must focus on whatever operational approach will offer the most cost-efficient and highest-quality service in a manner that is consistent with the organization's mission. They must also understand that only the provision of a service can be contracted for, not the responsibility for it. The ultimate accountability will always rest with the organization. Effective management of the contract services is the key to success.

Help! We Can't Do It All!

What situations trigger the desire to consider outsourcing services? Perhaps your organization is experiencing an operational or financial crisis. Are there significant personnel issues or cost that could be reduced? Perhaps a significant capital investment will be required that could be avoided. A change in leadership or management philosophy is another likely opportunity for an investigation into outsourcing. Whatever the reasons, the goal is usually the same: to meet the mission of the organization and improve both the level of customer satisfaction and financial performance. Outsourcing operations is often viewed as a way to get more for less, which can be true if careful, step-by-step planning is done from the outset.

Consider Your Costs and Needs

The first step in determining what would best suit your property is to define your costs and needs. If you currently have an in-house operation, consider both direct and indirect costs. Indirect costs are often left out of the equation when determining overall costs—to the detriment of the evaluation. Direct and indirect costs include the following:

Direct Costs	Indirect costs
Salaries and wages	Administrative overhead
Equipment and repairs	Employee benefits
Materials, supplies, and small tools	Insurance and workers compensation
Chemicals	Hiring, training, and labor relations
Fuel and oil	Information technology support
Communications, cell phones	Utilities and irrigation
Recycling, composting and disposal fees	Facility and office expense and maintenance
Uniforms	

Once you have determined your costs, the next step is to define your organization's needs and decide whether each is currently being met and if the operation is effective and efficient. As you evaluate the possibility of contracting, the following considerations may be useful:

- Consider the scope of a contract. What is the inventory of property and areas to be contractually maintained? Identify and list specific tasks to be accomplished.
- Define the quality of landscape maintenance desired. Refer to "Determining APPA Levels of Cleanliness in Buildings" (Chapter 7 of the *Custodial Operational Guidelines*) and include definitions and examples.
- Define the efficiency, quality, and stability of staff, and the level of service you expect.
- Define the degree to which you need to retain control and flexibility of staff. Who will employ them and who will supervise them? Will existing employees be retained or be offered positions with a contractor?
- Clarify relationships with other departments. Will there be shared staff and equipment? What are your expectations of public relations with customers and

employees? Who provides security? What will be an efficient use of space, equipment, storage, and so on?

- What will happen to existing equipment and other capital resources?

When you have identified your costs and needs, you will then be able to determine whether outsourcing services would be the best choice for your property.

All, Some, or None?

Do you need all services outsourced, or would contracting out a portion of the operations fulfill your needs? Grounds managers at some large organizations find that contracting out a portion of the operations works very well. Such operations as mowing, turf care, large tree work, and snow removal seem to be the most commonly outsourced services. Cemetery managers, for example, frequently outsource mowing. Bringing in large numbers of laborers to complete the job in one day enables them to eliminate "perpetual" mowing by in-house staff.

While outside contractors mark up their total costs in order to make a profit, the increase may be offset if they have a lower direct cost of labor, less overhead, or complete work faster using specialized crews and equipment. Further, they may be able to purchase materials and supplies more competitively because of their volume or relationships with their established suppliers. Therefore, large-scale landscape maintenance or installation projects or work requiring specialized equipment can often be outsourced for less.

But many institutions have significant expectations about the less tangible aspects of service, response time, and quality. Because these are more difficult to quantify, define, and ensure through a contract or because these institutions have other specialized needs, an in-house staff may be the only reasonable option. In addition, in-house staff is often essential to assist other departments for special events, graduations, emergencies, severe weather, complete grounds repair work after utility repairs, or other tasks. An in-house staff can also perform ongoing or extensive annual, perennial, or bulb plantings cost-effectively by purchasing directly from the grower, with no markup from an outside contractor.

No Surprise

It is no surprise that landscape contractors can offer advantages, primarily cost reduction and, in some cases, improved quality or convenience. When looking for outside contractors, you should investigate each company's experience, staffing levels training and expertise, scope of services, and business philosophy, as well as costs.

The increasing commitment to environmental sustainability, such as LEED certifications, the American College & University Presidents' Climate Commitment statement (http://www.presidentsclimatecommitment.org/), and goals of zero waste must now be incorporated into your outsourcing decisions. It is important for you to include these special requirements in your specifications and define the best green practices for your site. Look for landscape contractors who share your values and understand the importance of environmentally friendly horticultural practices such as integrated pest management, fertilizing only when deemed necessary by soil testing, using organic products, conserving water and managing stormwater, minimizing green waste, composting yard waste, recycling, using lower-emissions equipment, and reusing materials whenever possible.

Writing the Contract Specifications

Including all essential information in the specifications is imperative for a successful and workable contract. Your organization's attorney should always review contract specifications for proper legal information, insurance requirements, performance bonds, cancellation clauses, and so on. The general conditions should include the following:

- Detailed descriptions of all tasks to be performed
- Working hours
- Qualifications of workers
- Security issues
- Requirements or restrictions on any equipment, pesticides, materials, and methods that should or should not be used on the site.
- Sustainability requirements to meet set goals

Clear definitions of all spaces where tasks are to be performed are critical, including accurate maps of those areas. A schedule of when work is to be performed is also important. You should define expected frequencies and schedules. You should also identify, in the contract specification, the person who will be monitoring the contract and to whom the contractor will report. Figure 6.1 shows a suggested contract outline.

Figure 6.1: Contract Specifications and General Conditions

I. General Statement
II. Contract Term
III. Performance
IV. Contract Renewal
V. Utilities, Storage, and Work Space for Contractor
VI. Labor, Materials, and Equipment
VII. Supervision
VIII. Insurance
IX. Hold Harmless
X. Operations
    A. Turf
        i. Edging
        ii. Foundation Trimming
        iii. Fertilization
        iv. Lime
        v. Pre-emergent Control
        vi. Post-emergent Control
        vii. Aeration
        viii. Dethatching
        ix. Overseeding
        x. Topsoil, Sand, or Compost Topdressing
    B. Shrub care
        i. Pruning, Including Rejuvenation Pruning
        ii. Edging and Mulching
    C. Tree Care
    D. Flower Beds, Annuals, and Perennials

Figure 6.1: Contract Specifications and General Conditions, continued

E. Insects and Disease Control

   i. Tree and Shrub—Control Schedule

   ii. Turf—Insect Control

   iii. Plant Diseases

   iv. Integrated Pest Management Strategies

F. Weeding

G. Natural Areas

H. Recycling and Trash Removal

I. Leaf Removal, Composting

J. Snow and Ice Removal

K. Street Cleaning

L. Interior Plant Care

M. Special Services

N. Environmental Concerns

O. Waste Disposal

P. Changes in Scope of Work

Q. Permits and Licenses

R. Employees of the Contractor

S. Employee Conduct

T. Working Hours

U. Termination

Memorandum of Understanding

I. Definitions

II. Contractor-Employer Relations

III. Supervision by Contractor

IV. Standards of Performance

V. Extras

VI. Exclusions

VII. Flower Beds and Ground Cover

Figure 6.1: Contract Specifications and General Conditions, continued

- A. Definitions
- B. Flower Gardens, Bulbs
- C. Scope of Work
- D. Annual Bedding Plants
- E. Soil Preparation
- F. Plant Materials
- G. Plant Materials Guarantee

VIII. Tree Care
- A. General Condition Standards
- B. Pruning and Corrective Bracing, Staking
  - i. Preparation
  - ii. Application
    - a. Fertilization
    - b. Preparation
  - iii. Removals

IX. Shrub Care
- A. Shearing vs. Pruning (rejuvenation pruning)
- B. Fertilization

X. Natural Areas

XI. Contract Watering

Snow and Ice Removal

I. General Statement

II. Emergency Snow Removal

III. Lesser Snow and Ice Conditions

IV. Fee Schedule

Hourly Rates vs. Set Price Contract

Just as in-house staff individuals work at different paces, so do contract employees. With detailed specifications, a set price contract may save valuable administrative time on both your end and the contractor's, ultimately saving you money, time, and headaches. It is always good to include labor rates for extra services not specified in the contract. For a set price contract, it is critical to spell out expectations and results to avoid problems. Detailed information must be included, such as frequency of services, numbers of annual flower rotations, bulbs, and so on. Also specify materials such as soil amendments, fertilizers, mulches, deicers and other supplies.

Who Will Oversee the Contract?

Whether all or part of the grounds maintenance jobs will be contracted out, a trained in-house grounds manager is still required to oversee operations. Good communication is key to working with a landscape contractor. Frequent, positive communication between both parties will mean the difference between success and failure. Both parties should be familiar with the scope of the contract and knowledgeable about all tasks to be performed. Retaining a professional grounds manager who is well versed in all aspects of the services required is in the best interests of the organization.

Apples to Apples, Bananas to Oranges

With so many variables involved in selecting a contractor, comparing apples to apples on this subject is no easy task. If you need help obtaining an unbiased comparison, you may be able to retain a landscape consulting firm to review your options. If you decide to outsource, a landscape consulting firm can also manage your landscape contractor for you, as well as perform regular inspections and provide quality control reports.

Network, Network, Network!

Networking with other grounds managers through APPA, the Professional Grounds Management Society, or other green industry organizations is an ideal way to learn from the experience of others. Such contacts can also provide you with background checks and information you will need to make the best choice for your particular site. Many of these organizations have their own websites and helpful links. Take advantage of professional associations; education is their mission.

CHAPTER 7

Benchmarking Your Organization

By James B. Spengler and Fred Gratto

Campuses throughout North America struggle to understand and adjust to competition, variable public support, resistance to tuition increases, quality of campus life, public perception, accessibility, affordability, and dozens of other challenges. At the same time, society increasingly considers a college education essential to the notion of the good life, so the demand for higher education remains strong. Within this context, faculty seek higher salaries, greater security, and more autonomy. Students want better teachers, higher quality academic programs, lower costs, more attention to their needs, and great job prospects. The public expects better education without rising costs, and legislatures want to know how their money is being expended. Each of these expectations exerts pressure on the institution, impacts decision making, and changes priorities.

The challenge of managing our colleges, universities, and schools continues with new expectations, such as sustainability, but the issue of accountability remains an important factor in facilities management. In recent years, accountability has captured an increasing amount of time and attention, and this trend is not likely to change, as our constituents want to know how their money is being spent. Benchmarking helps with accountability because it allows us to measure our performance and see how others are doing similar things. It also increases credibility when stakeholders know that we are measuring our performance and making changes as necessary. Benchmarking also helps quantify results. In fact, the president of the United States recently demanded results in exchange for federal dollars by requiring grant applicants to set benchmarks for improvement.

Although colleges, universities, and schools have been comparing costs and productivity with one another for many years, there are increased efforts to do this. For example, one new effort to benchmark, called the College Portrait (http://www.

collegeportraits.org), allows institutions to share online data about students' academic progress. It allows prospective students, parents, state legislators, and others to compare the undergraduate experience among participating institutions and examine institutional performance and costs. The University of North Carolina system and the University of Wisconsin system are using it, as is the California State University system. Chancellor Charles B. Reed of California State University commented, "This will give us greater credibility and confidence to those who fund us." These are good outcomes, and we are looking for similar results in our maintenance organizations. Other areas of higher education that are being measured because of an increased call for accountability include the performance of college endowments, student learning, student engagement, and facilities management. Benchmarking can help organizations responsible for performance in these areas and assist in comparing and improving their performance.

Benchmark Your Organization

Organizations everywhere, big and small, private and public, urban and rural, and in every conceivable type of business are trying to get better at what they do. They are looking for ways to attain greater organizational effectiveness. One of the ways they do this is by observing facts and figures from other organizations, such as APPA's Facilities Performance Indicators (FPI), to see how well they are accomplishing their mission (http://appa.org/research/fpi).

By definition, benchmarking is the process of measuring activities considered critical to an organization's success. It directs attention to comparison and measurement to help discover opportunities and strategies for improvement. Benchmarking is one of the management tools that can contribute to improved performance. The International Benchmarking Clearinghouse identifies four reasons for looking outside your industry and organization for benchmarks:

1. To avoid reinventing an existing solution
2. To achieve breakthrough improvements and accelerate change
3. To drive and direct reengineering
4. To set stretch goals

Four steps are fundamental to success of benchmarking efforts: (1) know your operation, (2) know competitors in your industry who are benchmarking, (3) seek implementation of best practices in your organization, and (4) gain superiority. With these in mind, an investment in benchmarking can result in significantly improved results for your organization. Benchmarking includes an analysis of internal procedures to see how things are going. It is much more than comparing yourself with yourself; it includes external benchmarking. Benchmarking takes a broader view to see how you are doing in comparison to others. This broader view identifies and illuminates procedures, policies, and facts that, when implemented, can make your organization more productive and better able to provide quality products and services.

Four Types of Benchmarking

Different types of benchmarking have evolved as organizations have used the process.

1. Internal benchmarking compares functions and procedures in different operating units within the same organization. This type of benchmarking concentrates on internal customers. It is the easiest type of benchmarking to study and implement. Internal benchmarking usually leads to small performance improvements that might be translated into improved financial performance, streamlined operations, or enhanced customer satisfaction. With regard to grounds maintenance, an example of this type of benchmarking would be studying the process of mowing in two or more maintenance districts in the same department to determine the most efficient and effective method.
2. Competitive or external benchmarking looks at competitors. This type of benchmarking is the most difficult to accomplish because of the fact-finding process, which involves working with and depending on others. But it can result in performance improvement that is worth the effort. To perform this type of benchmarking, public and private maintenance companies competing in the same geographic area, for example, might study mowing processes to determine which methods are lower in cost but result in the highest quality. Another way to gain valuable comparisons is through industry measurements such as APPA's annual FPI survey, or APPA's Facilities Management Evaluation Program (http://appa.org/fmep).

3. Functional benchmarking analyzes dissimilar industries. The objective of this inquiry is to identify best practices in any organization that has a reputation for excellence in the specific functional area being investigated. Significant process improvements for the investigating organization are common. For example, to improve the speed and accuracy of estimating landscape projects, a facilities organization might study the inventory management and procurement processes at a bank and apply the findings to maintenance operations.
4. Generic benchmarking is a comparison of work practices that are not related. A facilities organization might, for example, use barcoding technology from the retail industry to improve a work order system and preventive maintenance operations. This type of benchmarking often pays big dividends by way of performance improvement, because entirely new ways of doing things are discovered.

Benchmarking Is an Effective Management Tool

Benchmarking has been a management and assessment tool since 1979. Xerox started using it when it discovered that Japanese companies were selling copiers at the price it cost Xerox to make them. Further investigation revealed that, in comparison to the foreign competition, Xerox had nine times as many suppliers, seven times as many product defects, took twice as long to develop and deliver products, and took five times as long to set up its production lines. Also, before benchmarking, unit costs and other targets at Xerox were set internally. To become more competitive, Xerox directed all units in the corporation to use benchmarks. The results of these inquiries and comparisons radically changed the fee structure in this organization. As these changes were implemented and noticed by others, benchmarking efforts began to spread to other industries.

Business experts now estimate that 60 to 70 percent of the largest U.S. companies have some kind of benchmarking program in place. A contributing factor to the exponential growth of benchmarking is the popular Malcolm Baldrige National Quality Award (http://www.baldrige.com), whose criteria include a strong benchmarking program. Criteria for the performance improvement award include a set of questions focusing on critical aspects of management that can help an organization realign resources; improve communication, productivity, and effectiveness; and achieve strategic goals. These are examples of the positive results to which benchmarking can contribute.

Benchmarking is usually not a one-time effort that checks performance at a moment in time and then goes away. Organizations usually use benchmarking to measure and direct things over a period of time, such as strategic planning, forecasting need for a product, searching for new ideas, comparing processes and procedures, and setting goals. Areas of focus in these periodic reviews include parts or products of the organization that touch internal and external customers. Just about any aspect of an organization that can be observed or measured can be benchmarked. The process is a powerful systems improvement tool because with new information, managers can go beyond making incremental improvements. External comparisons break the cycle of comparing current performance results with past results. This is good. With benchmarking, your organization is not judged against itself but against others, and this is an enlightening process. You may be convinced that you are doing all the right things, and maybe you are. But it is also safe to assume that at least one organization that does what you do is doing it better than you are. Benchmarking can provide this insight.

Benchmark comparisons give your organization the opportunity to test the value of its current practices. Looking at other companies in the same industry or in different industries gives management a meaningful report card. Benchmarking also allows an organization to move beyond the current time frame and consider the impact on services if changes and improvements are implemented. This is worthwhile because the role of a facilities manager is to make the most effective use of resources in delivering services that improve and enhance the campus landscape and meet customer needs. Benchmarking is a tool for gaining greater efficiency and effectiveness in operations—just what we want.

Process Management

Most landscape maintenance activities can be viewed as processes. For example, we know that great turf does not just happen by itself. Growing the turf expected on campuses is a complicated maintenance process. Providing annual color in plant beds is a process. Managing pedestrian traffic around campus is a process that involves a lot of observation and planning. Each process requires specific input in the form of labor, materials, and equipment. Each process also entails certain steps and has a measurable output or results. Facilities leadership manages processes, and the decisions made drive the efficiency and effectiveness of maintenance activities. Because grounds maintenance work involves process design, benchmarking can be a successful endeavor in an organization that is seeking continual improvement.

An external benchmark is a point of reference from outside the organization that serves as a model for improving methods inside the organization. The process involves learning what causes certain outcomes to occur. In addition, benchmarking is a comparison of two processes: yours and somebody else's, or a comparison of two others outside your organization, from which you can glean helpful information. A benchmarking analysis examines those process factors that help bring about improved performance. An organization involved in benchmarking is trying to learn from other organizations the processes and procedures that enable them to perform in an optimum way.

Benchmarking Steps

The first step in this important process is to identify what processes, components, functions, or divisions within an organization need to be improved. With regard to grounds maintenance, the following questions might start some interesting discussions:

- Which tasks are most critical to maintenance success?
- What maintenance activities cause the most trouble or negative feedback?
- What are the tasks that we don't consistently perform well?
- What maintenance services are provided to customers?
- What exactly do our customers expect?
- Which maintenance functions represent the highest percentage of costs?
- Which performance outcomes, such as mowing or tree trimming, must we improve?
- What else should we be doing?

One benchmarking goal, for example, might be to consider the real cost of service. To improve performance and reduce cost, an organization needs to eliminate actions that increase cost but do not add value. Costa increase when activities are included that do not need to be performed in order to generate a finished product or service. In other words, "Do we really need to do this?" "What would happen if we stopped doing it?" "Does it matter?" "Would anybody notice?" "Does this effort really add value in the eyes of the customer?"

Benchmarking would take a look at critical factors such as cost, quality, and time, perhaps quantified in cycle time of work orders. Another factor to consider in performance improvement is waste, which is time when the maintenance staff is not physically performing maintenance tasks. There are plenty of time wasters in grounds maintenance, such as the following:

- Breakdown...a mower breaks down and is out of service.
- Setup and adjustment...the cutting height of a mower deck must be calibrated.
- Idling and minor stoppage...an operator has to get off a mower to pick up trash.
- Travel time...getting from one place to another takes time.
- Quality defects and rework...a crew must be sent to a site to correct a problem that was not fixed correctly the first time.
- Start-up/setup time ... a crew must start and set up another project, such as an irrigation system.

A commitment to reduce or eliminate these losses, by comparison with other organizations, can lead to important benchmarking ideas and savings. There are plenty of maintenance practices that could be improved by benchmarking, such as mowing, litter removal, turf management, fleet maintenance, tree trimming, shrub pruning, painting, and repair of landscape features such as benches, tables, and bike racks.

After the areas for benchmarking have been identified, six important questions must be answered about the process under study:

1. Who is in charge of the process?
2. What is the purpose and expected result of the process?
3. What is the best sequence in the process?
4. Who are the customers of the process and what are their requirements?
5. What measures will be used to monitor the process?
6. What are the problems in the process?

Identify Benchmark Partners

A team of people must come together as stakeholders to benchmark a process. The team should consist of the process owner and key people who work in the process. The team clarifies the improvement objective to ensure that all members understand and agree. Next, the team identifies an external organization against which to benchmark, perhaps identified through previous studies, literature from national associations, or other sources. Benchmarking can be extremely time-consuming, so you may want to team with a nearby organization in the same industry, one that is similar in size to yours, one that has had similar experiences, or one that has characteristics similar to yours, such as operating budget or number of personnel.

Collect Data, Identify Performance Gaps, and Project the Outcome of Improvements

Based on the process to be benchmarked and the organizations selected as partners, the team then determines the data collection method. This is an especially critical step. When the data is collected, it should reveal a difference between the "as is" process and the "best of class"—in other words, a performance gap. This gap becomes the focus of analysis to identify process improvements. One option is to continue performing current processes as modified by the new methods and information discovered. Another option is wholesale process change. Projecting the benefits that are expected to accrue with either course of action becomes the rationale for changing the process.

Implement Change, Measure Results, and Adjust the Process

The methods and practices of a process must be changed to bring about different results, which is the main point of benchmarking. Implementation calls for a plan of action. This plan includes who, what, when, and how to implement the change. Once implemented, the process change must be validated. It is essential to know whether the expected results were achieved. The plan of action must also specify when this process will be examined again for additional improvements.

Pitfalls and Benefits of Benchmarking

The benchmarking effort must be specific. The team looks for specific processes where change can bring about measurable results. The methods to measure improvement should be determined before the project is started. When a project scope is too broad, the effort lacks focus, which makes it difficult to identify companies to benchmark and also makes it difficult to collect the most helpful data. In this scenario, benchmarking is no more than a data-gathering expedition. In the final analysis, explanations of performance gaps must be factual, not merely conjecture.

One perspective to keep in mind is that organizations should conduct benchmarking to improve processes and performance, not to place blame. If the team works in an atmosphere of faultfinding, the benchmarking effort will not be successful. In the end, for meaningful change to occur, the organization needs the commitment of employees, not just grudging compliance.

Performed correctly and accurately, benchmarking can serve as an important tool for the maintenance manager. When under way and rolling along toward specific outcomes, it helps set targets and creates internal tension for change. Benchmarking lets you know you how well you are doing by establishing a context and a new paradigm for the maintenance operation. The investigating organization needs to clearly see the benefits of change once the benchmarking study has shown what is really possible. It is helpful to keep in mind that if others are improving their organization, so can you. Positive results from benchmarking often prompt investigations into other areas in an organization where improvement is possible. Benchmarking requires a fair amount of time and resources; however, the results of these inquires can be significant, and perhaps, may change the course of your organization in a more positive direction.

CHAPTER 8

Snow Removal

By John Lawter

The removal of snow and ice during the winter months can be one of the toughest problems for grounds maintenance crews at institutions in northern climates. During recent years, increases in litigation resulting from slips and falls have only put additional pressure on this difficult assignment. Snow and ice removal that is not well handled can have serious public relations consequences for the facilities organization. A successful snow removal program that serves the institution well will be based upon clearly established and recognized priorities, and carefully developed planning and procedures.

Establishing Priorities

Although every person on campus would like a high priority placed on their parking space, building, or sidewalk, snow and ice removal can be successfully accomplished only by following clearly established priorities that meet recognized needs. These priorities typically follow a hierarchy of use, with arterial roads and major pedestrian walkways being first, followed by secondary roads, walks, and parking lots. But critical function areas must be considered first.

At institutions with medical centers that provide 24-hour emergency care, access to this service from major arterial roads and sidewalks is critical and always a top priority. Student health centers that provide similar emergency care would also have a high priority. Second priority is usually assigned to power plant service areas, then residence halls and food services areas. After high-priority areas and main roads and walks, the remaining main roads and walks serving classrooms and research buildings are cleared of snow. Handicapped ramps and curb cuts, a high priority for mobility of a limited number of people, are of no value until the surrounding streets and walks are in passable condition. Therefore, ramps and curb cuts should have the same priority as adjacent surfaces.

Widespread publication of the basic priorities and principles of the snow and ice removal plan can help to forestall much of the criticism and controversy that usually come with a major snow removal effort.

Employee Callback

A workable system of mobilization is of prime importance. The responsibility of initial notification rests with a department and specific individuals who are on campus during nonworking hours. If snow or ice conditions occur during working hours, the removal process can begin as needed. In the evenings, on weekends, and during nonbusiness hours, the responsibility for callback must be clearly established. The job is often assigned to campus police, as they are on duty 24 hours a day, every day. The police should be provided with current contact information for the person designated as the primary contact, and at least two backup contacts. Dispatchers should be updated on your callback procedures and expectations annually at the beginning of winter. The definition of when to call during a middle-of-the-night surprise snowstorm may vary and place the grounds crew in a difficult catch-up situation if not made early enough.

The grounds manager's decision to call out employees or contractors is difficult and must be based on experience as well as other readily available information. National and local weather forecast information and contacts with local agencies are important. Managers should consider establishing a procedure for communicating with the institution's top administrators if conditions warrant restricted movement or school closing. A good rule always is to err on the side of calling people back sooner than proves necessary, or calling back more staff than prove necessary. Once a major storm has gotten the upper hand, it can be almost impossible to recover.

Staffing Requirements

The personnel required to form crews for snow emergencies can come from several sources, and duties should be assigned to relate as closely as possible to normal assignments. Grounds maintenance employees, usually experienced with heavier equipment and equipment operation, should be responsible for snow removal from sidewalks and curb cuts. Street and parking lot snow removal may be assigned to grounds maintenance crews or to a campus service group that operates heavier equipment and trucks. Equipment maintenance personnel should be on duty to repair breakdowns and install plows. Frequently, custodial employees can remove snow and ice from entrances, steps, and landings, as this requires a great deal of labor campus-wide yet a minimal amount of labor for each custodian. Some institutions supplement their regular maintenance crews with part-time student workers during periods of heavy snowfall, and some institutions have standing contracts to use contractors and their equipment for snow removal.

A strong agreement on participation in emergency call-out procedures should be made with employees and their labor organizations, if applicable. Some employees may delay their response to emergency calls or not respond at all. The established policy should include method of contact, response time expected, payment for overtime or compensatory time granted, job responsibilities, and the consequences of nonresponse. Most institutions classify their grounds employees as essential personnel or emergency workers and clearly classify snow and ice removal as an emergency.

In the case of an emergency condition that could last for many hours or days, it is important to phase the working hours of available labor. Repetitive shifts in cold weather should last a maximum of about 12 hours. Beyond this, efficiency and safety capabilities decrease rapidly. Just before the first snow or ice conditions are expected, hold a brief meeting of all employees and contractors to explain or review the mission and expectations of the operation and delineate responsibilities of the various crews. It is helpful to ask various agencies on campus to send representatives. Interested groups include security, traffic, custodial, and general administration, as well as someone to represent accessibility issues. Problem areas can be discussed and special requests or expectations presented. Instruction and training in the use of equipment and distribution of salt is invaluable. Damage to the campus can be extreme if care is not taken. Plow damage becomes quite obvious as winter snows melt and grass does not grow.

Attention to details can make snow removal a success. In areas where snowfall or accumulation is deep, placing stakes at walk intersections to guide operators when the area is entirely covered helps to protect both the grounds and the equipment. Do not overlook the needs of the workers during the operations. Providing coffee, hot chocolate, snacks, or even meals for employees during long hours of overtime improves the operations efforts. During extreme weather conditions, employees who live in rural areas or without adequate transportation may not be able to return home to sleep between shifts. A backup plan such as transporting or providing local accommodations may become necessary, and it is best to have a contingency plan already in place.

Snow Removal Equipment and Operation

Equipment funding, staffing, policies, procedures, the physical characteristics of the snow removal areas, and especially local snowfall, all directly influence the types of snow control equipment best suited for each campus setting. For example, the snow throwers that are essential in high snowfall, northern, and mountainous areas may be essentially useless in the mid-Atlantic and southern regions, where snowfalls tend to be lighter, but are very wet and heavy. It is important that all of these factors be considered when evaluating equipment, as many varieties of equipment and materials are manufactured to clear, remove, and melt snow and ice.

Once policies, procedures, and staffing patterns are established, other factors can be considered, such as the physical characteristics of the snow removal areas. Characteristics such as street, sidewalk, and parking lot sizes; vehicle weight restrictions; snow emergency zones; street and sidewalk bollards; and bridges all are factors that need to be considered when purchasing or evaluating equipment. Because funding for equipment is generally limited, it is important to select equipment that will be cost-effective. For instance, will tractors, commercial lawn mowers, and dump trucks also be equipped for snow and ice control, and will the equipment handle the workload during severe weather conditions? Utilizing a piece of equipment that might otherwise sit idle in storage will greatly increase the equipment's return on investment and justify its purchase. If possible, the grounds manager may also want to consider contracting with state, county, or local public works departments to share equipment and routes.

Before purchasing equipment, these questions must be answered, manufacturers' recommendations studied, and various pieces of equipment demonstrated. It is also a good idea to visit nearby institutions to observe other snow control programs.

It is typically most efficient to assign each piece of equipment a route or area to maintain and identify the priorities by which to proceed. This works just as well with campus walks as it does with highways and roads. Assigning two employees to each piece of equipment is also a good practice, which ensures that they are both familiar with the equipment operation and the area where they are working. This can avoid damages and provide operations in shifts in order to keep essential equipment from being idle. Be sure to keep some equipment in reserve to cover breakdowns or problems areas that arise during the operation. All employees should be thoroughly trained on the equipment that they will use, and the training must be documented and retained on file.

Once equipment is selected and a program is established with equipment assignments, fine-tuning begins through a trial-and-error process. A piece of equipment and procedure that works in one area may not work in another. As the snow control program is carried out, meetings should be held to discuss and review the effectiveness of the snow control program. The supervisor should implement worthy suggestions from the staff and keep track of which techniques work well.

Be prepared. Organize the snow control program several months in advance. Ensure that supplies are ordered in a timely fashion. Have vehicle maintenance employees winterize equipment to be pulled from storage, and equip the tractor mowers and dump trucks with plows, tire chains, and salt spreaders.

Deicing materials vary in their effective temperature range, corrosiveness, impact on plant life and soil structure, availability, and cost. Be sure to research available products and identify the active ingredients in each one; otherwise you may be paying a lot for red coloring and fancy containers. Order snow-melting compounds suitable for the local conditions, and have them ready in their storage areas. The *Snowfighter's Handbook*, available from the Salt Institute, contains information pertaining to all phases of snow control. The American Public Works Association schedules an annual snow conference that can be a valuable training resource.

Snow and Ice Control Plan

As with any emergency procedure, careful advance planning is an essential element of a successful snow and ice control program. If this planning is to be effective, it must be written down in a well-organized and comprehensive way. Among the basic elements of a good plan are the following:

- Summary of basic policies and procedures for snow and ice control
- Establishment of priorities
- Organization for snow and ice control
- Control and communications
- Assignment of responsibilities
- Personnel assignments
- Delineation of equipment routes

To remain effective, a snow and ice removal plan should be reviewed and updated each fall, well in advance of winter weather, and the updated plan should form the basis for training all essential snow and ice control personnel.

Snow and Ice Removal Budgeting

Snow removal is difficult to plan and budget for due to the unknown quantity of the weather. However, if you are able to make reasonable assumptions based on historic information on your particular area, a snow work plan is a useful tool. A space inventory can determine the amount (square feet) and type of surfaces to be cleared, such as sidewalks and plazas, stairs, ramps, roads, and parking lots. Then the amount of square feet to be cleared is matched to the activity used to clear it, such as hand shoveling, brooming, salting, liquid deicing, and plowing.

A sample formula would be —

Frequency (# Events) x Surface Type (SF) x Method (HRS) = # Hours to complete task

Hours to complete task x Billing Rate ($) = Cost per year

When calculating frequencies, it is important to consider the clearing priorities noted in "Establishing Priorities." Tracking time for each task is an important component in adjusting the information on the snow work/budget plan. Historic information on budgets vs. actuals will make the plan more accurate as each year's adjustments are added.

The following spreadsheets show an example of using this method to calculate the labor hours, costs, and material expenses for annual snow removal at the University of Michigan. Each grounds maintenance operation, campus, equipment pool, and climate is unique and must establish its own unique values. However, once the basic calculations are completed, the values for the various spreadsheet elements, such as area, frequency, or wage rates, can be connected and allow the entire set of budget calculations to be adjusted easily.

Figure 8.1: Maintenance Estimating Worksheet
Campus Snow Removal Plan — Areas and Frequencies

Activities Involved	Qty	Unit	Min./ 1,000 SF	Time to Complete Activity 1x (hrs)	Frequency by Month Oct.	Nov.	Dec.	Jan.	Feb.	March	April	Freq. per Year
Horticultural Zone One: Areas and Frequencies												
Snow Removal: Lots												
Priority One Zone	7282	SF	4	0.5	0	2	5	7	7	4	1	0
Priority Two Zone	149126	SF	4	9.9	0	2	5	7	7	4	1	19
Priority Three Zone	13842	SF	4	0.9	0	2	5	7	7	4	1	19
Snow Removal: Roads												
Priority One Zone	0	SF	2	0.0	0	5	11	15	10	9	2	0
Priority Two Zone	16192	SF	2	0.5	0	5	11	15	10	9	2	36
Priority Three Zone	26804	SF	2	0.9	0	5	11	15	10	9	2	36
Snow Removal: Special Pavement												
Priority One Zone	30862	SF	4	2.1	0	5	11	15	10	9	2	0
Priority Two Zone	27430	SF	4	1.8	0	5	11	15	10	9	2	36
Priority Three Zone	0	SF	4	0.0	0	5	11	15	10	9	2	36
Snow Removal: Steps												
Priority One Zone	1922.5	SF	120	3.8	0	5	11	15	10	9	2	0
Priority Two Zone	6468	SF	120	12.9	0	5	11	15	10	9	2	36
Priority Three Zone	34	SF	120	0.1	0	5	11	15	10	9	2	36
Snow Removal: Walks												
Priority One Zone	115429	SF	2	3.8	0	5	11	15	10	9	2	0
Priority Two Zone	274315	SF	2	9.1	0	5	11	15	10	9	2	36
Priority Three Zone	16940	SF	2	0.6	0	5	11	15	10	9	2	36
Sidewalk Liquid Deicing												
Priority One Zone	115429	SF	1	1.9	0	5	11	15	10	9	2	0
Priority Two Zone	274315	SF	1	4.6	0	5	11	15	10	9	2	36
Priority Three Zone	16940	SF	1	0.3	0	5	11	15	10	9	2	36

Figure 8.2: Maintenance Estimating Worksheet
Campus Snow Removal Plan — Monthly Time Distribution

	Time Distribution by Month in Hours							Total Hours per Year
Activities Involved	Oct.	Nov.	Dec.	Jan.	Feb.	March	April	
Horticultural Zone One: Monthly Time Distribution								
Snow Removal: Lots								
Priority One Zone	0.0	1.0	2.4	3.4	3.4	1.9	0.5	12.6
Priority Two Zone	0.0	19.9	49.7	69.6	69.6	39.8	9.9	258.5
Priority Three Zone	0.0	1.8	4.6	6.5	6.5	3.7	0.9	24.0
Snow Removal: Roads								
Priority One Zone	0.0	0.0	0.0	0.0	0.0	0.0	0.0	0.0
Priority Two Zone	0.0	2.7	5.9	8.1	5.4	4.9	1.1	28.1
Priority Three Zone	0.0	4.5	9.8	13.4	8.9	8.0	1.8	46.5
Snow Removal: Special Pavement								
Priority One Zone	0.0	10.3	22.6	30.9	20.6	18.5	4.1	107.0
Priority Two Zone	0.0	9.1	20.1	27.4	18.3	16.5	3.7	95.1
Priority Three Zone	0.0	0.0	0.0	0.0	0.0	0.0	0.0	0.0
Snow Removal: Steps								
Priority One Zone	0.0	19.2	42.3	57.7	38.5	34.6	7.7	199.9
Priority Two Zone	0.0	64.7	142.3	194.0	129.4	116.4	25.9	672.7
Priority Three Zone	0.0	0.3	0.7	1.0	0.7	0.6	0.1	3.5
Snow Removal: Walks								
Priority One Zone	0.0	19.2	42.3	57.7	38.5	34.6	7.7	200.1
Priority Two Zone	0.0	45.7	100.6	137.2	91.4	82.3	18.3	475.5
Priority Three Zone	0.0	2.8	6.2	8.5	5.6	5.1	1.1	29.4
Sidewalk Liquid Deicing								
Priority One Zone	0.0	9.6	21.2	28.9	19.2	17.3	3.8	100.0
Priority Two Zone	0.0	22.9	50.3	68.6	45.7	41.1	9.1	237.7
Priority Three Zone	0.0	1.4	3.1	4.2	2.8	2.5	0.6	14.7

Figure 8.3: Maintenance Estimating Worksheet
Campus Snow Removal Plan — Monthly Costs

	Cost Distribution by Month							Total Cost per Year
Activities Involved	Oct.	Nov.	Dec.	Jan.	Feb.	March	April	
Horticultural Zone One: Monthly Cost								
Hourly rate Eq. Ops	$ 55.14							
Hourly rate Temps	$ 17.00							
Snow Removal: Lots								
Priority One Zone	$ –	$ –	$ –	$ 187	$ 187	$ –	$ –	$ 375
Priority Two Zone	$ –	$ 1,096	$ 2,741	$ 3,837	$ 3,837	$ 2,193	$ 548	$ 14,252
Priority Three Zone	$ –	$ 102	$ 254	$ 356	$ 356	$ 204	$ 51	$ 1,323
Snow Removal: Roads								$ –
Priority One Zone	$ –	$ –	$ –	$ –	$ –	$ –	$ –	$ –
Priority Two Zone	$ –	$ 149	$ 327	$ 446	$ 298	$ 268	$ 60	$ 1,547
Priority Three Zone	$ –	$ 246	$ 542	$ 739	$ 493	$ 443	$ 99	$ 2,562
Snow Removal: Special Pavement								$ –
Priority One Zone	$ –	$ 567	$ 1,248	$ 1,702	$ 1,134	$ 1,021	$ 227	$ 5,899
Priority Two Zone	$ –	$ 504	$ 1,109	$ 1,512	$ 1,008	$ 907	$ 202	$ 5,243
Priority Three Zone	$ –	$ –	$ –	$ –	$ –	$ –	$ –	$ –
Snow Removal: Steps								$ –
Priority One Zone	$ –	$ 327	$ 719	$ 980	$ 654	$ 588	$ 131	$ 3,399
Priority Two Zone	$ –	$ 1,100	$ 2,419	$ 3,299	$ 2,199	$ 1,979	$ 440	$ 11,435
Priority Three Zone	$ –	$ 6	$ 13	$ 17	$ 12	$ 10	$ 2	$ 60
Snow Removal: Walks								$ –
Priority One Zone	$ –	$ 1,061	$ 2,334	$ 3,182	$ 2,121	$ 1,909	$ 424	$ 11,031
Priority Two Zone	$ –	$ 2,521	$ 5,546	$ 7,562	$ 5,042	$ 4,537	$ 1,008	$ 26,216
Priority Three Zone	$ –	$ 156	$ 342	$ 467	$ 311	$ 280	$ 62	$ 1,619
Sidewalk Liquid Deicing								$ –
Priority One Zone	$ –	$ 530	$ 1,167	$ 1,591	$ 1,061	$ 955	$ 212	$ 5,516
Priority Two Zone	$ –	$ 1,260	$ 2,773	$ 3,781	$ 2,521	$ 2,269	$ 504	$ 13,108
Priority Three Zone	$ –	$ 78	$ 171	$ 233	$ 156	$ 140	$ 31	$ 809

Figure 8.4: Maintenance Estimating Worksheet
Campus Snow Removal Plan — Summary and Staffing Needs

Total Labor Hours Needed by Month for Each Maintenance Category

Activity	Jan.	Feb.	March	April		Oct.	Nov.	Dec.	Annual Hours
Zone 1	717.0	504.5	427.9	96.4		0.0	235.2	524.3	–
Zone 2	647.0	443.5	387.2	86.6		0.0	213.9	473.8	–
Zone 3	1003.1	711.5	598.2	135.0		0.0	328.2	733.1	–
Zone 4	1204.0	936.6	710.9	164.4		0.0	382.2	875.3	–
Zone 5	652.5	435.0	391.5	87.0		0.0	217.5	478.5	–
Zone 6	644.5	429.6	386.7	85.9		0.0	214.8	472.6	–
Zone 7	588.8	392.5	353.3	78.5		0.0	196.3	431.8	2,041.24
IH/Pres	40.0	27.5	23.9	5.4		0.0	13.2	29.3	139.43
Fam Hous	1647.3	1195.2	980.1	222.4		0.0	535.2	1202.5	5,782.67
Total	7144.2	5076.0	4259.7	961.5		0.0	2336.6	5221.2	24,999.13

Total Cost by Month for Each Maintenance Category

Activity	Jan.	Feb.	March	April		Oct.	Nov.	Dec.	Annual Cost
Zone 1	$ 29,893	$ 21,389	$ 17,704	$ 4,001		$ –	$ 9,702	$ 21,705	$ 104,394
Zone 2	$ 27,934	$ 19,292	$ 16,703	$ 3,744		$ –	$ 9,216	$ 20,447	$ 97,336
Zone 3	$ 40,279	$ 30,107	$ 24,716	$ 5,603		$ –	$ 13,509	$ 30,319	$ 144,532
Zone 4	$ 57,563	$ 45,760	$ 32,473	$ 7,528		$ –	$ 17,417	$ 40,001	$ 200,742
Zone 5	$ 29,077	$ 19,385	$ 17,446	$ 3,877		$ –	$ 9,692	$ 21,323	$ 100,800
Zone 6	$ 30,390	$ 20,260	$ 18,234	$ 4,052		$ –	$ 10,130	$ 22,286	$ 105,351
Zone 7	$ 19,854	$ 13,236	$ 11,912	$ 2,647		$ –	$ 6,618	$ 14,559	$ 68,826
IH/Pres	$ 1,612	$ 1,122	$ 883	$ 196		$ –	$ 490	$ 1,079	$ 5,382
Fam Hous	$ 69,564	$ 51,723	$ 41,280	$ 9,428		$ –	$ 22,424	$ 50,708	$ 245,129
Total	$ 306,167	$ 222,274	$ 181,351	$ 41,076		$ –	$ 99,198	$ 222,427	$1,072,492

Figure 8.4: Maintenance Estimating Worksheet
Campus Snow Removal Plan — Summary and Staffing Needs, continued

Estimated Staff Needed by Month for Each Maintenance Category									
Activity	Jan.	Feb.	March	April		Oct.	Nov.	Dec.	
Zone 1	4.8	4.2	3.6	0.6		0.0	2.0	4.4	
Zone 2	4.3	3.7	3.2	0.6		0.0	1.8	3.9	
Zone 3	6.7	5.9	5.0	0.9		0.0	2.7	6.1	
Zone 4	8.0	7.8	5.9	1.1		0.0	3.2	7.3	
Zone 5	4.4	3.6	3.3	0.6		0.0	1.8	4.0	
Zone 6	4.3	3.6	3.2	0.6		0.0	1.8	3.9	
Zone 7	3.9	3.3	2.9	0.5		0.0	1.6	3.6	
IH/Pres	0.3	0.2	0.2	0.0		0.0	0.1	0.2	
Fam Hous	11.0	10.0	8.2	1.5		0.0	4.5	10.0	
Total	47.7	42.3	35.5	6.4		0.0	19.5	43.5	

CHAPTER 9

Position Descriptions for the Green Industry

By Leonard O. Morrow, PhD, and Thomas Flood, MBA

Modern grounds maintenance procedures require diverse skills and abilities. Recycling of materials, for example, along with a variety of other responsibilities, is often handled by facilities management or grounds maintenance specifically. This chapter is based on a review of descriptions solicited from current employers, guidelines used by green industry leaders, and insights from various institutions, municipalities, and commercial businesses. Many position descriptions from this survey are available at www.appa.org.

Trends

Even a superficial examination of job descriptions reveals a lack of uniformity among employers. Some institutions have their own systems. Others may adhere to classification schemes used by the government agencies that fund them. Some organizations include specific information about the job, reporting systems, tasks, supervisory channels, and so on, while others provide a superficial description at best.

Compared with job descriptions circulated in past decades, however, more recent descriptions exhibit certain trends worth noting. Facilities and grounds managers are, indeed, becoming an increasingly high-technology, highly skilled professional group. Other trends include the following:

- *Accountability and responsibility:* In general, organizations are placing more emphasis on responsibility and accountability, rather than simply the completion of tasks. Expectations of some employers may be higher now than in past years, or perhaps employers are clarifying their expectations. For example, one institution includes the category "Consequences of Actions and Decisions" in its statement of classification factors.

- *Supervision:* Many descriptions clearly state both who an employee will supervise and who will supervise the employee. In general, position descriptions address the questions, "To whom does this position report?" and "Does this position include supervisory responsibilities for other employees?"
- *Intellectual attributes:* Recent descriptions often emphasize the human element. The wording attempts to communicate the need for workers who can perceive the environment, sort out opportunities from problems, and take action. Reading and math skills, some measure of a reasoning component, and an ability to communicate with others are all important requirements, some of which are explained in the descriptions. Within certain limits, an employee is then empowered to solve certain kinds of problems or make certain kinds of decisions. Note that many of these descriptions are quite specific. For example, consider this excerpt from a language skills statement: "Ability to read and interpret..."; Ability to write..."; "Ability to effectively present information...."
- *Educational requirements and skill levels:* Educational or experiential background for employees tends to vary depending on the level of the position. For leadership or management positions, organizations may prefer a Bachelor of Science degree in horticulture, while others require a two-year degree; and some look for experience rather than education. For entry-level skill jobs, most employers seem to look for one to two years or three to five years of on-the-job experience. For midlevel or higher positions, employers require a high school diploma or GED, a two- or four-year college degree, or a graduate degree. Anecdotally, it appears that organizations are requiring more education than they have in the past.
- *Certification:* Some organizations require certain kinds of certifications for employment, such as certification as an arborist, a pesticide applicator, a grounds manager or technician, or a nutrient manager. Some kinds of employment may require a driver's license; a special driver's permit for buses, trucks, and so on; or certification as a heavy equipment operator.
- *Networking:* The networking component within and outside of a given private or government organization has increasing importance. Nearly all descriptions now

include a category of "Working Relationships" or "Persons Contacted," which lists other people with whom the employee must deal, their status, and the frequency of contact.

- *Opportunities for advancement:* Many employers are emphasizing career development, in part as incentives to retain employees. Such opportunities may take the form of the potential for training in cardiopulmonary resuscitation, first aid, or similar skills; a career path in a technical skill area, such as tree trimmer 1, 2, 3 or equipment operator 1, 2, 3; or a career track in management toward becoming a team leader, supervisor, or department head.

Job Descriptions as Recruiting Tools

The wording of some descriptions suggests that the hiring agent is sampling the labor pool to find the right kind of person to whom job duties will be assigned. Such descriptions are sales or marketing pieces and may actually function as recruiting tools. The descriptions offer a good presentation of the employer and of the outcome of the job, without providing much detail about day-to-day responsibilities.

In contrast, some statements may be quite comprehensive, listing all necessary qualifications, duties, reporting channels, salary levels, and so on. In the extreme case, the description seems like a veiled warning that an unqualified individual who mistakenly takes the job will suffer appropriately. In a competitive market for employees, such descriptions may discourage those who are marginally qualified from applying for certain positions.

Job Descriptions as Contracts Between Employer and Employee

To some employers, the job description is a binding contract; the text may even contain statements that the duties and requirements must be met for continuing employment. For other employers, the job description is not a contract; the text may include wording that not all the duties to be performed are listed in the description. In either case, position descriptions should be clear, and employees should understand the duties and responsibilities expressed in their position descriptions. Ideally, during the employees' performance reviews, they would be evaluated against the fulfillment of duties and responsibilities described in their position description, not compared with other employees. Note, too, that most gender-specific references, such as "groundsman," have now been changed to gender-neutral titles such as "groundskeeper."

Some descriptions show breakouts of certain positions into specific duties, frequency, and percentage of work time. Such detail clearly communicates the major expectations of the position. For example, at one botanical garden, horticulturists are expected to spend 70 percent or more of their time on horticultural maintenance, plant care, and garden design.

Some organizations find benefit in increasing job specificity. For example, Michigan State University lists 15 nonexempt employee job descriptions engaged in horticultural work in its Landscape Services department. An organization with this number of positions typically provides a clear line of advancement opportunities and specific job descriptions. More traditionally, this is found in unionized work environments.

Conversely, some organizations prefer fewer and more generalized position titles. Elon University Landscaping and Grounds department has only six distinct nonexempt positions. This provides the employer more latitude in varying employee assignments and duties, hence avoiding the complaint that "that assignment is not in my job description."

In addition to the detailed job description itself, some organizations include precise statements of physical requirements and descriptions of the work environment. Undoubtedly, such statements have taken on greater importance with the increasing need to avoid discriminating based on age, gender, or disability. It becomes a clear description of the physical requirements of the job. Either you can fulfill them or you cannot.

Brigham Young University uses a standard worksheet as part of its job descriptions. The sheet is divided into three main sections: physical requirements, equipment and tools, and working conditions. These sections contain applicable descriptions that are checked off by the hiring agent.

One final responsibility that may or may not be included in job descriptions is the task of dealing with winter precipitation. At many institutions, snow shoveling or snow and ice removal are included in the written duties and responsibilities of groundskeepers. At Farmington Country Club in Charlottesville, Virginia, all staff members are involved in snow removal. At the Winterthur Museum and Gardens in

Delaware, snow removal is sixth on the list of priorities, accounting for an estimated 2 percent of workers' time annually. Undoubtedly, snow removal is an important task in other organizations, but has not been spelled out as such.

Snow removal or responding to other emergency situations, such as severe weather and natural or manmade disasters, is a requirement of most grounds management employees. Specifically including those duties and your expectations for unscheduled or immediate response will both make it clear to the employee what is expected and avoid numerous complaints afterward.

Position Descriptions in Your Organization

Obviously, position descriptions vary a good deal from one organization to another. Taking the time to write detailed position descriptions for your facilities management department is the first step in matching the right employees with the right jobs.

First, determine where the position falls in the organizational hierarchy. Most positions fall into one of three categories: entry level; midlevel, which involves additional skills and duties; or supervisory and/or administrative. In writing the rest of the description, be sure to include the following items:

- Title of the person who fills the position
- Reporting and/or supervisory channels
- Statement of general duties and responsibilities
- Specific requirements for the job, such as skills, academic degrees, professional certifications, government certifications, and so on
- A clear description of the career track that is open to the employee
- An explanation of applicable physical requirements and working conditions
- Any additional information specific to the job

Last, be aware that each organization may prefer a standardize position description format. In unionized work environments, union contracts or work agreements may take precedence. Check with your Human Resources department before initiating changes.

Examples

The following pages include a sampling of different position descriptions in the green industry. They range from Elon University's simple two-page position description to the University of Michigan's detailed competency profile. Many more are available on the APPA website at www.appa.org.

ELON UNIVERSITY
Position Description

POSITION TITLE: Assistant Sports Turf Manager

DEPARTMENT: Physical Plant, Landscaping and Grounds

REPORTS TO: Sports Turf Manager, Landscaping and Grounds

FLSA STATUS: __x__ Exempt (salaried employee) _____ Non-exempt (hourly employee)

SUMMARY OF POSITION

- This position assists the Sports Turf Manager in the management of allocated resources to ensure all University playing surfaces and surrounding areas are expertly conditioned to provide optimum performance and appearance. The incumbent carries out work through assignments to subordinate workers as well as hands-on involvement.

ESSENTIAL DUTIES AND RESPONSIBILITIES

- Plan and manage the sports turf maintenance activities and staff in the absence of the sports turf manager.
- Lead the daily maintenance of all inter-collegiate athletic fields and the surrounding landscape, totaling approximately 40 acres.
- Provide oversight of the recreations fields and facilities as assigned.
- Develop and implement short term maintenance programs based on field usage and specific requirements for individual sporting events.
- Prepare all fields of play dependent on their purpose including, but not limited to, mowing, aeration, fertilization, cultural practices, grooming and painting of individualized fields.
- Provide game day preparation and support for all ICA sports fields or other scheduled events as required by each sport.
- Enhance the present turf grass conditions to comply with the requirements and expectations of NCAA Division I athletic program.
- Maintain health and appearance of landscaping in areas surrounding playing fields and surfaces including, but not limited to, the athletic complex and Powell Tennis Center.
- Monitor and inspect equipment to ensure safe working condition; perform repairs as required.
- Prepare performance evaluations of subordinates and conducts appraisal reviews highlighting strengths and areas needing improvement, if any. Delegate and hold subordinates responsible for satisfactory performance of assignments.
- Provide assistance in snow removal and disaster preparedness/recovery operations as required.
- Perform other duties as assigned or necessary.

SUPERVISORY RESPONSIBILITIES

- Supervises two to four crew workers, providing assignments, inspection, evaluations and training. Supervisory authority may also be exercised over seasonal temporary workers.

EDUCATION AND EXPERIENCE

- Four to six years' related experience in maintaining athletic fields at an NCAA Division I institution or similar organization and demonstrated ability to provide effective employee and resource management is required. A bachelor's degree or an associate degree in turfgrass management is desired.

LANGUAGE SKILLS

- Ability to read, analyze, and interpret technical articles related to turf grass or landscape management. Position requires ability to verbally communicate effectively with the Sports Turf Manager and administrative or athletic personnel.

MATHEMATICAL SKILLS

- Ability to perform simple to medium complex calculations such as determining volume, area, percentages, and basic concepts of geometry.

REASONING ABILITY

- Must be able to discern the difference between symptoms and root causes of turf problems. Ability to analyze facts and data, apply common sense and agricultural experience in determining cause(s) of a problem and developing solutions with alternatives.

OTHER SKILLS REQUIRED

- Computer experience with PCs is desired; prefer knowledge and experience with Microsoft Office applications. Experience with equipment associated with the trade is essential; e.g., mowers, tractors, etc.

CERTIFICATES OR LICENSES

- Must possess a valid NC driver's license and be insurable by the University's carrier. A pesticide application license or the ability to obtain within six months of employment is required. A certification in turf management is desirable.

PHYSICAL DEMANDS

- Must be able to bend, crouch, climb movable or fixed ladders, and may be required to assist in safely lifting up to 50 lbs. of material. Employee must be in good physical condition as work may be arduous at times.

WORK ENVIRONMENT

- Work is primarily in the field, but may be in the office depending on the circumstances. Indoor work environment may be in an office (moderate noise), or in the field or shop spaces where loud noises may be encountered. Additionally, outdoor work may expose the incumbent to extreme heat or cold for significant portions of the workday.

MICHIGAN STATE UNIVERSITY
Arborist II

Abbreviation:	Grade:	Union	FLSA:	Code:	Job Group:
ARB II	19	1585	N	3102	1631

CLASSIFICATION: ARBORIST II

Basic Function

- Perform general tree and plant care, preservation, treatment, and maintenance operations.

Characteristic Duties And Responsibilities

- Perform general tree and plant care, preservation, treatment, removal, and related maintenance and pruning operations.
- Identify and treat tree and plant diseases, insect and other related problems.
- Operate and maintain power equipment such as stump grinders, chain saws, brush cutters, aerial towers, hydraulic sprayers, mist blowers, compressors, brush chippers, trucks and other vehicles.
- Climb and trim trees using ropes and safety saddles, ladders, spurs, handsaws, pole pruners, chain saws, gas powered brush cutters and aerial tower trucks.
- Cable, bolt, guy, and brace designated trees.
- Mix, spray and apply pesticides and fertilizers to trees and grounds.
- Remove trees and shrubs using cranes, trucks, front-end loaders and tractors.
- Amend soil around trees using hydraulic sprayers, power augers, and/or compressors.
- Clean, sharpen, and lubricate power equipment and hand tools.
- Clean and maintain work areas and equipment.
- Instruct assigned support employees in proper work methods and safety techniques.
- Erect street and pedestrian barricades and warning signs.
- Collect, haul, and dispose of plant refuse and debris.

Related Duties

- Perform related duties as assigned including, but not necessarily limited to, the following:
  - Participate in snow plan by shoveling, operating snow removal vehicles and equipment and applying ice melt products.
  - Assist in football tailgate cleanup.

Supervision Received

- Immediate supervision is received from a designated supervisor.

Minimum Qualifications

- Two years of satisfactory experience as an Arborist I or an equivalent combination of technical training and experience.
- Expert knowledge of tools, methods, materials, and equipment used in tree trimming and grounds maintenance.
- Expert climbing knowledge and ability using ropes and other safety equipment, and working at heights.
- Possession of a valid Michigan Commercial Pesticide Applicator Certification in categories Ornamental (3B), Right of Way (6) and Mosquito (7F).

- Possession of a valid Michigan Class B Commercial Driver's License with applicable endorsements (air brakes) and medical certificate to comply with State of Michigan requirements. Applicant must have a good driving record and submit their operator's license number on their application form for a motor vehicle check.
- Possession or attainment of a MSU Forklift Operators Permit, CPR and First Aid Certification prior to completion of applicable probation or trial period.
- Arborist certification by the International Society of Arboriculture prior to completion of applicable probation or trial period.
- Must drive University vehicle to perform job duties of this classification.
- The ability to work in variable or severe weather conditions.
- Participation in Campus Snow Removal Plan.
- This position requires significant after-hours, weekend and holiday work.
- Frequent lifting of 26 to 75 lbs. with occasional lifting of over 75 lbs.

Additional Requirements

- May require valid operator, chauffeur, or commercial driver's license(s) with applicable endorsements and medical certificate in order to comply with State of Michigan requirements.
- This position requires, or will require prior to the completion of the probationary period: knowledge of basic personal computer terminology and operations, and the ability to use e-mail and the Internet.

"This description is intended to indicate the kinds of tasks and levels of work difficulty that will be required of positions that will be given this title and shall not be construed as declaring what the specific duties and responsibilities of any particular position shall be. It is not intended to limit or in any way modify the right of any supervisor to assign, direct, and control the work of employees under his or her supervision. The use of a particular expression or illustration describing duties shall not be held to exclude other duties not mentioned that are of similar kind or level of difficulty."

Date: 3/2010

MSU is an affirmative-action, equal-opportunity employer.

Competency Profile
HR Job Title
Groundskeeper II

****

G&WM Job: Groundskeeper (Horticulture Zones)

- A Groundskeeper II a.k.a. Groundskeeper (Horticulture Zones) installs and maintains hardscapes and landscapes within zones to ensure a safe, and beautiful environment for the students, visitors, and staff of the University of Michigan.

G&WM Job: Groundskeeper (Horticulture Zones)					
Duties	Tasks				
A - Provide Customer Service	A1- Educate our clients (This should be a much larger task)	A2- Build rapport with the clients	A3- Identify the real client	A4- Check that all commitments made to the customers are kept	A5- Make ourselves available to our clients
	A6- Build a specific maintenance plan for each location with individual building managers (Not currently done)	A7- Provide consistent customer service planning	A8- Keep the customer informed of any changes if possible	A9- When the customer asks for specific individuals, provide them when possible	
B - Install New Beds	B1- Survey site	B2- Remove existing material	B3- Spray pesticides	B4- Amend soil	B5- Edge bed (Outline the Bed)
	B6- Install metal edging	B7- Install weed guard	B8- Follow the horticulture & landscape architect design	B9- Water plants	B10- Grade the Bed
C - Maintain Landscape	C1-Mechanically weed the landscape	C2- Chemically weed the landscape	C3- Water the landscape	C4- Install additional plants	C5- Clean up garbage & debris
	C6- Rake leaves from bed	C7- Divide plants & replant	C8- Prune the trees, shrubs, bushes, etc. (Plants)	C9- Monitor the site	
D - Leaf Removal	D1- Use the Smith Co. to collect leaves	D2- Maintain and Clean the Smith Co.	D3- Use and maintain the Goosen Vac.	D4- Rake and bag leaves	D5- Remove and dispose compost
E - Bulb Care	E1- Plant bulbs according to plan	E2- Rotor till soil	E3- Operate mechanical rotor tiller	E4- Operate hand rotor tiller	E5- Mark the Bed
	E6- Remove the bulbs after season				
F - Maintain a Zone	F1- Maintain the tool crib	F2- Inventory tools & materials	F3- Maintain spray sheets	F4- Identify zone damage (daily) and find solution	F5- Meet with manager and construction on a regular basis

G&WM Job: Groundskeeper (Horticulture Zones)					
Duties	Tasks				
G - Hardscape Clean Up	G1- Sweep stairs, walkways, entrance way, ramps, etc.	G2- Blow off stairs, walkways, entrance ways, ramps, etc.	G3- Remove graffiti	G4- Remove posters, or any posted signs	G5- Remove gum
	G6- Sweep up cigarette butts	G7- Unflip the concrete benches	G8- Spray for weeds on stairs, walkways, entranceways, ramps, etc.		
H - Remove Snow	H1- Shovel crosswalks, sidewalks, steps and spread ice melt	H2- Install the plow on the truck	H3- Plow snow and broom snow	H4- Operate powered snow removal equipment	H5- Spray liquid deicers
	H6- Remove snow by priority area	H7- Clean and maintain all equipment	H8- Chop ice	H9- Clear drains	H10- Mark drains and fire hydrants, and Siamese connectors
	H11- Load the salt truck	H12- Squeegee areas of low water	H13- Order, receive and put away bags of salt (by hand)	H14- Truck snow to holding areas	H15- Pre-treat area with deicer (stairways, entryways, sidewalks)
	H16- Be available 24/7 for snow removal				
I - Maintain Lawns	I1- Inspect the lawn for debris before mowing (Walk the lawn)	I2- Aerate the lawn	I3- Apply fertilizers as required	I4- Reseed the lawn (top-dress)	I5- Thatch the lawn
	I6- Apply weed killers to the lawn	I7- Mow the lawn to the correct height by turf standard (by supervisor)	I8- Water the lawn	I9- Check the lawn for grubs and insects	I10- Protect the lawn from chemicals i.e. gas, calcium chloride
	I11- Apply organic pesticide to the lawn	I12- Rake the lawn	I13- Lay sod	I14- Edge the lawn	I15- Fence off the lawn
	I16- Weed whip around obstacles	I17- Repair damaged lawns caused by people's negligence			
J - Use and Maintain Equipment	J1- Utilize hand tools e.g., rakes, trowels, shears, drills	J2- Maintain mowers e.g., clean, gas up, grease and sharpen blades	J3- Clean and maintain tillers and attachments	J4- Maintain and repair hoses and reels	J5- Maintain the truck i.e. check fluids, clean
	J6- Use, maintain and repair small power tools	J7- Use, maintain and repair spray equipment	J8- Clean out the sprayers for chemical changes	J9- Use and maintain the spreaders	J10- Trouble- shoot equipment (Repair or replace)

G&WM Job: Groundskeeper (Horticulture Zones)					
Duties	Tasks				
	J11- Sharpen blades	J12- Suggest modifications	J13- Wash equipment	J14- Inform heavy equipment mechanics when maintenance is due	J15- Make service calls
K - Training	K1-Train seasonal employees on specific pieces of equipment and locations (On the job training)	K2- Check that new employees are correctly using safety equipment	K3- Obtain "CDL", Forklift license, med card license, manufacture specific training on all equipment		
L - Gather and Dispose of Waste and Recyclables	L1- Load one ton truck manually and deposit garbage in dumpsters or compactors	L2- Follow the daily schedule for trash pick-up	L3- Pick up recycling materials	L4- Separate recycling materials and place in appropriate containers	L5- Suggest replacement containers for damaged units
	L6- Operate the compactors	L7- Clean up completed area	L8- Move recycling containers in and out of the buildings	L9- Keep the truck clean (should be done daily)	L10- Re-bag garbage and police garbage storage areas
M - Maintain Plants	M1- Inspect outdoor plants and soil	M2- Prune dead, damaged or diseased branches	M3- Water plants as necessary	M4- Fertilize plants as required	M5- Mulch plants as required
	M6- Weed plantings	M7- Assist in cultivating plantings	M8- Pull and replace dead or diseased plants	M9- Assist in dividing plants and bulbs	M10- Stake, tie or guide plants as needed
N - Maintain Trees and Shrubs	N1- Transplant shrubs as required	N2- Prune new growth as required	N3- Train and guide trees	N4- Prune small trees	N5- Choose appropriate chemicals and concentrations
	N6- Cut down small trees	N7- Plant trees and shrubs	N8- Water the trees and new plantings	N9- Remove fallen trees	N10- Pick up and deliver plants and supplies
	N11- Deadhead bushes or shrubs				
O - Special Occasions	O1- Park cars	O2- Shuttle people	O3- Pick up, deliver and set up floral arrangement	O4- Move-in and move-out	O5- Provide extra policing of area
	O6- Provide attention for special occasions	O7- Distribute and recollect trash cans	O8-Install/Remove holiday lights	O9- Obtain extra materials, e.g., flowers	
P - Suggest Equipment, Services and Supplies	P1- Place orders and receive goods	P2- Source new equipment and supplies (more often)	P3- Maintain files	P4- Evaluate all tools and equipment (should happen pre-season)	P5- Maintain an orderly storage area

G&WM Job: Groundskeeper (Horticulture Zones)					
Duties	Tasks				
	P6- Consult with landscape architects on specific landscape issue (should happen)				
Q - Perform Winter Tasks	Q1- Rake and mulch leaves	Q2- Install fencing	Q3- Paint, assemble, and install garbage cans	Q4- Block off low traffic areas	Q5- Intial burlap fence
R - Perform Other Job-Related Duties	R1- Remove graffiti	R2- Clean up litter and posters	R3- Maintain community relations	R4- Install no-roost	R5- Attend meetings
	R6- Supervise students / assist students	R7- Transplant flowers from special events	R8- Give lectures and advice on horticulture	R9- Account for time- complete work orders	R10- Attend classes and seminars
	R11- Install Christmas trees	R12- Remove Christmas trees	R13- Pick up gas and diesel fuel	R14- Load and unload trucks, supplies and equipment	R15- Clean up pigeon droppings
	R16- Deliver and pick up broken and repaired equipment	R17- Follow manufacturers guidelines for equipment maintenance	R18- Verify that all power equipment is safe and operational before taking it out	R19- Clean all tools and return them to their proper locations	R20- Winterize equipment
	R21- Check all fluid levels as required daily	R22- Evaluate pedestrian and animal accessibility i.e. theft, vandalism	R23- Assist plan the new installation	R24- Clean and prepare the new site	R25- Re-evaluate the installation and suggest adjustments
	R26- Make daily inspections of the grounds	R27- Report to supervisors and building managers as required	R28- Rectify small problems with the grounds or plantings immediately	R29- Unload and transport plant materials	R30- Paint and repair chain and post
	R31- Assist tree crew cutting up	R32- Assist/Fill gator	R33- Assist with water main break	R34-Clean drains	R35- Assist with fountain installation
	R36- Loan out tools	R37- Defend the Zones	R38- Call authorities to remove unwanted people	R39- Report vandalizing	
S -Administrative	S1- Fill out timecards	S2- Check and respond to email	S3- Fill out hauling sheets	S4- Attend conferences and seminars	S5- Have department meetings
	S6- Fill out medical reports	S7-Take physicals	S8- Fill out vacation request reports	S9- Fill out accident reports	

Skills and Knowledge

- Knowledge in the techniques of landscape grooming
- Knowledge in efficient weed control techniques
- Skill in accessing what an area needs and the skill to lead by example and the ability to communicate

Traits and Attributes

- Self-motivators
- Positive Attitude
- Sense of Humor
- Cooperative
- Safety minded
- Team Player
- Comfortable
- Flexible
- Willing to get dirty

Requirements (i.e. Physical and others)

- The work of this position focuses on litter picking, weed removal (by mechanical and or chemical), and other manual maintenance items
- Physical dexterity
- Endurance rather than brute strength
- Mental dexterity
- The ability to focus mentally and to be mentally flexible

Licenses, Certifications and Degrees

- CDL
- Pesticides
- Fork Lifts
- Case Loader
- Health Card

Tools & Equipment

- Basic hand tools
- Basic power tools
- Tractors and mowers
- Holders
- Spray rigs
- Fork lift
- Hydro seeder
- Leaf sucking or blowing
- Trailers
- Red Max
- Edger
- Trimmer
- Tiller (Mantis)
- Toro Rotor Tiller
- Walk Behind Mower
- Ride on Mower
- Power Hedge Trimmer
- Pole Saw
- Chain Saw
- Daihatsu
- Trucks to 5 yards
- Front End Loader
- Skid Steer Loader
- Kabota Broom
- Toro Sprayer
- Salt Spreader Truck
- Snow Plow
- Smith Co.
- Goosen Vac.
- Weed Wacker
- Hearing and eye protection
- Glasses
- Gloves
- Respirators/suits

Training Needs

Hard Skills	Soft Skills
Basic Horticulture e.g., Plant Pruning, Plant Identification, Seasonal Questions, Misc.	Train the Trainer
Manufacturer-based training on all equipment	Interpersonal Skills Training
General landscape/ horticulture training	***Do Not Start Training Programs If You Don't Intend To Let Us Finish Them!!!***

APPENDIX A

Case Study: Quality Appearance Program

By Joseph Jackson

At Duke University, the Grounds and Sanitation Services Unit has implemented a new program that involves a process of self-evaluation and embraces the concept of perpetual and continuous improvement. It is called the Quality Appearance Program (QAP). Obviously, the use of this acronym is an embellishment from the Quality Assurance Program concept, but with a twist to grounds management improvement strategies.

Over the years, the Grounds Unit has employed many practices bearing technical significance as well as traditional management perspectives. We have devised grounds standards, conducted peer inspections, established training plans, formulated work measurements and metrics, and even won national grounds awards. When you examine our campus with a trained or untrained eye, however, there are areas that just don't look "as good as they should." These landscaped areas may have been installed as intended, maintained properly, and contain thriving plant material, yet the areas simply do not look very pleasing.

Like many aspects of quality, aesthetics is a difficult thing to quantify. It is true that beauty is in the eye of the beholder. So when an area does not look as good as it should, is that a matter of opinion, preference, or definition? The Duke QAP initiative is an attempt to address this visual disconnect more specifically and definitively. It is the collective creation of the department's grounds supervisors. It was determined that such a program should be a full-circle, continuous process (Figure A.1, next page).

- **Step 1. Identify:** Locate the landscaped area for consideration.
- **Step 2. Analyze:** Determine shortcomings and deficiencies.
- **Step 3. Effectuate:** Implement improvement measures.
- **Step 4. Evaluate:** Monitor and document success of upgrades.

Figure A.1: QAP Full Circle Implementation Process

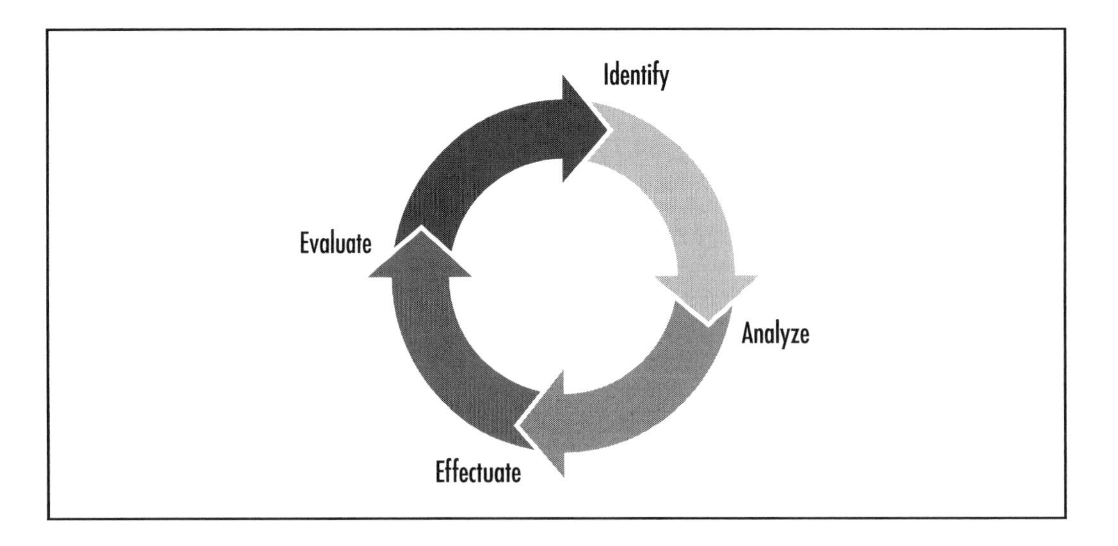

This four-step process created the framework for evaluating areas.

With a conceptual understanding of how the program should work, it became necessary to define what a quality grounds area should really look like. Three descriptive criteria were chosen and defined:

1. **Beautiful:** The landscape must capture the eye, stir the imagination, and cause one to pause momentarily, with the realization that this may be the only opportunity to create an unforgettable memory.
2. **Appealing:** The landscape must attract favorable and pleasant attention to the campus and must maximize the tantalization of human senses.
3. **Diverse:** The landscape must be an assorted, multifarious place that offers a rich, distinctive, and exciting world and brings forth the stimulation of good design, colors, and shapes.

With these general descriptive criteria in place, the next exercise was to develop a systematic way to assess and weigh the worthiness of an area or project being evaluated. A rubric was established that could be used to rate areas based on a set of conditions that, when met, would effectively integrate and visually display the best qualities of these three criteria (Figure A. 2).

Employees can submit areas for QAP awards, and department managers rate the areas according to the rubric, with only the highest rated areas receiving an award. The QAP is an incentive program designed to encourage area supervisors and employees to improve the appearance of their areas and motivate all employees to

Figure A.2: QAP Rubric Chart

	4	3	2	1
Turfgrass Management	Turf is in exceptional visible health. Species are properly matched to environment. Turf is free of weeds, debris, disease & pest injury. Outstanding color, density & uniformity. Borders are edged and kept crisped.	Turf is in good overall health. Good uniformity in species, color, and appearance. Very limited number of weeds. Minimal signs of stress from drought, insects, disease, or wear. Borders kept crisped & edged.	Moderate signs of damage from insects, disease, traffic or drought. Nonuniformity is present in species, color, height, and overall appearance.	Significant evidence of poor turf health. Turf is lacking color, density, and quality appearance. Significant levels of irreversible damage from insects, disease, or mechanical injury.
Landscape Management	Plants are vigorous with no symptoms of pests, disease, or infertility; thoughtfully pruned using proper methods. Beds are weed-free, definitively edged, and freshly mulched to proper depth with appropriate materials. Irrigation is working and programmed for optimum effectiveness.	Plants are healthy overall with sporadic symptoms of pest or disease, adequately pruned to achieve neat appearance. Beds have occasional weeds that do not detract significantly. Mulch is sufficient to conserve water and suppress weeds. Irrigation is working effectively.	Plants exhibit some signs of pests or disease. Pruning is somewhat inadequate or incorrect. Beds are not uniformly edged. Mulch is not fresh and weeds are visible throughout. Irrigation may not provide adequate water at all times or may be inefficient.	Plants have significant damage from pests or disease. Pruning is inadequate or incorrect to the point of being detrimental. Weeds are rampant and mulch is insufficient. Irrigation is inoperable and ineffective. Landscape is unappealing. Debris and dead material are present.
Landscape Design	Landscape exhibits rich diversity of plants well suited to the local micro-environment. Design is appealing and cohesive in form and function with thought given to management issues and mature size and spacing.	Landscape meets functional requirements of site. Plant material is sufficiently suitable to achieve viability but lacks some diversity. The design allows for reasonable management inputs.	Landscape does not meet all functional criteria. Plant materials lack diversity or are inappropriate for site. Design causes management to be unnecessarily challenging.	Landscape is neither functional nor cohesive. Plant choices and design show no consideration of management issues or sustainability. Overall effect is unappealing.
Challenges	Maintenance strategy shows high level of success in overcoming high levels of usage, soil compaction, poor soil profile, and harsh micro-climate through efficient optimization of resources.	Moderate success has been achieved through sound management practices with varying degrees of soil compaction, moderate to heavy use, and less than ideal climatic conditions.	Visible signs of a highly thought out and executed management strategy. Although site is aesthetically pleasing, few obstacles were overcome to achieve high level of success, i.e., ideal soil profile, low usage rates, and ideal growing conditions.	Site is aesthetically poor. Management plan has not been executed due to less than ideal growing conditions. Site is compact and has constant use, and the utilization of resources is minimal.

monitor their sites, make improvements, and submit them for a quality award. Areas submitted for a QAP that do not win can be reassessed, improved, and resubmitted later. Areas that receive a QAP designation are to be seen as examples to other employees of ways they can improve.

The intent of this program is not to correct all the ills and misfortunes that produce landscape eyesores on campus, nor is it intended to force the landscape design process to move in a certain direction. Such notions would be sophomoric at best and imbecilic at worst. It is, though, another measure to add to our existing arsenal of initiatives for the purpose of reaching excellence in our Grounds Services Unit. It is intended to take a landscape space that we have been given, in whatever form or with any set of inherited problems, and make that section of our whole landscape as visually rewarding as possible.

Figure A.3: Quality Assurance Award Winners

Before

After

APPENDIX B

Glossary

Compiled by Dennis L. Swartzell

ACCRETION – The buildup of land along a beach or shore by deposits of waterborne or airborne sand, sediment, or other material.

ADJUSTMENT FACTOR – A method by which a weekly multiplier is determined. For example, if a task is required to be accomplished once per week, it is assigned an adjustment factor of 1.00. If the task is altered to be accomplished every other week or biweekly, then the factor becomes 0.50.

AERATE – The process of making holes or slits in turf to improve or alter the physical soil conditions and to stimulate plant growth. Aeration increases air infiltration, water percolation, and plant nutrient mobility into the root zones. A cultural practice used to correct soil compaction.

AERIAL LIFT – Hydraulically operated aerial tower used for ascent and tree entry, usually mounted on a large truck. Line crews use some as short as 35 feet for clearing cables and streetlights. Most forestry departments use towers of 45 to 55 feet for trimming and removal operations. Sometimes used to replace burned-out floodlights at ballparks. Also known as a cherry picker.

AERIAL RESCUE – The process of getting help for and bringing down a tree worker who has been injured aloft.

AEROSOL – A fine spray produced by pressurized gas that leaves very small droplets of solids or liquids suspended in the air.

AGREEMENT – (1) A legally enforceable promise or promises between two or among several persons. (2) On a construction project, the document stating the essential terms of the construction contract that incorporates by reference the other contract documents. (3) The document setting forth the terms of the contract between the architect and owner or between the architect and consultant.

ALTERATION – A change or rearrangement in the structural parts of a building or in its facilities. An alteration may include repairs and replacements but is distinguished from them by the fact that repairs and replacements do not entail a change in partitions or in other parts of the structure.

AMENDMENT – A chemical or mineral element added to the soil to improve soil characteristics, such as porosity, aeration, drainage, pH, and moisture retention.

AMERICANS WITH DISABILITIES ACT (ADA) – An act signed into U.S. law on July 26, 1990, that prohibits discrimination on the basis of disability with regard to employment, programs, and services provided by state and local governments; goods and services provided by private companies; and in commercial facilities. The ADA contains requirements for new construction, for alterations or renovations to buildings and facilities, for improved access to existing facilities of private companies that provide goods or services to the public, and for state and local governments to provide access to programs offered to the public. The ADA also covers effective communication with people who have disabilities, establishes eligibility criteria that may restrict or prevent access, and requires reasonable modifications of policies and practices that may be discriminatory.

ANNUAL FLOWERS – Herbaceous plants that live one year or less, during which time they grow, flower, produce seed, and die.

ANNUALS – Herbaceous plants characterized by abundant flowering that live for one year or less, during which time they grow, flower, produce seed, and die.

APPROVED EQUAL – Material, equipment, or method approved by the client for use by the contractor as being acceptable as an equivalent in essential attributes to the material, equipment, or method specified in the contract documents.

AQUATIC LIFE – A plant that must live partly or entirely in water for at least part of its life cycle.

ARBOR – A light, open structure of trees, shrubs, or vines closely planted, twined together in a self-supporting manner or supported on a light, latticework frame.

ARBORETUM – A place where trees and related plants are grown for the purposes of education, research, or display.

ARBORICULTURE – The growing of, and caring for, trees for aesthetic purposes, such as specimen trees, street trees, and shade trees.

ARBORIST – A position that provides expertise in the field of tree maintenance practices, including but not limited to pruning, planting, pest and disease diagnosis, and fertilization. Typically, this position functions as a working lead or supervisor of a tree crew or as the tree specialist for an organization. This position generally requires a moderate to extensive education, experience, and certification in the field of arboriculture.

ASEXUAL PROPAGATION – Plant reproduction without the use of seed, as with cuttings, budding, layering, and grating.

ASPHALT – (1) A dark brown to black cementitious material, solid or semisolid, in which the predominating constituents are bitumens that occur in nature. (2) A similar material obtained artificially in reining petroleum, used in built-up roofing systems as a waterproofing agent. (3) A mixture of such substances with an aggregate for use in paving.

ASPHALTIC CONCRETE, Paving, Blacktop – A mixture of asphalt and graded aggregate widely used as paving material over a prepared base; it is normally placed, shaped, and compacted while hot but can be mixed and placed without heat.

ATTORNEY-IN-FACT – A person authorized to act for or in behalf of another person or organization, to the extent prescribed in a written instrument known as a Power of Attorney.

AVULSION - (1) A tearing away or separation by the force of water. (2) Land that is separated from upland or adjacent properties by the action of a stream or river cutting through the land to form a new stream bed.

BALANCED FERTILIZER - A balanced-ratio fertilizer that contains equal amounts of the primary elements nitrogen, phosphorus, and potassium.

BALLED AND BURLAPPED (B&B) - Plants prepared for transplanting by digging them so that the soil immediately around the roots remains undisturbed. The ball of earth is then bound up in burlap or similar mesh fabric.

BANKED TURF - A turf area that occurs on a slope considered too steep to mow with standard mowing equipment.

BASE MAP - A map indicating the significant existing features of an area, such as the streets, rivers, parks, and rail lines, that serves as the foundation for subsequent mapping and planning.

BELOW - Warning call given by tree trimmer or topper when dropping a piece of brush or wood.

BENCHMARK - A relatively permanent object, natural or artificial, bearing a marked point with an elevation that is known above or below an adopted datum. Usually designated as a BM, such a mark is sometimes further qualified as a permanent benchmark (PBM) or a temporary benchmark (TBM). Benchmarks serve as references for topographical surveys and tidal observations.

BENCHMARKING - The process of measuring activities considered critical to an organization's success.

BERM - A mound of earth, with a length greater than its width, constructed as a barrier or an aesthetic landform.

BID - A complete and properly signed proposal to do the work or designated portion thereof for the sums stipulated therein, supported with data called for by the bidding requirements.

BID BOND – A form of bid security executed by the bidder as principal and by a surety. See also Bid Security.

BID DATE – The date established by the client for the receipt of bids.

BID FORM – A form furnished to a bidder to be filed out, signed, and submitted as the bid.

BID SECURITY – The deposit of cash, certified check, cashier's check, bank draft, money order, or bid bond submitted with a bid and serving to guarantee to the owner that the bidder, if awarded the contract, will execute the contract in accordance with the bidding requirements and the contract documents.

BIDDER – One who submits a bid for a prime contract with the owner; distinct from a subbidder who submits a bid to a prime bidder. Technically, a bidder is not a contractor on a specific project until a contract exists between the bidder and the owner.

BIDDING DOCUMENT – The advertisement or invitation to bid, instructions to bidder, the bid form, and the proposed contract documents, including any addenda issued before receipt of bids.

BIENNIALS – Herbaceous plants that produce leafy growth, often in a rosette, from seed the first growing season, followed by dormancy during the winter months. The second season, the plants develop stalks with flowers and seeds, then die. Typically, biennials live more than 12 months but less than 36 months.

BIOLOGICAL CONTROL – The control of pests by means of naturally occurring agents, such as parasites, predators, and disease-producing organisms.

BITUMEN – An asphalt of naturally occurring substances.

BODY THRUST – An ascent method in which the climber pre-crotches a line and pulls himself or herself into the tree. The climber is either belayed or secured by a tautline hitch.

BOSUN'S CHAIR – A nautical term for a wooden seat used by a climber in place of a saddle or bowline when an extensive amount of work must be done. A seat or "swingboard" is put into a bowline or double-bowline (one loop goes around the waist). The free end is used to tie a tautline hitch on the up-rope so that the climber may control his or her position in the tree. Originally used aboard ships and adopted by early arborists. Also known as a swingboard.

BROADCAST MAINTENANCE – The deployment of specifically trained crews that each perform specific groundskeeping tasks and that move from one area to another of a site, such as a park or campus, doing all work of a particular type as needed. Examples include a tree crew or an irrigation crew.

BROADLEAF PLANTS – Plants with leaves in which the veins are almost never parallel. These plants tend to have wider leaves than grasslike plants such as lilies, irises, palms, and orchids. Typically, these plants are dicotyledons (dicots).

BRUSH CHIPPER – A specialized piece of equipment designed for shredding brush and limbs into small chips.

BRUSH CONTROL – Control of woody plants and brush, usually by herbicides, weed killers, or mechanical methods.

BUCKSTRAP – Leather strap or 5/8-inch-diameter rope fastened onto a climber's safety belt or tree saddle. Has a large snap-hook to fasten onto a D-ring after being passed around the tree limb or pole.

BULB – A highly compressed subterranean stem having fleshy scales, such as an onion, lily, or tulip.

BULL LINE (BULL ROPE) – Work rope, often 3/4 to 1 inch in diameter, used to pull up and lower large limbs or sections of trees. Used with snatch block and truck for heavy loads. Light loads often pulled by two or three workers with another snubbing the running part of the rope around the trunk of a nearby tree. Use of hydraulic crane units and towers has eliminated much of the need for this technique.

BULL SAW – A heavy-duty saw used by a climber. Teeth usually include both cutters and rakers, as in a crosscut saw. Lightweight, one-person chainsaws have taken the place of most such saws.

BUTT ROPE – Work rope, 3/8 or 1/2 inch in diameter depending on size of limb; tied with a clove hitch or running bowline 6 inches above the cut line on a limb to be cut. When the cut is made, this rope enables the butt end to be lowered easily from a crotch or controlled by using a pull rope.

CABLE STRETCHER – A piece of equipment that is used in installing cable in trees. When hardware has been properly placed on an eyebolt, the cable stretcher is fastened with ropes to the other limb just below the eye. The cable is placed in the come-along clamp of the cable stretcher, and the handle is worked on a ratchet (such as a bumperjack) until the cable is pulled properly snug. Then the other end is spliced around the lag or eye and the cable stretcher is removed. Also known as a cable grip.

CAD (Computer-Aided Design) – A specialized application of computers primarily for the purpose of designing and precisely drawing architectural or engineering projects.

CALCIUM CHLORIDE – A granular salt-based chemical sometimes applied to earthen paths and roads to settle dust. Also used as a deicing agent on pavement. This material is toxic to plants and should be applied with care in their proximity.

CALIPER – (1) Tool for rolling and lifting logs (with two cant hooks). A heavy handle has an iron hook hinged about 8 inches above an iron-shod tip. Similar to a peavey but has a flat tooth instead of a pike point. (2) May denote the diameter, or thickness, of a tree. Typically reserved for smaller nursery stock.

CAPILLARY WATER – Water held in the capillaries or small pores of the soil that occurs either when free water passes through the soil or by capillary attraction from a wetter stratum.

CAPITAL IMPROVEMENT – Any substantial physical facility built by the public or any major nonrecurring expenditure. The construction of schools, highways, and sewer and water systems and the landscaping of a park are all capital expenditures, as distinguished from operating costs.

CARRYING CAPACITY – Level of use that can be accommodated and continued without irreversible impairment of the productivity of natural resources, the ecosystem, and the quality of air, land, and water resources.

CATCH BASIN – A receptacle used for collecting surface drainage that is connected through drains or conduits to a stormwater system.

CEFP (Certified Educational Facilities Professional) – Advanced facilities management credential developed and offered by APPA.

CEMENT – A material or a mixture of materials (without aggregate) that when in a plastic state, possesses adhesive and cohesive properties and hardens in place.

CGM (Certified Grounds Manager) – Advanced grounds management certification developed and offered by the Professional Grounds Management Society.

CGT (Certified Grounds Technician) – Certification program developed and offered by the Professional Grounds Management Society.

CHANGE ORDER – A written order to the contractor signed by the owner and the architect and issued after the execution of the contract, authorizing a change in the work or an adjustment in the contract sum or contract time. The contract sum and contract time may be changed only by change order. A change order signed by the contractor indicates his or her agreement therewith, including the adjustment in the contract sum or the contract time.

CHERRY PICKER – Hydraulically operated aerial tower used for ascent and tree entry, usually mounted on a large truck. Line crews use some as short as 35 feet for clearing cables and streetlights. Most forestry departments use towers of 45 to 55 feet for trimming and removal operations. Sometimes used to replace burned-out floodlights at ballparks. Also known as an aerial lift.

CHLOROSIS – A condition in which a plant or portion of a plant, particularly the leaves, is light green or yellowish, often cause by a nutrient deficiency.

CLAY – (1) A minute soil particle less than 0.002 millimeters in diameter. (2) Soil material containing more than 40 percent clay, less than 45 percent sand, and less than 40 percent silt.

CLIMBER – Arborist term for one who works aloft in a tree.

CLONE – An individual plant propagated asexually from another plant.

COASTAL SHORELANDS – Areas immediately adjacent to the ocean, all estuaries and associated wetlands, and all coastal lakes.

COMPETITIVE BENCHMARKING – A method by which a company seeks legal ways to learn about its competitors without their cooperation, then tries to implement some of the competitors' practices or processes.

COMPLETE FERTILIZER – A fertilizer that contains all three of the primary elements, nitrogen, phosphorus, and potassium, not necessarily in a balanced ratio.

CONCENTRATE – A condensed formulation usually diluted with water or oil before use. Also, in a product name, the strongest commercially available formulation of the active ingredient.

CONCENTRATION – The amount of active ingredient in a given weight of a mixture or volume of a solution. Recommendations and specifications for concentration of agricultural chemicals are frequently made on the basis of pound per unit volume of mixture or solution.

CONCRETE – A composite material that consists essentially of a binding medium within which are embedded particles or fragments of aggregate; in portland cement concrete, the binder is a mixture of portland cement, water, sand, and stone.

CONCRETE BLOCK – A hollow or solid concrete masonry unit consisting of portland cement and suitable aggregates combined with water.

CONSERVATION – Management in a manner that avoids wasteful or destructive uses and provides for future availability; the act of conserving the environment.

CONTOUR INTERVAL – The vertical distance between adjacent contour lines on a topographical map.

CONTOUR LINE – A line on a topographical map or drawing connecting points on a land surface that have the same elevation.

CONTRACT – An agreement between two or more parties to do or not to do a particular thing.

CONTRACTOR – The bidder awarded the contract for the work.

CONTROLLED-RELEASE FERTILIZER – A fertilizer composed of elements that have been treated to release all or part of the nutrients over a controlled or long period of time. The process may be chemical or physical in nature and varies in length of time.

CORM – A vertical, thickened, solid underground stem, such as is borne by a crocus or gladiolus.

CORRECTIVE CONTROL – The application of chemical or mechanical controls designed to eliminate observed problems.

CORROSION – The deterioration of metal or concrete by chemical or electrochemical reaction resulting from exposure to weathering, moisture, chemicals, or other agents in its environment.

CREOSOTE – (1) An oily liquid obtained by distilling coal that is toxic to fungi, insects, plants, and people; used to impregnate wood (as a preservative), to waterproof materials, and to retard weathering and checking of wood. (2) A plant native to the southwest United States that is occasionally used for landscaping.

CROTCH – An arborist's term for the junction formed by two limbs or where a limb originates from the trunk of a tree.

CROTCHED IN – Safety climbing rope or work rope passed through an open crotch (so the rope will move freely without burning) high in the tree. From a well-chosen crotch, a climber can swing from one part of the tree to another in relative safety.

CROWN – The upper portion of a tree from the lowest branch on the trunk to the top.

CROWN CLEANING - The removal of dead, diseased, crowded, weakly attached, and weak branches.

CROWN LIFTING - The removal of the lower branches of a tree to provide clearance for vehicles, pedestrians, or buildings or site clearance (signs, vistas). Sometimes referred to as crown raising or elevating.

CULTIVAR - A variety of plant denoting an assemblage of cultivated individuals that are distinguished by a significant characteristic and that when reproduced (sexually or asexually), retains its distinguishing feature. Derived from "cultivated variety."

CULTURAL CONTROL - Control measures that modify the methods by which crops are grown and aid in preventing pest damage rather than focusing on elimination of the pest.

CUT AND FILL - The process of excavating and moving the excavated material to another location to use as fill to adjust the surface grade.

CUTTING - A severed part of a plant for rooting to form a new plant. See Clone.

DATUM - A point used as a basis for calculating or measuring.

DEADWOODING - The removal of dead, weak, or dying branches from a tree. Often considered a hazard reduction.

DECIDUOUS - Plants that lose all their leaves at the end of the growing season.

DEFOLIANT - A material that causes the leaves to fall from plants; for example, a spray used to remove leaves from cotton plants just before harvest.

DETAIL DRAWING - A drawing, at a larger scale, of a part of another drawing, indicating in the detail the design, location, composition, and correlation of the elements and materials shown.

DETHATCHING - The reduction of an excessive amount of thatch accumulation, usually with mechanized equipment, such as a vertical slicer.

DEVELOPED AREA - An area of land on which site improvements, such as grading and utility installation, have been made and buildings are erected.

DIAMETER BREAST HEIGHT (DBH) – The diameter of a tree trunk measured at breast height, or 4 feet, 6 inches (54 inches) from the ground. The measurement is taken this high to avoid the flaring effect of the buttress roots on the methods used for estimating the amount of lumber in a tree. The diameter can be measured with calipers or a diameter tape.

DITCH CHECK – A small damlike structure built transversely to the ditch centerline for the purpose of reducing discharge velocities and associated soil erosion.

DORMANCY – A seasonal recession of plant growth, normally caused by shortness of days (during winter), cold, or drought. Unless accompanied by extreme or adverse conditions, this annual "hibernation" is essential to the best growth of many perennial plants.

DORMANT – Not in an actively growing condition but capable of becoming so under proper conditions.

DORMANT OIL – A spray applied when plants are in a dormant condition.

DOUBLE-CROTCHING – When a climber has tied into one crotch then uses the tail (opposite end) of the climbing rope to tie in around another crotch on the other side of the tree. This technique enables the climber to move across the top of the tree (as one must in installing cables) without a lot shinnying. Double-crotching is also used to provide a more stable work position for extensive tree work.

DRAINAGE AREA – A horizontal area in a watershed, contributing to a specific point on the channel.

DRESSED SIZE – The dimensions of a piece of lumber or a timber after sawing and planking; usually about 3/8 inch (.95 cm) in thickness or 1/2 inch (1.27 cm) in width less than the indicated size.

DROP-CROTCHING – Technique of trimming used when the top of a tree must be reduced for any reason. Instead of clipping the tops off at a certain level, the cuts are made to a lower crotch so that the vigor of the tree continues to flow into the limb that assumes the role of the removed branch. The wound left from drop-crotch pruning heals much faster with less chance of invasion by wood-rot fungi than the stubs that are all too often left with the "butchering" type of pruning. This method also avoids the common witch's broom effect. Although more radical than thinning, drop-crotching is considered superior to heading back or topping.

DUE CARE – The degree of care that a reasonably prudent person would exercise under the same or similar circumstances.

EASEMENT, Conservation – An easement acquired by the public and designed to protect privately owned lands for recreation purposes or to restrict the use of private lands to preserve open space and protect certain natural resources.

EASEMENT, Scenic – The grant or sale by a landowner to an agency of the right to use his or her land for scenic preservation or enhancement. The easement bars the owner from changing the use or appearance of the land without the agency's consent.

ECOLOGY – The branch of biology that deals with the mutual relations among organisms and between organisms and their environment.

ECOSYSTEM – The living and nonliving components of the environment that interact or function together, including plants and animal organisms, the physical environment, and the energy systems in which they exist. All the components of an ecosystem are interrelated.

EFFLORESCENCE – An encrustation of soluble salts, commonly white, deposited on the surface of stone, brick, plaster, or mortar; usually caused by free alkalis leached from mortar or adjacent concrete as moisture moves through it.

EFFLUENT – The water solution discharge from a sewage treatment plant. This term may also refer to any liquid being discharged from a holding area.

EFP (Educational Facilities Professional) – Facilities management certification program developed and offered by APPA.

ELEVATION – (1) The altitude of a given point in relation to a given datum. (2) Drawing of a building or other development from a horizontal view without perspective.

EMINENT DOMAIN – The power or right of a federal, state, or local government unit to take private property for public use with just compensation to the owner.

EMULSIFYING AGENT – A material that helps to suspend globules of one liquid in another (e.g., oil in water).

EMULSION – A material in which one liquid is suspended in minute globules in another liquid (e.g., milk or an oil preparation in water).

EPIDEMIC – The widespread and severe outbreak of a disease.

EQUIPMENT OPERATOR – A position that provides expertise in the operation of a variety of pieces of equipment generally related to landscape maintenance operations. This position usually requires a moderate education and experience in the maintenance and operation of equipment. The size of the equipment determines the rating of the operator, such as heavy equipment operator.

ETHICS – Usages and customs regarding the moral and professional duties of a professional toward others.

EVERGREEN – A plant that retains green foliage throughout the year.

EXFOLIATE – To peel off in scales, layers, or thin plates, as bark from a tree trunk.

EXOTIC – A plant or other organism that has been introduced from other regions. The opposite of indigenous.

EXPANSION JOINT – (1) A joint or gap between adjacent parts of a building, structure, or concrete work that permits their relative movement caused by temperature changes (or other conditions) without rupture or damage. (2) An expansion bend.

EXPOSED AGGREGATE FINISH – A decorative finish for concrete work; achieved by removing the outer skin of mortar, generally before the concrete has fully hardened, and exposing the coarse aggregate.

FALSE CROTCH – A pulley, block, sling, lashing, or metal ring affixed to a tree's leader or limb to provide an anchorage for rigging or climbing.

FERTILIZATION – The application of required nutrients, such as nitrogen, phosphorus, and potassium, by a variety of means, including but not limited to the following:
(1) Liquid injection: fertilizer introduced into the soil by means of a probe
(2) Granular broadcast: fertilizer applied typically by means of a mechanical spreader
(3) Trunk injection: fertilizer injected directly into the trunk of a tree

FERTILIZE – To add a natural or manufactured material to the soil to supply one or more nutrients.

FERTILIZER – A natural or manufactured material added to the soil to supply one or more nutrients. In the trade, the term is generally applied to largely inorganic material other than lime or gypsum soil. See also Balance Fertilizer, Complete Fertilizer, and Controlled-Release Fertilizer.

FILL – The placement of sand, sediment, or other material, usually in submerged lands or wetlands, to create new uplands or raise the elevation of land.

FINE AGGREGATE – That portion of an aggregate that passes through a 4.76-mm (no. 4) sieve and is predominantly retained on a 74-m (no. 200) sieve.

FINISH GRADE – The top surface of lawns, walks, and drives or other improved surface after completion of construction or grading operations.

FIXED RETAINING WALL – A retaining wall that is rigidly supported or laterally braced at its top and bottom, enabling it to withstand higher pressures than a freestanding wall.

FLOOD FREQUENCY – A period of time within which the probability exists that a discharge equal to or greater than the discharge under consideration will occur.

FLOODPLAIN – The area adjoining a stream, tidal estuary, or coast that is subject to intermittent flooding.

FLOODWAY – The normal stream channel and the adjoining area of the natural floodplain needed to convey the waters of a regional flood.

FLOWER BEDS – A collection of showy annual or herbaceous plants that form a bed or planter; typically defined by a border.

FOOTING – That portion of the foundation of a structure that transmits loads directly to the soil; it may be the widened part of a wall or column, the spreading courses under a foundation wall, the foundation of a column, or a similar part of the structure. The footing is used to spread the load over a greater area to prevent or reduce settling.

FOOTLOCK – A method of ascent using a doubled-suspended rope. The rope is passed under one foot and clamped on by the other foot. The use of a Prusik loop or an ascending device is required to ensure safety during the ascent.

FORMAL SHRUB PLANTING – Pruning that develops a rigid, unnatural shape by the nonselective shearing or pruning of all the branches or leaves to a predetermined point. Often used in topiary to create a variety of shapes.

FOUNDATION – (1) Any part of a structure that serves to transmit the load to the earth or rock, usually below ground level. (2) The entire masonry substructure. (3) The soil or rock on which the structure rests.

FOUNDATION PLANTING – Plants massed close to the foundation of a structure.

FRIABLE – Soil or other material that is easily crumbled, pulverized, or reduced to powder.

FUMIGANT – A substance or mixture of substances that produces gas, vapor, fume, or smoke intended to destroy insects, bacteria, or rodents. Typically, fumigants are intended for use in enclosed or confined areas so that the fumigant may be retained for the intended purpose.

FUNCTIONAL BENCHMARKING – A process that analyzes dissimilar industries to recognize best practices regardless of product or service.

GAFFS – Pieces of sharp metal fastened to spurs or climbing irons. They are designed to penetrate easily, not to "cut out" to the side, and to come out easily when the climber takes another step. Considered for use on valuable trees only in the event of a climber emergency or a tree removal.

GARDENER – (1) A position that provides expertise in the maintenance of landscape operations and often functions in a lead or supervisory role over other groundspersons or groundsworkers. Generally, this position requires a moderate to considerable education in horticulture with a specified level of experience and/or certification. (2) A generic term for one who performs landscape maintenance tasks, such as mowing, trimming, or fertilizing.

GENERAL CONDITIONS – That portion of a contract for construction that remains essentially the same for every project.

GENERAL CONTRACT – The principal or prime contract in a construction project. The agreement between the owner and the general contractor.

GENERIC BENCHMARKING – A process that compares unrelated work practices.

GEOGRAPHIC INFORMATION SYSTEM (GIS) – A system of hardware, software, and procedures designed to support the capture, management, manipulation, analysis, modeling, and display of spatially referenced data to solve complex planning and management problems.

GIN POLE – A tall section of a tree to be removed that has one or more strong open crotches. It should be as close to the center of the tree as possible to aid in roping down sections of the tree. With large sections, a bull-rope is used with a snatch block. A dependable gin pole may be impossible to find in a dead or dying tree. Hydraulic crane units are now used in much the same way and are much safer for dealing with dead, dying, or storm-damaged trees.

GINK – The number-two worker on a tree crew. This worker is one of the most experienced crew members and usually takes the place of the foreperson if he or she must leave the job for a while.

GIRDLE – A circle made by removing or constricting the bark around the main trunk of a tree. Because it severs the xylem and phloem, which conduct the fluid, nutrients, and sugars of the tree, a girdled tree usually dies.

GIRDLING ROOT – A root that has changed normal direction and grown around the trunk or larger roots of a tree. The pressure exerted can become great, and the "tourniquet effect" cuts off the flow of fluids and nutrients down through the inner bark (phloem) and up through the sapwood (xylem). Often, this condition happens naturally, but care is needed in planting a bare root tree to avoid bending roots when turning a tree into position. When planting a container-grown tree, some roots will usually be found growing around the edge of the can. These should be cut or straightened to prevent eventual girdling.

GIS – See Geographic Information System.

GLOBAL POSITIONING SYSTEM (GPS) – A system originally funded, controlled, and designed for the U.S. military now in common use. GPS provides specially coded satellite signals that can be processed in a GPS receiver, enabling the receiver to compute its location in the grid coordinate system.

GRANULAR BROADCAST – Fertilizer typically applied by means of a mechanical spreader.

GRADIENT – (1) The degree of inclination of a surface, road, or pipe, often expressed as a percentage. (2) A rate of change in a variable quantity, such as temperature or pressure. (3) A curve representing such a rate of change.

GRAFFITI – Drawings or writing that is placed on walls or other smooth surfaces. Typically applied with spray paint and found in public places.

GRAFT – Asexual method of plant propagation in which a growing part of one plant (called the "scion") is affixed on the growing stock of another. For success, the two cambium layers must join. The plant produced is a clone, faithful to the characteristics of the scion.

GREEN DESIGN – A type of design that embraces sustainable practices and is considered friendly to the environment.

GREEN INDUSTRY – A general term used for the profession of growing and maintaining plant life and related businesses that support this industry. This term may embrace all forms of landscape and tree maintenance, as well as the greenhouse and florist trades.

GREENSKEEPER – A position that provides expertise in the maintenance of golf courses, including tees, greens, fairways, and roughs. This position generally requires moderate education in agronomy and turf grass with a specified level of experience and/or certification.

GREYWATER – A by-product of common campus activities such as bathing, dishwashing, and laundry. It is termed grey because the wastewater is not derived from toilets and does not contain any human waste. Greywater may be recycled for the purpose of refilling toilet tanks, landscape irrigation, or to supply wetlands.

GRID – In surveying, two superimposed sets of equidistant parallel lines intersecting at right angles.

GROUND COVER – A broad term used to describe low-growing vegetation, typically a vine or succulent plant that is used to cover a large area. Often used as an alternative to turf grass, particularly under the canopy of large trees.

GROUNDSKEEPER, GROUNDSPERSON, GROUNDSWORKER – Considered the entry-level position in landscape maintenance operations. A generic term for one who performs landscape maintenance tasks, such as mowing, trimming, or fertilizing.

GROUT – (1) Thin mortar used for filling in the joints of masonry, brickwork, or brick or stone pavements. (2) Thin mortar pumped into the ground to rectify expansive clay problems or to seal off subsurface drainage.

GRUNT – Slang for a groundsworker who picks up brush and services the climber with tools and equipment.

GUARANTEE – A pledge that ensures a standard of performance.

HANGER – A storm-broken limb or one cut by a trimmer or topper that does not fall to the ground but remains hanging in the tree as a possible hazard to people, vehicles, houses, or utility wires. Such storm-broken limbs should receive priority over broken limbs on the ground. One of the last things a tree trimmer should do is to make a final check to be sure that all hangers from the trimming or line clearing have been removed from the tree.

HARDINESS – The capability of a plant to survive in a given environment.

HARDPAN – A hardened, relatively impervious layer of soil.

HARDSCAPE – A landscape term for areas that are composed of brick, concrete, or other hard surfaces. May be absent of softscape features.

HEADING BACK – Cutting back limbs to a stub, bud, or lateral branch that is not large enough to assume the terminal role. Sometimes referred to as "topping."

HEADS UP – Warning call given by the tree trimmer or topper before he or she lets a piece of brush or limb wood fall to the ground.

HEDGES – A collection of woody shrubs or low trees that are arranged in a dense row; often used to create a fence or boundary.

HERB – A flowering plant with aboveground stems that are destitute of woody tissue and perish when the flowers and fruit (seed) mature.

HERBACEOUS – A stem that is not woody like those of trees and shrubs.

HERBACEOUS PLANT – A plant that remains soft or succulent and does not develop woody tissue.

HERBICIDE – A pesticide used to kill herbaceous or other plants. Any compound used to kill or inhibit the growth of a plant.

HIGH-INTENSITY RECREATION – Recreation that uses specially built facilities or occurs in such density or form that it requires or results in a modification of the area of resource. Campgrounds, golf courses, public beaches, campus quads, and marinas are examples of high-intensity recreation.

HIGH WATER – The flood stage of a stream or lake that is the measurement of the actual height of the water surface above the stream banks during the maximum flow of the water. The historic high water mark is called stage recorded. The design high water is used for design purposes and is usually based on the empirical frequency of recurrence or history of flood cycles.

HORTICULTURE - The science and art of growing plants, such as fruits, vegetables, and ornamental plants. Intensified agriculture.

HORTICULTURIST - One who practices the science and art of horticulture. One who maintains fruit or vegetable production or ornamental gardens and landscapes.

HUMUS - Decomposed or partially decomposed organic matter in or on the soil; frequently of a dark color.

HYDRAULIC - Pertaining to water in motion and the mechanics of motion.

HYDRAULIC PROCESSES - Actions resulting from the effect of moving water or water pressure on the bed, banks, and shore lands of water bodies (ocean, estuaries, streams, lakes, and rivers).

HYDROLOGIC - Pertaining to the cyclic phenomena of waters of the earth, successively as precipitation, runoff, storage, and evaporation; quantitatively as to distribution and concentration.

INCREMENT BORER - Tool that has a T-handle, a sharpened hollow bit, and a core remover. It is used to take out a small core of wood about 3/16 inch in diameter. From this core, the annual rings can be counted to determine rate of growth, or used to diagnose disease, such as wetwood, verticillum wilt (green or brown spots), and Dutch elm disease (brown spots); and to determine extent of wood rot.

INDIGENOUS - Native or belonging to a region or an area. The opposite of exotic.

INFORMAL SHRUB PRUNING - Pruning that allows the shrub to develop in a natural shape defined by the species of the plant. Such pruning may be accomplished by thinning or selectively removing branches in the interior of the plant.

INFRASTRUCTURE - The necessary components that allow an entity, such as a park or other facility, to function. These items may include potable water, irrigation water, power, sanitary and storm sewers, and roadways and walkways.

INORGANIC - Substances occurring as minerals in nature or obtainable from those minerals by a chemical means. Generalized to refer to fertilizer that is not derived from plant or animal matter.

INSPECTION – An examination or careful scrutiny to ensure compliance.

INTEGRATED PEST MANAGEMENT (IPM) – A system that uses all the appropriate methods and techniques to control pest populations at levels below those that cause economic injury. This system may include cultural practices, natural remedies, and selective pesticides.

INTEGRITY – The quality or state of being complete and functionally unimpaired; the wholeness or entirety of a body or system, including its parts, materials, and processes. The integrity of an ecosystem emphasizes the interrelatedness of all parts and the unity of its whole.

INTERNAL BENCHMARKING – A process that concentrates on benchmarking internal customers.

INTERNODE – The region of a stem between two successive nodes.

IRRIGATION – The artificial application of water to the land or soil to assist in the maintenance of landscapes, growing of crops, and to supplement water needs during periods of inadequate rainfall.

LABOR AND MATERIAL PAYMENT BOND – A bond of the contractor in which a surety guarantees to the owner that the contractor will pay for labor and materials used in the performance of the contract. The claimants under the bond are defined as those who have direct contracts with the contractor or any subcontractor.

LANDSCAPE – The surroundings of a site, which may or may not include hardscape (walks and plazas) and softscape (lawns and plantings).

LARVICIDE – A pesticide that is used to kill insect larvae.

LEACHING – (1) The washing out of soluble nutrients from the soil. Occurs naturally in areas of high rainfall. May require replacement of nutritive elements (especially nitrogen) and correction of acidity, which comes from the leaching out of alkaline salts. Leaching is sometimes done intentionally to rid soil of a detrimental salt or overdose of inorganic nitrogen. (2) The subsurface disposal of septic tank effluent into the ground (i.e., leach field disposal).

LEED® – The acronym for Leadership in Energy and Environmental Design, a green building certification system developed by the U.S. Green Building Council, providing third-party verification that a building or community was designed and built using strategies aimed at improving performance in energy savings, water efficiency, CO2 emissions reduction, improved indoor environmental quality, and stewardship of resources and sensitivity to their impacts.

LETTER OF INTENT – A letter signifying an intention to enter a formal agreement, usually setting forth the general terms of such agreement.

LIABILITY – An obligation that one is bound in law or justice to perform; the condition of being actually or potentially subject to an obligation.

LIEN – An enforceable right against specific property to secure payment of an obligation.

LIFE-CYCLE COSTING – Considering all relevant costs during the life of a product or facility. Used to decide whether to make a given investment or to choose between alternative courses of action.

LINEAR MEASUREMENT – A measure of length, such as feet or miles.

LION-TAILING – The removal of all the inner lateral branches and foliage from a limb. This process hollows out the interior foliage, which may lead to a weakened branch.

LIQUID INJECTION – Fertilizer introduction into the soil by means of a probe.

LIQUIDATED DAMAGES – A sum specified in a contract whereby damages in the event of breach are predetermined. In construction contracts, liquidated damages usually are specified as a fixed sum per day for failure to complete the work within a specified time. If set at a level consistent with a reasonable forecast of actual harm to the owner, liquidated damage clauses will be upheld and will preclude use of standards for computation of damages that would otherwise be imposed by law. If the amount prescribed for liquidated damages is unreasonably high, the provision will be denominated an illegal "penalty" by the courts and held invalid; in such cases, damages will be determined pursuant to otherwise applicable rules of law.

LITIGATION – A lawsuit or judicial controversy.

LITTORAL DRIFT – The material moved, such as sand or gravel, in the littoral zone (shallow water near shore) under the influence of waves and currents.

LOAM – The textural class name for soil that has a moderate amount of sand, silt, and clay. Loam soils contain 7 to 27 percent clay, 28 to 50 percent silt, and less than 52 percent sand.

LOW-INTENSITY RECREATION – Recreation that does not require developed facilities and can be accommodated without change to the area of resource. Boating, hunting, hiking, wildlife photography, and beach or shore activities are examples of low-intensity recreation.

MACADAM, TARMAC, TARMACADAM – (1) A paving for roads or other surfaces, formed by grading and compacting layers of crushed stone or gravel. The top layer(s) are usually bound by asphaltic material, acting to stabilize the stone, provide a smoother surface, and seal against water penetration. (2) The crushed stone used in a macadamized surface.

MAINTAIN – Support, keep, and continue in an original state or condition without decline.

MAINTENANCE IMPACT STATEMENT – An assessment process used to document impacts on an agency's maintenance operating budget and organization in terms of dollar costs of operating and maintaining a proposed facility or program. Provides a focus beyond the initial investment on the long-term financial and organizational impact of each option considered.

MAINTENANCE PERFORMANCE – A measure of the effectiveness of labor; calculated as a ratio of time allowed divided by time taken on a series of jobs completed during a given period. For example, if a job is determined to require 10 hours to complete, yet the workers take 20 hours, the performance is only 50 percent.

MAINTENANCE REQUIREMENTS – Specific criteria established for guidance in carrying out maintenance tasks.

MAINTENANCE STANDARDS – Activities or individual work elements that support maintenance requirements.

MANAGEMENT UNIT – An area or group of areas that is managed under a single management plan.

MATRIX – A rectangular array of mathematical elements that can be combined to form sums and products.

MECHANIC – A position that provides expertise in the maintenance of a variety of pieces of equipment generally related to landscape maintenance operations. This position usually requires a moderate to extensive education and experience in the maintenance and repair of equipment.

MECHANIC'S LIEN – A claim that attaches to improvements on real property and to the land itself for the purpose of securing priority of payment for the value of work, labor, or services performed or materials furnished in making improvements to the property.

MEDIATION – The act of a third person who attempts to persuade two or more parties to a dispute to adjust or settle their problem.

MINIMUM TURNING RADIUS – The radius of the path of the outer front wheel of a vehicle making its sharpest turn. A dimension often used in the performance of grounds maintenance equipment, such as mowers, to denote ability to make tight turns in the process of mowing.

MONKEYFIST – Type of knot tied in the end of a throw line (1/4 or 3/8 inches) to make it easier to throw over a limb or through an open crotch. This knot has been virtually replaced by shot pouches and other throwing weights.

MOUNTABLE CURB – A curb that can be climbed readily by a moving vehicle.

MULCH – A layer of organic or inorganic material put on the soil for one or more of the following reasons: to reduce the evaporative loss of water from the soil, reduce runoff, reduce compaction, help to control weeds, add organic matter to the soil, protect plants from mowers or equipment, moderate soil temperature fluctuations, or for ornamental purposes.

NEGLIGENCE – The failure to exercise that degree of care that a reasonably prudent person would exercise so as not to submit others to unreasonable risks of harm. Contributory negligence is the want of ordinary care on the part of the person injured that concurred with a defendant's negligence and was a cause of the injured party's damage. Comparative negligence is a doctrine of law wherein the concurrent negligence of a plaintiff and a defendant are compared and the plaintiff's damages are diminished proportionally to his or her fault.

NEGOTIATION – The official notice included in a proposal for inviting bids for a proposed improvement.

NODE – An enlarged region of the stem that is generally solid, where leaves are attached and buds may be located. Stems have nodes, but roots do not.

NONSELECTIVE HERBICIDE – A chemical that is generally toxic to all plants without regard to species.

NONSYSTEMIC HERBICIDE – A chemical or formulation that works without being ingested into the plants, generally without residual results.

NOTCHING – Technique used in felling trees or in cutting off large limbs so that the log falls in a certain direction. Two saw cuts are made, the first horizontal cut from 1/3 to 1/2 of the diameter. The second cut is made from above at about a 45-degree angle to meet the first so that a wedge-shaped section is removed. When the wood on the opposite side is cut (back cut), the tree will begin to lean and the remaining wood will start to break. The tree or log will fall at about 90 degrees to the base of the notch. If the back cut is made at a slight angle so that more wood is left on the left or right side, the tree will swing in that direction before it breaks off.

NOVATION – The substitution of a new contract for an existing valid contract between the same or different parties.

NOXIOUS WEED – A weed or plant defined as being especially undesirable, troublesome, or difficult to control.

OILS – References are usually to aromatic or paraffinic oils used in formulating such products as diluents or carriers for herbicides. Dormant oil is used to smother insects that overwinter on a plant.

ORNAMENTALS – Plants that are used to enhance landscapes and gardens.

OVERHAUL – The transportation of excavated material beyond a specified limit.

OVERSEED – A process by which grass seed is applied over top of an existing stand of turf, often for the purpose of increasing plant density or creating a temporarily green, viable sports surface during winter months. Common on golf tees and greens, as well as sports fields.

PEAVY – Tool for turning, rolling, and lifting logs, especially when floating in water. Has a heavy hook hinged about 8 inches above an iron-shod tip; similar to a cant hook except that it has a pike point on the end instead of a flat-toothed plate.

PERENNIAL FLOWERS – Plants, typically herbaceous, that grow more or less indefinitely from year to year and usually bear seed each year.

PERENNIAL ROOT – A root that lives over winter and initiates the stem growth from buds. Such a root must be large enough to store enough food to start the new growth in the spring.

PERENNIALS – Plants that live more than two years and that can persist indefinitely in specific climatic ranges. A plant that is a perennial in one climate may be used as an annual in another climate.

PERFORMANCE BOND – A bond of the contractor in which a surety guarantees to the owner that the work will be performed in accordance with the contract documents. Except where prohibited by statute, the performance bond is frequently combined with the labor and material payment bond.

PERGOLA – Open garden structure enclosing part of a path or walk. Vines or pleached trees are often trained overhead.

PERMEABILITY – (1) The property of soil, rock, or mantle that permits water to flow through it. (2) The property of a porous material that permits the passage of water vapor through it.

PEST – Any organism that is injurious to humans, their property, or the environment.

PEST CONTROL SPECIALIST – A position that provides expertise in the control of pests and diseases, including but not limited to plant disease, insects, vertebrate pests, weeds, and disorders that hinder the production of food crops or ornamental plants. This position generally requires considerable education in pest control and a specified level of experience and/or certification.

PESTICIDE – As defined by the U.S. Federal Insecticide, Fungicide, and Rodenticide Act (FIFRA), an economic poison (pesticide) "means any substance or mixture of substances intended for preventing, destroying, repelling, or mitigating any insects, rodents, nematodes, fungi, weeds, or any other forms of life declared to be pests; and any substance or mixture of substances intended for use as a plant regulator, defoliant, or desiccant."

pH – The measure of acidity or alkalinity, expressed as the negative logarithm of the hydrogen-ion concentration. With a pH of 7 denoted as neutral, a value less than 7 indicates acidity; a value higher than 7 indicates alkalinity.

pH MAINTENANCE – The management of the pH of soil or a solution by the application of alkaline or acidic products.

PLAN, Graphic – A two-dimensional graphic representation of the design, location, and dimensions of the project or parts thereof, seen as a horizontal plane viewed from above.

PLANTING EASEMENT – An easement for reshaping roadside areas and establishing, maintaining, and controlling plant growth thereon.

PLEACH – To train and interlace the tops of trees or other plants to form an archway over an alley or walkway.

PLOT CONDITION – A rank of relative condition, as in excellent to poor.

PLUG – (1) Short piece of limb left when a large limb is removed by the three-cut method. See Stub. (2) That portion of the soil and turf removed during the core aerating process.

POLICING – A general term for the hand removal of litter, debris, and rubbish from landscape and hardscape areas.

POST-EMERGENT HERBICIDE – A herbicide that is applied after the appearance of a specified weed or plant.

POST-EMERGENT TREATMENT – Treatment made after a plant emerges. Contact pre-emergent treatment is made after weed emergence but before crop emergence.

POTABLE WATER – Water that is fit for human consumption and satisfies the standards of the appropriate health authorities.

POWER OF ATTORNEY – A legal instrument authorizing one to act as the attorney or agent for another party.

POWER TAKEOFF (PTO) – A supplemental mechanism (as on a tractor) enabling the power of the engine to be used to operate nonautomotive apparatus, such as a pump or spreader.

PRECAST CONCRETE – A concrete member that is cast and cured in other than its final position.

PRE-EMERGENT HERBICIDE – A herbicide that is applied to control specific weeds before the emergence of the weed or a crop.

PREVENTIVE CONTROL – A scheduled chemical or cultural program designed to prevent significant damage.

PREVENTIVE MAINTENANCE – A technique of planning for maintenance using a system of periodic inspections and routine replacement of critical parts to identify and correct faulty conditions. The objective is to minimize breakdowns and maximize availability.

PRIORITY – A rank of priority relative to visibility, such as in high to low visibility.

PROFESSIONAL STANDARD OF CARE – That degree of skill or care usual in a particular profession.

PROGRAM – Proposed or desired plan or course of proceeding and actions.

PROPOSAL – An offer. A proposal becomes a contract when the terms and conditions of the proposal have been accepted by the other party.

PRUNE – To remove dead, diseased, unnecessary, or unwanted twigs, branches, lowers, fruits, and roots from plants for shaping or ornamental purposes.

QUALITY – A description of the condition expected on completion of assigned work. Quality is derived from many factors, such as aesthetics and orderliness, health and cleanliness, safety, and properly functioning equipment and facilities, as well as conservation and sound environmental practices.

RATE OR DOSAGE – These terms are synonymous. Rate is the preferred term and usually refers to the amount of active ingredient material applied to a unit area (such as 1 acre or 1,000 square feet), regardless of the percentage of the chemical in the carrier.

REAL PROPERTY – Land, everything growing on it, and all improvements made to it. Usually includes rights to everything beneath the surface and at least some rights to the airspace above it.

"REASONABLE MAN" – The fictitious person used to measure the standard of care that must be exercised to avoid negligence.

REBAR – A steel bar that has ribs to provide greater bonding strength when used in reinforced concrete.

REHABILITATION – The restoration or improvement of deteriorated areas, structures, public facilities, or neighborhoods to bring them up to an acceptable standard for use.

REMONTANT – Blooming a second time in a season.

REPOSE, Angle of – The gradient or slope at which a given material will establish itself if dumped freely from grade.

RESIDUAL – A product that is capable of having a continued effect over a period of time, such as a pesticide.

RESIDUAL PESTICIDE – A pesticide that can destroy pests or prevent them from causing disease, damage, or destruction for a specified duration past the time of application.

RESTORATION – Revitalizing, returning, or replacing original attributes and amenities, such as natural biological productivity or aesthetic and cultural resources, that have been diminished or lost by past alterations, activities, or catastrophic events. Specific remedial actions might include removing fills, installing water treatment facilities, rebuilding deteriorated urban waterfront areas, rehabilitating strip-mined areas, reestablishing prairies, and so on.

RESURFACING – A supplemental surface or replacement placed on an existing surface to improve its surface conformation or increase its strength.

RETAINING WALL – A wall, either freestanding or laterally braced, that bears against an earth or other fill surface and resists lateral and other forces from the material in contact with the side of the wall.

RHIZOME – A prostrate, more or less elongated stem growing partly or completely beneath the surface of the ground and usually rooting at the nodes and becoming upcurved at the apex.

RIGHT OF WAY – The areas existing or acquired by permanent easement for highway, utility, or other purposes; also, the areas acquired by temporary easement during the time the easement is in effect.

RIPRAP – (1) Irregularly broken and random-sized large pieces of quarry rock; individual stones ranging from very large (2 to 3 cubic yards, approximately 1.5 to 2.3 cubic meters) to very small (1/2 cubic foot, approximately 0.014 cubic meters); used for foundations and revetments. (2) A foundation or parapet of stones thrown together without any attempt at regular structural arrangement.

RISER – (1) The vertical face of a step or stepped ramp. (2) In irrigation, a short piece of pipe used to connect the irrigation head with the water supply line.

ROADBED – The graded portion of a highway within top and side slopes prepared as a foundation for the pavement structure and shoulder.

RODENTICIDE – A substance or mixture of substances intended to prevent, destroy, repel, or mitigate rodents.

ROLLING – Compacting turf or soils, usually by mechanical means; leveling uneven turf or soil surfaces.

ROOT – The descending axis of the plant, without nodes and internodes, that absorbs nutrients and moisture from the ground and may store food.

SADDLE – Safety equipment that is worn around the waist with loops for the legs of the climber. Originally made of rope with padding around the back and under the legs. Now made in various styles of canvas, nylon, and leather, equipped with D-rings or other means for attaching the climbing rope and/or buckstrap. Other rings or snap fasteners are used to attach a handsaw in scabbard, a paint can, and sometimes chisels and other tools for surgery and repair. Should be inspected daily for signs of damage or wear.

SANITARY SEWER – A sewer intended to carry only domestic sewage.

SEAL COAT – A surface seal for application on asphalt surfaces on which chips of coarse sand or limestone are spread before the seal has lost its tack or stickiness.

SEDIMENT – Deposit made by suspended material settling out of a liquid.

SELECTIVE HERBICIDE – A herbicide that is more toxic to some species of plants than others.

SHINNY – Method of climbing used when a tree has no limbs to climb on. Unlike climbing with spurs, in this method, the body is kept close to the trunk. First, the climber reaches high and grasps trunk or limb with both arms; then, pulling up with his or her arms, the climber arches the back and grasps the trunk with the legs. One leg goes around the opposite side of the trunk and the calf of the leg is pressed against the trunk. The other leg is placed with the knee and thigh against the trunk. The shinbone (hence, "shinny") and ankle are placed against the near side of the trunk with the foot extending around opposite the knee. The climber grips the trunk with the legs to take the weight off the arms, which are extended as the body straightens and a fresh grip is taken. The climber repeats the process until he or she reaches a limb from which to work.

SHORELINE – The boundary line between a body of water and the land, measured on tidal waters as the mean highest high water mark and on nontidal waterways as the ordinary high water mark.

SHOT POUCH – A lead-filled throw weight used for placing a throw line into a tree. This device often replaces the older monkeyfist.

SHRUB – A woody plant smaller at maturity than a tree and usually with several basal stems.

SHRUB BED – A collection of fairly low-growing woody plants that form a bed or planter, typically defined by a border.

SITE DRAINAGE – Removing water from a site by surface or subsurface drainage.

SITE PLAN – A plan of a construction site showing the position and dimensions of existing structures or structures to be erected, and the dimensions and contours of the property and improvements.

SLOPE RATIO – The relation of horizontal distance to vertical rise or fall; for example, 2 feet horizontal to 1 foot vertical is designated 2 to 1 or 2:1.

SLUDGE – The solid part of sewage water treatment. Can be used as a soil amendment because of organic content and fertility.

SNATCH BLOCK – A special block constructed so that the casing can be opened on one side to receive a loop of rope around the pulley. This configuration eliminates the need to thread the rope through the block. These blocks are used with a bull rope to "pull up" large sections of a tree during removal operations. The block is chained to the trunk. The rope is tied onto the limb, run through the crotch of the gin pole and down through the snatch block, and fastened to the grounds maintenance vehicle used to pull up the limb after it has been cut part way off. Once the limb is pulled up, it is completely cut off. Often a butt rope is used to help guide the limb as the vehicle slowly moves forward to let it down.

SNOW AND ICE REMOVAL – The physical or chemical removal of accumulations of ice or snow from transportation or parking surfaces, often by means of one of the following:
(1) Sodium/magnesium chloride: a granular salt-based chemical sometimes applied to earthen paths and roads to settle dust. Also used as a deicing agent on pavement. This material is toxic to plants and should be applied with care in their proximity.
(2) Calcium chloride: a granular salt-based chemical sometimes applied to earthen paths and roads to settle dust. Also used as a deicing agent on pavement. This material is toxic to plants and should be applied with care in their proximity.
(3) Urea: a nitrogen-based fertilizer that is used as a deicing agent on pavement.

SNUBBING – Technique used to control a work rope. The running end of the rope is given one or two turns around a limb or the trunk of the tree. The friction of the rope absorbs the pull of the limb being lowered to the ground so that the climber or ground worker can control a weight that could not be held with the arms alone. Care must be used so that the friction does not "burn" the rope. Snubbing is also used in "pulling up" limbs. In this case, the bull rope is pulled up a few inches at a time and the "snubber" takes up the slack and holds it while the workers who are pulling get a fresh grip or rest.

SODIUM/MAGNESIUM CHLORIDE – A granular salt-based chemical sometimes applied to earthen paths and roads to settle dust. Also used as a deicing agent on pavement. This material is toxic to plants and should be applied with care in their proximity.

SOFTSCAPE – A landscape term used for areas that are composed of lawn or ornamental plantings. Often absent of hardscape features.

SOIL AMENDMENT – A chemical or mineral element added to the soil to improve soil characteristics, such as porosity, aeration, drainage, or moisture retention.

SOIL AUGER – Tool for boring into the ground. It is usually about 1-1/2 inches in diameter and 3 feet long and may be shaped to take a wooden T-handle that is about 2 feet long. It can also be made for use with a power drill. The soil auger is used to take soil samples, to check for fill or other changes in the normal soil profile that could affect aeration and drainage around and through the root system of an existing tree, or to make a quick check of a proposed planting site. It can be used to check for a suspended subsoil gas leak or to make holes for fertilizer, deep watering, or, when filled with peat moss, to improved aeration.

SOIL COMPACTION – The process of increasing soil density primarily as a result of excessive wear. In compacted soils, particles are pressed or packed together with few large air pores or interstices.

SOIL CONDITIONER – A material that when added to compacted soil, tends to make it loose, crumbly, or porous.

SOIL FERTILITY – The ability of a soil to supply nutrients in sufficient quantity to meet the growth requirements of plants when other growth factors are favorable.

SPECIAL PROVISIONS – Specific directions, provisions, requirements, and revisions of the specifications peculiar to the work under consideration that are not satisfactorily provided for in the specifications. Special provisions set forth the final contractual intent as to the matter involved. The special provisions included in the contract shall not operate to annul those portions of the specifications with which they are not in conflict.

SPECIFICATIONS – The body of directions, provisions, and requirements authorized and printed by the contracting entity, together with written agreements and all documents of any description made or to be made pertaining to the method or manner of performing the work, the quantities, or the quality of materials to be furnished under the contract.

SPRINKLER OR IRRIGATION SPECIALIST – A position that provides expertise in the installation and maintenance of irrigation systems. This position generally requires considerable education in hydraulics and a specified level of experience and/or certification.

SPURS – Tools used for climbing. Developed and used by line workers for climbing utility poles, these climbing irons are often worn by climbers for removing trees or in the event of emergency. Because the gaffs leave a wound in the tree at every step, they should not be used for trimming or repair work. Spurs are fastened to the inside of the leg below the knee with the straps at knee and ankle. The gaff is in position on the inside of the instep. The climbing technique with spurs is almost the opposite of that used by a climber who is shinnying up a tree. When climbing with spurs, the knee is inclined away from the trunk or limb to prevent the gaff from "cutting out."

STATUTE OF LIMITATIONS – Statute declaring that no suit shall be maintained on a cause of action unless brought within a specified period of time after the right to bring suit accrues.

STERILANT – A pesticide that kills all forms of a particular organism in a certain area.

STERILIZATION – The act of treating an area with a chemical or other agent to kill every living organism.

STEWARDSHIP – The duties and responsibilities required to properly manage a property with regard to the environment and the rights of others.

STILLING BASIN – An energy or velocity dissipater of water that uses a stilling pool for primary dissipation.

STOMATA – Small openings, bordered by guard cells, in the epidermis of leaves and stems.

STORM SEWER – A sewer for conveying storm and surface water only.

STORMWATER – Water that originates during precipitation events. May be harvested and recycled for landscape purposes.

STRATEGIC PLANNING – A method by which organizations are able to facilitate improvement to enhance productivity, communication, morale or motivation, team spirit, sense of purpose, and confidence. The plan relies on clear objectives with a common understanding by all the participants.

STRICT LIABILITY – Liability without negligence.

STRUCTURE – Anything constructed, installed or portable, the use of which requires a location on a parcel of land.

STUB – Short piece of limb left when a limb or twig is removed by a pruner or a saw when using the three-cut method. Also used to describe the standing trunk after the foliage and limbwood have been "topped out."

SUBBASE – The layer or layers of specified or selected material of designated thickness placed on a subgrade to support a rigid slab or base course.

SUBGRADE – (1) The soil prepared and compacted to support a structure or a pavement system; the base portion of any surfaced area, the elevation of which is lower than that of the finished grade. (2) The elevation of the bottom of a trench in which a sewer or pipeline is laid.

SUBSOIL – The bed or stratum of earth that lies immediately below the surface or topsoil.

SUMP – (1) A pit, tank, basin, or receptacle that receives sewage or water and must be emptied by mechanical means (pumping). (2) A reservoir sometimes forming part of a roof drain. (3) A depression in a roof deck where the roof drain is located.

SURETY BOND – A legal instrument under which one party agrees to answer to another party for the debt, default, or failure to perform of a third party.

SUSTAINABILITY – This term refers to a system, program, or condition that meets the needs of the present without compromising the ability of future generations to meet their own needs. It requires the reconciliation or balance of environmental, economic, and social demands. Used in reference to a program or site that is in ecological balance.

SWINGBOARD – A nautical term for a wooden seat used by a climber in place of a saddle or bowline when an extensive amount of work must be done. The seat or "swingboard" is put into a bowline or double-bowline (one loop goes around the waist). The free end is used to tie a tautline hitch on the up-rope so that the climber may control his or her position in the tree. Originally used aboard ship and adopted by early arborists.

SYSTEMIC PESTICIDE – A chemical that is absorbed and translocated throughout the plant or animal, making it toxic to pests.

TASK MAINTENANCE – The deployment of specifically trained crews that each perform specific groundskeeping tasks and that move from one area to another of a site, such as a park or campus, doing all work of a particular type as needed. Examples include a tree crew or an irrigation crew.

TASKS – A combination of the operations and activities required to accomplish the work defined in the task descriptions.

TAUTLINE HITCH – The standard climbing knot used by arborists to tie in.

TAXONOMY – That branch of science dealing with description, naming, and classification of types or kinds of plants.

TERRESTRIAL – (1) A plant growing in the air with its basal parts in wet or dry soil. (2) A term related to land.

THATCH – An intermingled layer of living and dead stems, leaves, and roots of grasses that develops between the layer of green vegetation and the soil surface.

THINNING – The selective removal of branches in the crown by removing a branch at the point of attachment or to a large lateral. This process typically includes crown cleaning. It increases light penetration and air movement in the crown.

THREE-CUT METHOD – Technique for removing limbs when pruning to prevent the limb from peeling the bark down the trunk and creating a larger wound. First, the limb is undercut about a foot from the trunk. The rule of thumb is to "cut until the saw pinches." The next cut is made from the top a few inches farther out. If the limb is heavier than the climber can hold, a butt rope should be tied on and snubbed to the trunk or to another crotch nearby. This cut is made until the limb breaks off, leaving a stub or "plug." The final cut is made close to the trunk to promote rapid healing of the wound. Because new growth takes place parallel to the sap flow, the flush cut heals easily from the edges. Very little healing will take place when a stub is left.

THROWING KNOT – A knot made in the end of a light work rope (1-1/4 to 3/8 inch in diameter) or climbing rope (1/2-inch diameter) so that it may be thrown high into the tree or from one part of the tree to another. Weight is needed to carry the rope through foliage and let it drop down through a crotch to the ground. Two types of knots are used. The first is the "closed knot," such as the monkey fist, that remains tied and weights the end of the rope as it is whipped through the crotch, gradually dropping the rope within reach. The second is the "open" or slipper knot, in which (a) the rope is wound onto the arm a sufficient number of turns, then (b) a half-dozen wraps are taken around the loops to hold them, and finally (c) a loop is pulled through the top of the loops. This loop becomes the throwing handle and pulls out (or is pulled out) once the rope is through the crotch. This action releases the wrapping turns, and the rope unwinds and falls to the ground (or within reach without the need of whipping a long length of rope through the crotch).

TILTH – Refers to cultivated soil that is easily crumbled and has a good organic content or to the physical condition of the soil.

TIMBER-R-R – This warning cry of the woods is well known but is still functional in alerting people in the area that a tree, trunk, or large section is to be dropped. It is an important safety measure because the results of several tons of wood hitting the ground are unpredictable.

TIME – This term represents the average time necessary for a qualified craftsperson or an adequately qualified individual working at a normal pace, following prescribed methods, working under capable supervision, and experiencing only normal delays to perform a defined amount of work of a specified quality.

TIME OF CONCENTRATION – The time required for storm runoff to flow from the most remote point.

TOLERANCE – The relative capacity of a plant or species to withstand cold, heat, wind, sunlight, and so on.

TOOL ROOM COORDINATOR – A position that conducts inventory, maintenance, and distribution for a collective tool system.

TOP OUT – Technique involving the removal of brush and pole wood, leaving only the trunk and main scaffold of branches standing. This technique is used during storm emergencies so that once the broken tree is "safe," the crew moves on to another emergency. It may also be used when the trunks are to be removed, stumps and all, by bulldozer as part of a construction process. Finally, crews may be organized for greater efficiency by using a task force of climbers with a tower truck to top out and another crew with a crane truck to fell the trunk and load the logs.

TOPDRESSING – Spreading a thin layer of material over an existing area of turf. This layer may include inert materials, such as good-quality sand or calcined clay, and mixtures of inert materials with organic materials, such as compost. Topdressing is frequently used on golf course greens and other sports fields that require a smooth surface.

TOPIARY – The cutting and trimming of shrubs and trees, especially evergreens, into odd or ornamental shapes, thus producing an effect entirely different from that produced by the natural growing habits of the plant. A formal pruning method.

TOPOGRAPHIC SURVEY – The process of determining the configuration of a surface, including its relief and the locations of its natural and manmade features, usually recorded on a drawing showing surface variations by means of contour lines indicating height above sea level.

TOPPER – A term (often used in a derogatory manner) for one who indiscriminately prunes the tops out of trees.

TOPPING – Cutting back limbs to a stub, bud, or lateral branch that is not large enough to assume the role as the terminal branch. Sometimes referred to as heading back, stubbing, pollarding, or hatracking.

TOPSOIL – (1) The surface or upper layer of soil, as distinct from the subsoil; usually contains more organic matter. (2) A broad term for imported soil for landscape purposes.

TORT – Any civil wrong, not arising out of contract, for which the law provides a remedy, such as negligence, defamation, assault and battery, and so on.

TORT FEASOR – A person or entity who commits or is guilty of a tort.

TOXIC – A poisonous chemical factor that is injurious to animals or plants through contact or systemic action.

TRACING – Trimming the edges of a wound with a hooked knife, sometimes a mallet and chisel as well, back to "tight" bark. All loose ends should be removed. This technique not only removes shelter for insects and lodging places for fungus spores but also removes the temptation for children to grasp the loose end and rip loose a greater piece. General practice indicates that tracing the wound to an oval with "pointing" at top and bottom makes a good-looking job. Recent studies of healing, however, indicate that rounder tracings heal faster.

TRANSLOCATED – The process by which items such as a pesticide are moved in a plant or animal from the site of entry.

TRANSPIRATION – The process by which a plant gives off water in vapor form into the atmosphere, mainly through its stomata.

TREE – A woody plant of considerable stature at maturity with one or a few main trunks.

TREE SPECIALIST – A position that provides considerable expertise in the field of tree maintenance practices, including but not limited to pruning, planting, pest and disease diagnosis, and fertilization. Typically, this position functions as the arborist for an organization. This position generally requires extensive education, experience, and certification in the field of arboriculture.

TRIMMER – A slang term used for one who prunes trees.

TRUNK INJECTIONS – Fertilizer injected directly into the trunk of a tree.

TUBER – A thickened subterranean stem; typically has numerous eyes, such as a potato.

TURF – An area completely covered with a thick mat of grass plants, often used for sports fields and park areas. Turf areas are mowed with standard mowing equipment.

TURF RENOVATIONS – A broad term used to describe various methods used to improve the condition of an area of turf.

UNIT OF WORK – The quantification, in standard units of measurement, such as individual numbers, acres, miles, square feet, or square yards, of the amount (volume) of work for which the standard applies.

UREA – A nitrogen-based fertilizer that is used as a deicing agent on pavement.

VACUUM BREAKER – A device that will prevent the creation of a backflow causing vacuum in a water supply system.

VALVE – A device that regulates the low of a fluid.

VALVE, Check (Back-Pressure Valve, Reflux Valve) – An automatic valve that permits liquid to flow in only one direction.

VANDALISM – The willful or malicious destruction or defacement of property.

VEGETATIVE PROPAGATION – The propagation of plants through asexual means, such as budding, cuttings, division, grating, layering, and so on; distinct from sexual production by seed or spores or bulbs.

VERTICAL MOWING, VERTI-CUTTING – Cutting slices in the turf with a machine that has blades mounted in a vertical manner on a rotating shaft. This practice is considered an important method of thatch reduction.

VIABLE – Fertile, in terms of a plant's capacity to germinate or grow; alive. A viable seed will sprout under moist or other special conditions, according to the type of seed.

VINE – A plant climbing or scrambling on some other support. Such a plant may attach itself by tendrils or aerial roots.

WAIVER OF LIEN – The voluntary relinquishment of one's lien rights.

WATER DEPENDENT – A use or activity that can be carried out only on, in, or adjacent to a water area because the use requires access to the water body for transportation, recreation, or energy production or as a source of water.

WATER LANCE – Tool for watering tree roots below the surface of sod or packing. Made of 1/2-inch pipe with a faucet handle and a T-handle capped at one end and equipped with a fitting for a power sprayer or garden hose at the other. With a sprayer, liquid fertilizer can be applied directly to the feeder root zone.

WATER RELATED – Uses that are not directly dependent on access to a water body but that provide goods or services that are directly associated with water-dependent land or waterway use. If such uses are not located adjacent to water, the result is a public loss of quality in the goods or services offered. Except as necessary for water-dependent or water-related uses or facilities, residences, parking lot spoil and sump sites, roads and highways, restaurants, businesses, factories, and trailer parks are not generally considered dependent on or related to water location needs.

WATER TABLE – The upper surface of groundwater.

WEDGE AND SLEDGE – Technique for removing stumps. The roots are chopped back with 5-pound axes, then slabs are split off using iron wedges and 12-pound sledges. This technique is often much harder than it sounds. Some stumps are twisted, are full of rocks or even iron nails, or present other challenges. In most areas, this method has been replaced by the use of power stump cutters.

WEED – A plant growing where it is not desired; in other words, a weed is a plant out of place. In practice, we understand a weed as wild, not intentionally sown or planted. A plant that grows between cultivated plants and is harmful because of competition for light, moisture, and nutrients.

WEED CONTROL – The process of chemically or physically inhibiting weed growth and limiting undesirable plants from areas that may include turf, shrub beds, or ground cover beds or within other landscape or hardscape features.

WEEP HOLE – (1) A small opening in a wall or window member through which accumulated condensation or water may drain to the building exterior, as from the base of a cavity wall, a wall lashing, or a skylight. (2) A hole near the bottom of a retaining wall, backfilled with gravel or other free-draining material, to permit water to drain to the outside of the wall and prevent the buildup of pressure behind the wall.

WET FEET – Plant roots trying to grow in soil that is continually saturated with water. Although bog plants can usually survive under such conditions, most garden plants will perish.

WETLANDS – Land areas where excess water is the dominant factor determining the nature of soil development and the types of plant and animal communities living at the soil surface. Wetland soils retain sufficient moisture to support aquatic or semi-aquatic plant life. In marine and estuarine areas, wetlands are bounded at the lower extreme by extreme low water; in freshwater areas, by a depth of 6 feet. The areas below wetlands are submerged lands.

WETTING AGENT – A substance capable of lowering the surface tension of liquids, facilitating wetting of solid surfaces and permitting penetration of liquids into the capillaries.

WIDOWMAKER – Usually the result of poor planning when felling trees, this name is given to a tree that does not fall clear to the ground when cut but catches the twigs and branches (hangs up) in a nearby tree or trees. This situation can occur because of improper notching at an unseen rotted spot, an unexpected gust of wind, or similar unexpected circumstances. The tree is a menace if left hanging and is more dangerous than ever to the workers who must finish removing the tree. Such trees often result from storm breakage.

WILDFLOWERS – A broad term for plantings of wild or uncultivated plants, typically sown from seed and allowed to naturalize.

WINTERIZE – A broad term used to describe tasks associated with preparing the landscape for the extremes of winter. Typically, this term refers to the required purging of the subterranean water lines of an irrigation system to avoid freezing, but it could include other activities, such as mulching beds and withholding fertilizer.

WOOD PRESERVATIVE – A chemical used to prevent or retard the decay of wood, especially by fungi or insects.

WOODY – A perennial stem that has had time to produce woody tissue, a characteristic bark that is often gray to tan, and buds that produce the next season's growth.

WOODY PLANT – A plant that develops woody tissue, retaining its essential shape from season to season, with normal growth. The opposite of a herbaceous plant, the top of which dies to the ground in winter.

WORK ORDER SYSTEM – A system of initiating and prioritizing maintenance tasks in which precise instructions for commencement of work, cost control elements, and the feedback mechanism for department record keeping are present.

WORK PROGRAM – A description of what work is to be done, how much is to be done, and when it is to be accomplished.

WORK STANDARDS – The level to which work should be performed to accomplish assigned tasks in the most efficient manner that produces both quality and quantity.

XERISCAPING – The process of landscaping with minimal water use. It is based on the use of water-efficient plant materials (preferably native) strategically placed for best utilization.

ZONE MAINTENANCE – The routine assignment of the same crew, comprising the same people and supervision, to the same specific area of a site, such as a park or campus, for which they have the responsibility to perform all the groundskeeping tasks.

ZONING, Aesthetic – The regulation of property by zoning in the interest of beauty.

APPENDIX C

Professional Organizations and Associations

American Forests
Washington, D.C.
202-955-4500
www.americanforests.org

American Horticultural Society
Alexandria, Virginia
www.ahs.org

American Public Works Association
Kansas City, Missouri
816-472-6100
www.apwa.net

American Society of Golf Course Architects
Brookfield, Wisconsin
262-786-5960
www.asgca.org

American Society of Landscape Architects
Washington, D.C.
202-898-2444
www.asla.org

APPA - Leadership in Educational Facilities
Alexandria, Virginia
703-684-1446
www.appa.org

Arbor Day Foundation
Nebraska City, Nebraska
888-448-7337
www.arborday.org

Association for the Advancement of Sustainability in Higher Education
Denver, Colorado
303-605-3537
www.aashe.org

Association of American Pesticide Control Officials
Milford, Delaware
302-422-8152
www.aapco.org

Association of Professional Landscape Designers
Harrisburg, Pennsylvania
717-238-9780
www.apld.com

Botanical Society of America
St. Louis, Missouri
314-577-9566
www.botany.org

Building Owners and Managers Association International
Washington D.C.
202-408-2662
www.boma.org

Building Owners and Managers Institute International
Arnold, Maryland
410-974-1410
www.bomi-edu.org

Campus Consortium for Environmental Excellence
Boston, Massachusetts
978-281-5020
www.c2e2.org

Campus Safety Health and Environmental Management Association
Bloomington, Indiana
812-245-8084
www.cshema.org

Clean Air-Cool Planet
Portsmouth, New Hampshire
603-422-6464
www.cleanair-coolplanet.org

Council of Educational Facility Planners International
Scottsdale, Arizona
480-391-0840
www.cefpi.org

Environmental Association for Universities and Colleges
Cheltenham, Gloucestershire, UK
www.eauc.org.uk

Environmental Design Research Association
McLean, Virginia
703-506-2895
www.edra.org

Golf Course Superintendents Association of America
Lawrence, Kansas
785-841-2240
www.gcsaa.org

International Erosion Control Association
Denver, Colorado
303-640-7554
www.ieca.org

International Facility Management Association
Houston, Texas
713-623-4362
www.ifma.org

The Irrigation Association
Falls Church, Virginia
703-536-7080
www.irrigation.org

The Lawn Institute
East Dundee, Illinois
www.thelawninstitute.org

National Association of Industrial and Office Parks
Herndon, Virginia
703-904-7100
www.naiop.org

National Parks Conservation Association
Washington, D.C.
800-628-7275
www.npca.org

National Pest Management Association
Fairfax, Virginia
703-352-6762
www.pestworld.org

National Recreation and Park Association
Ashburn, Virginia
703-626-6772
www.nrpa.org

National Wildlife Federation
Reston, Virginia
703-438-6000
www.nwf.org

Professional Grounds Management Society
Baltimore, Maryland
410-223-2861
www.pgms.org

Society for College and University Planning
Ann Arbor, Michigan
734-764-2000
www.scup.org

Society of American Florists
Alexandria, Virginia
703-836-8700
www.safnow.org

Sports Turf Managers Association
Lawrence, Kansas
800-383-3875
www.stma.org

Tree Care Industry Association
Londonderry, New Hampshire
603-314-5380
www.tcia.org

Urban Land Institute
Washington, D.C.
202-624-7000
www.uli.org

Water Environment Federation
Alexandria, Virginia
800-666-0206
www.wef.org

APPENDIX D

Bibliography and Resources

Allen, Ralph. "Environmental Health and Safety." In APPA's Body of Knowledge (BOK), *www.appa.org/bok,* retrieved July 7, 2011.

APPA. *Creating a Service Culture: Making the Customer Connection.* Alexandria, Virginia: APPA, 2005.

------. *Facilities Performance Indicators (FPI) Report.* Alexandria, Virginia: annual online report, *www.appa.org/research/fpi.cfm.*

------. *Operational Guidelines for Educational Facilities: Custodial.* Alexandria, Virginia: APPA, 2011.

------. *Operational Guidelines for Educational Facilities: Maintenance.* Alexandria, Virginia: APPA, 2011.

APPA and Campus Safety Health and Environmental Management Association. *Environmental Compliance Assistance Guide for Colleges and Universities, second edition.* Alexandria, Virginia: APPA and CSHEMA, 2008.

Bartlett, Peggy F., and Geoffrey W. Chase, eds. *Sustainability on Campus: Stories and Strategies for Change.* Cambridge, Massachusetts: MIT Press, 2004.

Brandon, R., and A. Spruch. "Inspired Landscapes." *American School and University,* November 2008.

Brown, Stewart. *Sports Ground Management: A Complete Guide.* Ramsbury, Marlborough, England: The Crowood Press Ltd., 2009.

Buckingham, Marcus, and Curt Coffman. *First, Break All The Rules.* New York: Simon & Schuster, 1999.

Campbell, Jeffrey L. *Facility Management Shared Services: The Balance Between In-House Services and Outsourcing.* Alexandria, Virginia: APPA, 2009.

Carson, Rachel. *Silent Spring.* Boston: Houghton Mifflin Co., 1962.

Chickering, A., and L. Reisser. *Education and Identity.* San Francisco: Jossey-Bass Publishers, 1993.

College Portrait of Undergraduate Education. www.collegeportraits.org

Eagan, David, and David Orr, eds. *The Campus and Environmental Responsibility,* New Directions in Higher Education Series, no. 77. San Francisco: Jossey-Bass Publishers, 1992.

Franko, Donna, Jay Klingel, and Betty Wooding. "From Risk-Takers to the Model *of* Success: University of Virginia's Apprenticeship Program Celebrates 25 Years." *Facilities Manager,* May/June 2008.

Goldstein, Philip J., Daphne E. Kempner, and Sean C. Rush. *Contract Management or Self-Operation: A Decision-Making Guide for Higher Education.* Alexandria, Virginia: APPA, 1993.

Gratto, Fred. "Give Me Liberty or Give Me Brick." *Facilities Manager,* May/June 2009.

Hansen, Jim. "The 800 Pound Gorilla: The Threat and Taming of Global Climate Change." *Facilities Manager,* March/April 2008.

Jackson, Joe. "Duke University's Quality Appearance Program." *Facilities Manager,* May/June 2008.

Lawter, John, Rob Doletzky, Chad Godfrey, and Bruce Morrison. "Grounds Maintenance and Operations." In APPA's Body of Knowledge (BOK), *www.appa.org/bok,* retrieved July 7, 2011.

Levine, A., and J. Cureton. "Collegiate Life: An Obituary." *Change,* no. 30, May/June 1998.

MacIntyre, Stephen, Kelly Meade, and Melissa McEwen. "From Campus Tug-of-War to Pulling Together: Using the Lean Approach." *Facilities Manager,* July/August 2009.

Marchese, T. "A New Conversation about Undergraduate Teaching: An Interview with Professor Richard J. Light, Convener of the Harvard Assessment Seminars." *AAHE Bulletin 42,* no. 9, 1990.

Mayer, Frederick, and William A. Daigneau. "Infrastructure Planning." In APPA's Body of Knowledge (BOK), *www.appa.org/bok,* retrieved August 15, 2011.

Melnick, Phillip. "Solid Waste and Recycling." In APPA's Body of Knowledge (BOK), *www.appa.org/bok,* retrieved July 7, 2011.

Orr, David W. *Earth in Mind: On Education, Environment, and the Human Prospect.* Washington: Island Press, 1994.

Professional Grounds Management Society. *Grounds Maintenance Estimating Guidelines, eighth edition.* Baltimore, Maryland: PGMS, 1998.

------. *Grounds Maintenance Management Guidelines, sixth edition.* Baltimore, Maryland: PGMS, 1998.

------. *Grounds Management Forms & Job Descriptions, sixth edition.* Baltimore, Maryland: PGMS, 1998.

Qayoumi, Mohammad H. *Benchmarking and Organizational Change, second edition.* Alexandria, Virginia: APPA, 2011.

Reeve, John R., and Marion B. Smith. *Planning for Master Planning.* Alexandria, Virginia: APPA, 1995.

Reynolds, Gary L., and David A. Cain. *The Impact of Facilities on the Recruitment and Retention of Students.* Alexandria, Virginia: APPA's Center for Facilities Research, 2006.

Salt Institute. *The Snowfighter's Handbook.* Alexandria, Virginia: Salt Institute, 2007.

Simpson, Walter, ed. *The Green Campus: Meeting the Challenge of Environmental Sustainability.* Alexandria, Virginia: APPA, 2008.

Strange, C., and J. Banning. *Educating by Design.* San Francisco: Jossey-Bass Publishers, 2001.

United States Environmental Protection Agency. Washington, D.C., *www.epa.gov.*

------. *Clean Cities' Guide to Alternative Fuel and Advanced Medium- and Heavy-Duty Vehicles.* Washington, D.C.: U.S. EPA, 2010.

------. *Clean Cities' Guide to Alternative Fuel Commercial Lawn Equipment.* Washington, D.C.: U.S. EPA, 2010.

Voluntary System of Accountability Program. *www.voluntarysystem.org.*

Van Yahres, Mike. "What Should Stay Put? Campus Landscape Planning for the Long Term." *Facilities Manager,* September/October 2000.